ASPECTS OF
SHAKESPEARE'S 'PROBLEM PLAYS'

ASPECTS OF SHAKESPEARE'S 'PROBLEM PLAYS'

ARTICLES REPRINTED FROM *SHAKESPEARE SURVEY*

EDITED BY

KENNETH MUIR

EMERITUS PROFESSOR OF ENGLISH LITERATURE
UNIVERSITY OF LIVERPOOL

AND

STANLEY WELLS

GENERAL EDITOR OF THE OXFORD SHAKESPEARE
AND HEAD OF THE SHAKESPEARE DEPARTMENT
OXFORD UNIVERSITY PRESS

CAMBRIDGE UNIVERSITY PRESS

CAMBRIDGE
LONDON   NEW YORK   NEW ROCHELLE
MELBOURNE   SYDNEY

Published by the Press Syndicate of the University of Cambridge
The Pitt Building, Trumpington Street, Cambridge CB2 IRP
32 East 57th Street, New York, NY 10022, USA
296 Beaconsfield Parade, Middle Park, Melbourne 3206, Australia

This collection © Cambridge University Press 1982

This collection first published 1982

Printed in Great Britain
at the University Press, Cambridge

Library of Congress catalogue card number 81-9985

British Library Cataloguing in Publication Data
Aspects of Shakespeare's 'problem plays'.
1. Shakespeare, William – Criticism and interpretation
I. Muir, Kenneth   II. Wells, Stanley
822.3′3   PR2976
ISBN 0 521 23959 1 hard covers
ISBN 0 521 28371 X paperback

CONTENTS

List of Plates   *page* vii

Preface   ix

Directing Problem Plays
    by JOHN BARTON and GARETH LLOYD EVANS   I

'All's Well That Ends Well' *by* NICHOLAS BROOKE   10

The Design of 'All's Well That Ends Well'
    by R. L. SMALLWOOD   26

Why Does it End Well? Helena, Bertram, and the Sonnets
    by ROGER WARREN   43

The Renaissance Background of 'Measure for Measure'
    by ELIZABETH POPE   57

The Unfolding of 'Measure for Measure'
    by JAMES BLACK   77

'The Devil's Party': Virtues and Vices in 'Measure for Measure'
    by HARRIETT HAWKINS   87

'Troilus and Cressida' *by* KENNETH MUIR   96

'Sons and Daughters of the Game': An Essay on Shakespeare's 'Troilus
    and Cressida' *by* R. A. YODER   III

The Problem Plays, 1920–1970: A Retrospect
    by MICHAEL JAMIESON   126

A selection from reviews of the three plays:

RICHARD DAVID: 'All's Well That Ends Well' (1953)   136

JOHN RUSSELL BROWN: 'All's Well That Ends Well' (1959)   139

RICHARD DAVID: 'Measure for Measure' (1950)   141

PETER THOMSON: 'Measure for Measure' (1970)   144

ROGER WARREN: 'Measure for Measure' (1978)   146

RICHARD DAVID: 'Troilus and Cressida' (1956)   148

JOHN RUSSELL BROWN: 'Troilus and Cressida' (1960)   149

ROGER WARREN: 'Troilus and Cressida' (1976)   152

PLATES

All's Well That Ends Well

1. Act I, scene iii.   Helena and the Countess, 1959.   *page* 22
2. Act II, scene iii. Helena and the Lords, 1955.   23
3. Act II, scene iii. Lafeu and Parolles, 1967.   23
4. Act III, scene v.   Watching the army pass by, 1951.   24
5. Act IV, scene iii. The unmasking of Parolles, 1959.   24
6. Act V, scene iii.   Bertram, Helena and the King of France, 1959.   25
7. Act V, scene iii.   Bertram kneels before Helena, 1967.   25

Measure for Measure

8. Act I, scene ii.   Lucio and Mistress Overdone, 1974.   74
9. Act I, scene ii.   Lucio and Mistress Overdone, 1970.   74
10. Act II, scene ii. Angelo assumes the Duke's authority, 1970.   75
11. Act II, scene iv. Isabella hears Angelo's declaration, 1970.   75
12. The Duke with prisoners, 1950.   76
13. Act III, scene i. Isabella begs Claudio to preserve her chastity, 1962. 76
14. Act V, scene i.   'Justice, O royal Duke', 1950.   76

Troilus and Cressida

15. Act III, scene i.   Pandarus' song, 1960.   108
16. Act III, scene ii. Pandarus brings Cressida to Troilus, 1968.   108
17. Act III, scene ii. Troilus and Cressida plight their troth, 1976.   109
18. Thersites and Achilles, 1968.   109
19. Act V, scene ii.   Cressida and Diomedes watched by Troilus
                        and Ulysses, 1960.   110
20. Act V, scene viii. Hector surrounded by the Myrmidons, 1960.   110

All the illustrations are from productions at the Royal Shakespeare Theatre, Stratford-upon-Avon. Grateful thanks are due to the Governors of the Royal Shakespeare Theatre, Stratford-upon-Avon, for permission to reproduce plates nos. 1, 2, 4, 5, 6, 8, 9, 10, 12, 13, 14, 15, 16, 17, 19, 20; to Thomas Holte for nos. 3, 7, 11, 18.

PREFACE

Until the present century the plays discussed in this volume were regarded with some embarrassment. During the nineteenth century they were scarcely performed, and those critics who paid them any attention found them so distasteful that they supposed that Shakespeare must have written them after some grave crisis in his own life and that in them he gave expression to his temporary disgust with sex – 'sex nausea' is their favourite diagnosis. The change of attitude to the plays came after the First World War when returned veterans found that their own feelings seemed to be reflected in *Troilus and Cressida*, and when the sexual frankness of all three plays appealed to that generation, as well as to our more permissive society.

A performance of *Troilus and Cressida* by the Marlowe Society at Cambridge in 1922 and a production of *Measure for Measure* at Sadler's Wells in 1933 (with Charles Laughton and Flora Robson) revealed that the plays worked on the stage, while G. Wilson Knight and R. W. Chambers began their critical rehabilitation. Their later fortunes are discussed in Michael Jamieson's article. Since he wrote it there have been two more books on *Measure for Measure*, by Rosalind Miles (*The Problem of 'Measure for Measure': A Historical Investigation*, 1976) and Darryl J. Gless ('*Measure for Measure*', *the Law and the Convent*, 1979).

In the present collection we have tried to illustrate the fortunes of the three plays in the theatre by photographs of productions, by reviews, and by the interview with John Barton who has directed them all. The articles, written over the past thirty years, are part of the continuing debate on the problem plays. Happily no one now regards them as evidence of the author's breakdown, whether psychological or artistic.

With *All's Well That Ends Well*, the least successful of the three, the debate centres on the question of tone; and R. L. Smallwood, Nicholas Brooke and Roger Warren seek to establish what Shakespeare was trying to do, and how successful he was in the attempt. With *Troilus and Cressida* the central question is one of genre. Is it a comical satire (as Oscar J. Campbell supposed) or is it rather a tragical satire? Kenneth Muir and R. A. Yoder in their different ways take the latter view. With *Measure for Measure* the controversy has sometimes been acrimonious between those who regard it as Shakespeare's most Christian play and those who think it cynical. The difficulty here has been that each article on the play published in *Shakespeare Survey* has been followed by an indignant rejoinder. The opening pages of a number of recent articles have been devoted to a summary of the damnable errors they seek to confute. Elizabeth Pope and James Black in their different ways support a 'Christian' interpretation, while Harriett Hawkins wittily demonstrates that the play is not without ironies and ambiguities. Indeed, the impression we get from the essays on all three plays is that more than one interpretation can be based squarely on the text, not because of a failure of communication, nor because they are flawed masterpieces, but rather because their ambiguity is a sign that Shakespeare's mind, in Keats's phrase, was 'a thoroughfare for all thoughts, not a select party'.

K.M.
S.W.W.

DIRECTING PROBLEM PLAYS: JOHN BARTON TALKS TO GARETH LLOYD EVANS

G.L.E. John Barton, you are, I think, one of the few directors who have produced all of the so-called Problem Plays. Do you find this a useful label?

J.B. No, I don't really. I hate categorising plays, and find it difficult to say what is a tragedy, what is a comedy, what is a romance, etc. But if I did, I think I would link *All's Well That Ends Well* and *Measure for Measure* with *Twelfth Night*. I believe that they carried through something that was coming to the boil in *As You Like It* and *Twelfth Night*, i.e. Shakespeare's very conscious split between the 'happy-ever-after' world of romantic comedy and his sense of what life and people are really like. I see it in *As You Like It* to some extent, and even more so in *Twelfth Night* where what happens at the end to Malvolio and Belch and Maria is set against the conventional romantic ending given to Olivia, Orsino, Viola and Sebastian. That sense of reality breaking in on convention goes further in *All's Well* and *Measure for Measure*, where a wry sense of what life's really like and what people are really like is at odds with what the story-line dictates. I think that *Troilus* is a much profounder, more complex, and richer play. If I had to align it with any, I suppose I would do so, as other critics have done, with *2 Henry IV* and with *Hamlet*. I mention those two partly because of the common disease imagery in the three plays. I think that there is also a difference in Shakespeare's overall attitude in *Troilus*. I take it to be on the whole wry, tolerant and accepting in

Twelfth Night, *All's Well*, and *Measure for Measure*, and to be more disturbed and disillusioned about human beings and human life in *Troilus*, which seems to me to lead towards the extreme disillusion of *Timon*. So I personally would hesitate to group the 'problem plays' together, but I would also hesitate to put labels on them at all. When directing such plays, I do not think 'Are they tragedies or comedies?'. Such a question does not arise when I am trying to bring them to life in the theatre. Nevertheless, there are of course certain common features which the three plays share. They are magnificently summed up in *Angel with Horns*. A. P. Rossiter's summary of the peculiar quality of the plays is, for me, the most perceptive and helpful piece of critical writing yet made about them.

G.L.E. I understand what you are saying and, indeed, I agree with it. I'm interested that although you're not prepared to come down absolutely on one side or the other about this, you do, in effect, make a distinction between *Twelfth Night* – and I presume plays of that ilk – which you refer to as wry, tolerant and accepting, and *Troilus and Cressida* which you describe as disturbed and disillusioned. Do you think that it's quite fruitless to ask the question why this happened? In your heart of hearts, do you think that there is a personal reason inside Shakespeare for this, or has it something to do with the conditions of the theatre at the time, or what?

J.B. I think one should be very suspicious of

drawing autobiographical conclusions about Shakespeare. But, even so, I do have a picture of Shakespeare himself, which I mostly derive from his sonnets. These confirm what I feel about him in studying his plays. They show him responding to the common subject of love in so many different ways; sometimes he's humorous and frivolous, sometimes romantic and idealistic, sometimes sardonic to a degree, sometimes hurt, sometimes disillusioned, sometimes cynical and sometimes savage. Whatever the date span of the sonnets, I see him responding in them to love in such totally different ways, that I feel that his response to everything in life was shifting, unsettled, volatile and un-codified. I doubt if there was a simple historical and autobiographical development in him. I think that the subject matter of a given play rather dictated his attitude, but I also believe that there is some autobiographical content, not in terms of hidden biographical detail, but in overall mood and tone. I certainly believe that his sense of what life and men are really like increasingly made him break forms and conventions.

G.L.E. Can I go back now to *Troilus and Cressida*? When the Old Vic revived *Troilus and Cressida* after the First World War, *The Times* said it was inevitably dull, and when Charles Laughton played Angelo to Flora Robson's Isabella, T. S. Eliot lamented in a letter to that paper, about the small audiences. How do you account for the lack of popularity of these plays till round about 1935?

J.B. Well, I think the popularity of a particular play depends enormously on its being well done by a given group of actors and a director. But I think also something of the taste and climate of the age comes into it. For instance, the Victorians loved *Romeo and Juliet* and totally dismissed *Troilus*. Today, however, I think anyone would agree that to bring off a *Romeo and Juliet*, to make an audience sympathise with those two characters and that world, is far harder

than to bring off a *Troilus*. I think that the sardonic, wry, realistic portraiture of human beings in the play is much more in tune with the taste of the last twenty or thirty years than it was in Victorian times. I think there's no doubt whatsoever – and it's something I've often discussed with my fellow directors – that a certain play can become more or less viable at a given time. I think, for instance, that it's very difficult to bring off *Richard II* today. I think that a self-pitying King, indeed the very subject of a King's fall, has far less import than it would have had for the Elizabethans. I think that modern taste, the modern response to life, immediately makes *Troilus* a popular play in a way it never was in the eighteenth and nineteenth centuries. I myself believe that it's one of his greatest plays, but that may be because of what I am, rather than of what the play is. I would hesitate to make an absolute judgement, but it's extraordinary to me that anybody could think of *Romeo and Juliet*, for instance, as being a better play than *Troilus and Cressida*.

G.L.E. Would it be right then to say that the kind of society we've got today is more amenable to a rather darker-hued production of a play, even of a comedy, than, let us say, forty or fifty years ago; that it's easier to put on, let us say, even a *Comedy of Errors* or *Love's Labour's Lost*, or *Twelfth Night*, with a wry-ness in it, even possibly, a disillusion in it – that it's easier to do this kind of thing today than it was?

J.B. Oh, I think it is, very definitely.

G.L.E. In the 1930s there were protests at, of all places, Melton Mowbray, and indeed Buxton, about performances of *Measure for Measure*. Now the revival of interest, certainly for scholars and critics, in the play, was due to the work of Wilson Knight, R. W. Chambers, and Muriel Bradbrook. The Wilson Knight interpretation, most particularly, is of course very much a religious interpretation. In your 1970 production of *Measure for Measure*, in which

Ian Richardson played Angelo, and Sebastian Shaw played the Duke, were you reacting against such religious interpretations?

J.B. Not primarily. I read the critics, but basically what I try to bring out in a play is what I myself find in it. I think that, without doubt, one has to take religion into account in that the religious background is strong in the play, but – may be this is just a matter of personal taste – I don't like taking a symbolical or allegorical or philosophical or metaphysical view of the play, mainly because I'm a director working with actors. What I have to do is to answer their questions about the individual characters: what is his intention? what is he really doing or thinking, or feeling behind a given line? When a director explores a play he is bound, primarily, to be doing so in terms of character and psychology, even though he may – indeed must – remind the actors that this is not necessarily what Shakespeare always demands of them. The exploration of character is not the only objective of rehearsals, but it is at the heart of the acting tradition in England, and one has to work within that tradition. There are, for instance, two ways in which one can look at the Duke; one can take him as a symbolic figure, but it's very difficult for an actor to bring a symbolic figure to life. If one is rehearsing *Measure for Measure*, rather than just studying it, one has to answer questions about what the Duke's really like, and what's going on inside him, and that leads to finding out about a human being rather than defining an allegory.

In practice, I did not find any particular critic especially helpful about the play. Critical opinion is usually as diverse and divided as a series of productions of the same play by different directors would be. This is particularly true of *Measure for Measure*, where critics in the last thirty years have been totally divided on the question, for instance, of how we are meant to view the Duke. I find this division of opinion more significant about the play than any one particular view of it. I in fact made an abstract for the actors of the views of some ten critics, and suggested that the truth might lie somewhere in between. I urged that if they depended on one view only, e.g. Wilson Knight's, they would be taking too narrow a view.

One thing, however, did seem to emerge in rehearsal and performance. It has often been pointed out how, on reading the play, one finds it splitting down the middle. At the point Isabella leaves Claudio after her interview with him in prison, and is left alone with the Duke, the level of the writing changes. The Duke for the first time goes into prose, and into plotting the bed-trick; and the play, which has in the first half been poetically intense and psychologically subtle, is then worked out on a lower, almost fairy-tale level. The change is obvious enough in the study; but in the theatre, I think that the difference disappears. This is because the actors, if they have brought their characters to life in exploring the first half, can carry through that life into the play's more superficial resolution. I felt, in fact, that what seemed a problem in the study largely melted away in the theatre, when those characters were embodied by living actors.

G.L.E. Yes ... I don't know whether you quite realise (perhaps you do) what a great shock you gave quite a lot of people because, in your production, Isabella quite firmly did not agree to marry the Duke. I would be very interested to know why this was so – if indeed you intended it to be so. It seemed so deliberate that I must believe that it was an intention. Now, did she in fact not agree to marry the Duke because the Duke was older than usual (as indeed he certainly looked), or because she couldn't forgive him for pretending that Claudio was dead and was, as it were, indulging in a kind of feminine umbrage; or was it because Isabella found sex repugnant?

J.B. Well, all those thoughts occurred to us in rehearsal, but that's not quite the way in which we tackled it. Again, what we did was to ask the question 'What would Isabella have done when the Duke made his proposal?' Shakespeare himself leaves it open-ended in the sense that he gives her no lines whatsoever in reply to the proposal. This is a situation which comes up again and again in rehearsal: Shakespeare doesn't provide a certain answer and one has to find one. One tends to do so by trying to deduce what a character's response would be from everything that we know about that character elsewhere in the play. What I actually intended was that Isabella's response should be open-ended. I suggested to Estelle Kohler, who was playing the part, that she was in no state at that moment to accept the proposal, and I asked her to reject it and yet think about it. The last thing that I presented on the stage, when everybody had gone off at the end of the play, was Isabella wondering, puzzling about what she should do.

G.L.E. The evidence seems to be that in the past Parolles was regarded as one of the greatest comic characters, as indeed I believe Shylock was. Would you agree that audiences nowadays don't find him as funny as apparently they did in the past ... Parolles I mean, not Shylock?

J.B. No, I wouldn't agree with that at all. I think that whether he is funny or not depends simply on how good the actor is who plays it. There are many parts in Shakespeare which may seem to be dreary if they are not brought alive by the individual talents of the actor. But provided that Parolles is well acted, I am sure he is still funny in the theatre today.

G.L.E. I remember with a great deal of pleasure – I don't know whether you do – Guthrie's production of *All's Well*. I felt both affronted and delighted at the same time. I suppose it could be said, although I wouldn't necessarily say so myself, that Guthrie seemed to be implying, in the way he directed the play,

that it could not really appeal to a modern audience, so something pretty drastic had to be done; so, for example, he introduced an amount of farcical business, including a microphone. Some might say that this kind of behaviour clashed with, for example, great performances such as Edith Evans gave us as the Countess Rousillon. Do you think that *All's Well* is viable to a modern audience – without gimmicks?

J.B. I certainly came to think so after doing the production. At first I was afraid of directing the play, and hadn't originally been going to do it. I had to take it over quickly because a director dropped out. I remember saying to the actors at the outset, 'Let's try and trust this play, explore it and find out how it works, and stage it simply without gimmicks.' We then found after a couple of frightened, doubtful weeks, that the play was coming alive. I believe, from that experience, that the play does work without jazzing-up, though I wasn't sure whether it did when I embarked on it. I ended by thinking the play much finer and more cohesive than I, or, indeed, most people had ever suspected. I think that what Guthrie did was brilliant; but he was always more a man of immense theatrical imagination, a giver of great delight, rather than someone who really tried to explore the content of a play. I think he overlaid plays with much creative invention but did not always try to realise their actual contents. As far as gimmicks are concerned, I think the question is whether an individual piece of business is an inventive overlay, or whether it's a truthful bodying-out of what's implicit in the text. But perhaps in the end it rather comes down to a question of taste.

G.L.E. Would you agree that the difference between Guthrie's attempt to make *All's Well* speak to the twentieth century and your own (or indeed the Royal Shakespeare Company's attempt to make a play speak to the twentieth century), is between what you've described as

Guthrie's inventive overlay and what you would accept as a matter of principle? Does that make sense? In other words, whereas Guthrie seems to try to speak to the twentieth century by a kind of sensationalism, or theatrical effect, you personally, and the Royal Shakespeare Company, would attempt to make Shakespeare speak to the twentieth century on the basis of a certain attitude, a certain set of principles, a certain philosophy about the twentieth century, that you yourself or the Company have?

J.B. I never personally think very much about the twentieth century. I simply read the play intensively in the study, and then work on it in the rehearsal room by responding to what the actors offer. My response is as often intuitive as it is analytic or rational. I say 'Wouldn't it be good if . . . ?' and then try to test a particular idea in terms of whether it tallies with what I take to be the play's meaning. I never consciously take a twentieth-century approach to the play. It's very difficult to define the process that goes on in the rehearsal room: instinct is a great matter – directors and actors work together on instinctive ideas which bubble up from day to day, which they then test with their reason. We sometimes cut things out because we think they are an overlay on the text, and sometimes leave them in, hoping and trusting that they are an embodiment of something implicit in the text. This process is certainly influenced by the fact that we are people living in the twentieth century. But as often as not we also try to modify our modern responses by asking 'What does Shakespeare *really* mean here? Are we distorting him by doing something which we *want* him to mean, because it appeals to us?'

G.L.E. Do you regard the ending of *All's Well That Ends Well* as a cynical one, or do you think that Bertram has learnt from experience? Indeed, what has he learnt?

J.B. I don't think Bertram's learnt very much; he's grown up a bit, he's learnt to value Helena more than he valued her at first, he's seen through Parolles, but he's still a pretty selfish and stupid man. I think that 'cynical' isn't quite the right word for the ending: the tone is more one of a worldly tolerance of people. There's no certainty that Bertram and Helena live happily ever after. Bertram ends with a couple of very spare lines which don't tell us much: 'If she, my lord, can make me know this clearly,/I'll love her dearly ever, ever dearly.' Their surface meaning is clear enough, but in the context of the whole scene, they also contain shame, awe of the King, and a resolve, at that moment, to make the best of things. Whether Bertram did in fact love her dearly ever is something which is surely made questionable by all we know of him from the play as a whole. And the end situation is well summed up in the text itself when the King says 'And if it end so meet/ The bitter past, more welcome is the sweet.'

G.L.E. May I turn back again to *Troilus and Cressida*? Do you agree with Oscar Campbell and Alice Walker that it's a comical satire? Now, some of the satire in your production was brilliant, but it could be argued that it would be possible to produce it as a tragical satire – that is, with Hector and Troilus as tragic heroes. In your estimation, what kind of satire is it? Tragical or comical?

J.B. I think there is satire in it, but I certainly don't think for one moment that the play is basically a comical satire. I think that people in it are too raw, too hurt, too bruised for it to be labelled on that superficial level. It is also comical, heroical, tragical, romantic – as a whole, it is a mixture of all these things. There is no play which I would less willingly tie down with a label. It continually invites a varying response. For much of it, it asks us to respond comedically, and at times one is drawn to say 'Ah, a "black comedy!"' But what happens, by the end, to Troilus and Cressida and Hector is not comic. The contrast, for instance, between what Hector professes and aspires to and what he does seems to me to be very sad. And I feel a great compassion for what becomes of Troilus and Cressida. If I had to give it a label, I would say it was closer to tragedy than to anything else, but I just don't believe those labels are useful. I've never understood myself what exactly it is that defines a tragedy; I don't think that way. *Troilus and Cressida* is unique and brilliant and resists labelling; one confines it terribly, and minimises its richness if one tries to categorise it.

G.L.E.   And yet, don't you think that Shakespeare himself would have had, in the Elizabethan way, a rather more formal notion of the kind of play he was writing? I agree with you that it is very difficult, and indeed probably for us not profitable, to think in these rather strict terms of Tragedy, Comedy, History, and so on, but is it not possible that Shakespeare himself would have been more inclined to than we are? If so, in what direction do you think his imagination would have been going in *Troilus and Cressida*? To make people laugh, or to make them feel bitter, or to make them, in fact, cry?

J.B.   I think he was trying to do all these things. I think there are bits of the play which are very comic, even farcical, bits that are very moving, bits that are horrifying, bits that are epic, and bits that are domestic and trivial. I think that he invites a much more mixed and complex response than other dramatists. One can categorise Jonson, for instance, far more easily than one can Shakespeare. I think that's true of Shakespeare throughout his career, but never more true than with *Troilus*. I think that it is one of his greatest plays precisely because of the way in which he invites in the course of a single play all the different kinds of response one can have in the theatre, which are normally isolated from one another. He invites tragic, comic, satiric, intellectual and compassionate responses almost at the same time. I believe that is how he himself responded to life. This shiftingness of view is also embodied in the play's presentation of character. There is a very remarkable difference between the declared intentions of the characters and the actual deeds done by them. Again and again a character enunciates certain intentions and beliefs which are confounded by his actions. Hector in the Trojan Council expresses a moral view of what the Trojans should think about the rape of Helen, but immediately after makes a volte-face for the slenderest of reasons. Cressida's declaration of faith and truth with Troilus is broken by what she does with Diomed. Ajax is presented as an oaf and a lout; and yet he is the one person who, in the Greek camp, utters a simple expression of grief and compassion for Hector's death, which is something one wouldn't have expected from what one sees earlier in the play. Again and again, a character who seems to be foolish or cruel or stupid turns up with something completely the opposite to one's first view of him; and that seems to me to be not a chaotic view of human nature, but a truthful and realistic one. It is something which Shakespeare tapped in a way that no writer before him had done, except fitfully.

G.L.E.   Do you mean something more than the old critical concept of appearance and reality? Is there a difference between your words 'declared intention' and 'action done' and this critical concept?

J.B.   I think there is a connection, though I haven't actually thought of it. I only want to make the simple point about the shiftingness of most of the characters. We see it around us all the time in life; we all say we believe something, and then in practice we do something quite different. This is of course a fact which most dramatists take into account to some extent, but I think no play exemplifies it so fully as *Troilus and Cressida* does.

G.L.E.   What about the later Jacobean dramatists – Massinger, Marston, and so on? Do you feel that they may have learnt something from

Shakespeare in this respect? I'm thinking of plays like *Women Beware Women*, which are rather later than the plays we are talking about now. Do you feel that these may have been influenced by Shakespeare in this particular context?

J.B.   Yes, I do think so.

G.L.E.   Despite the obvious theatrical differences which would tend to produce a different kind of play at a given time, I sometimes feel that, in fact, certain thematic pressures that Shakespeare has in this kind of play, do go forward. We tend to think of Shakespeare being wiped away by these later Jacobean dramatists, but I don't think he is, and I'm interested to know what you think.

J.B.   Yes, I think that's quite true. But I think also that when Shakespeare wrote his plays he often did things that no other dramatist had done and I think that this particular way of looking at people is both something new and something quite essential in his view of life. It is even more remarkable in one of the plays Shakespeare wrote soon after *Troilus*: in *Othello*, the Moor himself shifts from one point of view to another within the context of a single speech (for example, 'let her rot and perish and be damned tonight, for she shall not live; no, my heart is turned to stone; I strike it, and it hurts my hand. O, the world hath not a sweeter creature, she might lie by an emperor's side and command him tasks.' Or 'My relief/ Must be to loathe her' followed a few lines later by 'If she be false, O heaven mocks itself, / I'll not believe it'.) Of course, Shakespeare had done this earlier, as with the character of Richard II (in III, iii), but I have come to notice that it is often one of the most central facts about the way in which he presents character. I notice it particularly in the rehearsal room, where it often gives the actor great difficulty. The counsel I offer, 'Accept the inconsistencies without trying to iron them out' may be good; but it sets the actor great problems.

G.L.E.   Would you be prepared to agree that the kind of difference between *Troilus and Cressida* and the other two so-called 'problem plays', which you yourself are insistent upon, is indicated by the difference between Thersites and Lavache? Have you anything to say about those two characters? It seems to me that there is something of the Fool in Thersites, but he is 'not altogether fool'; he is much more and much less than Fool, and that this in itself indicates a difference.

J.B.   Maybe I would say that the difference in intensity in the two characters marks a difference in the two plays. They are both immensely disillusioned and sardonic. But Lavache doesn't probe very deeply, whereas Thersites is anguished by what he sees life to be – 'Still wars and lechery, nothing else holds fashion'. I think that Thersites's passion, and his whole response to life, is much more extreme, much more violent than it is in Lavache.

G.L.E.   As you know, the general tendency of modern criticism of Shakespeare has been to stress the options open to critics and directors. This emerged at the 1971 Shakespeare Vancouver Conference. Nevertheless, nearly all the critics and directors choose a particular interpretation when they are writing their criticism or directing their play, and therefore exclude all others. Do you think it is possible, or even desirable, for a director to present a play in such a way as to leave all the options open? Or is this just a pipe dream?

J.B.   I think it's certainly impossible, and I question whether it's desirable. It's impossible because, as I've said, you have to be specific with actors. Actors have got to know what effect they're trying to make with a given line, what they mean and what they feel. When one reads the play in the study one can say again and again of a given line, 'I'm not sure what Shakespeare intends here; it could be this or it could be that'. But, however unsure one may be, one can't leave things uncertain for the actor; he has to be specific. When there is a textual crux, where there are many editorial explanations, one's got to choose a specific reading for the actor to play. I think that what a given actor or director does with a play is very like what a given critic does when he is writing about it. He selects what seems to him the most important points, what seems to need bringing out the most, and in so doing he is very, very selective; he cannot write down everything. That is not even possible in a variorum edition. A given piece on a play is only the tip of an iceberg. And so it is in the theatre, especially with a dramatist as rich and complex as Shakespeare.

In practice, I think that the theatre's work is actually more open-ended than the critic's for a completely different reason. Whatever the actor and director decide that they are trying to do, they can't completely control the audience's response. I've often found that where an actor and myself have set out to define something, it has meant something quite different in performance to someone who was seeing it, and, indeed, something quite different to different members of the audience. To sum up, I think the only point at which the play can be said to be absolutely open-ended is when it exists as a mere text waiting to be performed or studied.

An example of an audience's response taking something in a different sense from what an actor and myself intended is the interpretation of Achilles which Alan Howard and I attempted in *Troilus*. We were attacked for presenting Achilles as an effeminate homosexual, which was something that had never entered our minds. We saw him as bisexual, a view which is surely embodied in Shakespeare's play and is also the view which an Elizabethan audience would have taken. Shakespeare shows him both with Patroclus and in love with Polyxena. What we did do was show him *playing* at effeminacy and homosexuality in order to mock and outrage the Greek generals. The real man we saw as

embodied in the aggression and destructiveness which surges from him when he confronts Hector ('In what part of his body shall I destroy him?') and when he finally appears on the battlefield. We hoped that we had made that plain enough, especially as Alan played most of the part with great vocal virility and power. But if it came over to members of the audience differently, then one must allow that what they thought they saw was perhaps of more weight than our intentions.

G.L.E. May I, as a final question, ask you to think yourself back into either the area of preparation for the production of a play, or, if you like, the period of rehearsal of the play, and ask you this question? As an academic and also as a distinguished theatre director, do you find that your academic knowledge of the plays, and indeed of the criticism about the plays, and *your* theatrical know-how, are in any sense at war? If you do, can you say what the nature of the war is? If you don't, what is happening in a rehearsal?

J.B. I think that they are deeply different. I think that, whatever one thinks about the play academically or privately, it becomes something completely different when one's working with the living actor. When I work on a play, I first of all read and think about it very hard. But when I go into rehearsal, my initial step is to say to the actors 'Do something; let's put the scene on its feet; you give me something and I will respond to it'. I find that when I do that, new thoughts come that have never occurred to me in the study; I call into question things that I had previously believed, or decide that they are wrong for a particular actor because his persona cannot embody it. Studying and directing a play are completely different experiences. I think the critic exists in an at times enviable isolation where there is just himself and the text and he can respond directly to it. Whereas a director is responding to individual human beings, to the invention and imagination and instincts of the individual actor, and that's the raw material he's got to deal with. He has to accept it, before he tries to mould it. And though his previous knowledge of the play helps him in defining it, in shaping it for the actor, the basic starting-point is not just a text. It's a text plus the creation and invention of the actors; which makes it a completely different experience.

A production of course gives a more impure, but possibly a richer and more complex reading of a play than a critic can provide. A book or an article consists of what the critic wants to say. A production, being a complex of design, music, movement, business, direction, and all that suggests itself in the voice and personae of the actors, is never one man's vision. It is a kind of anthology on the play made by all its participants. It is thus less precise than what the critic offers, and thus less easily pinned down. I always find after doing a production that it contains things which do not represent my preferred view of some detail in the play, but which are rather interpretations arrived at in rehearsal as the best solution to a particular problem for a particular actor. I don't regret this. A production finally belongs to the actors and not to the director, who is more a chairman than a dictator. All directors find their initial views modified by the independent interpretative powers of the actors they work with. I find I learn more from the actors than I could ever do by reading a variety of critical opinions.

© GARETH LLOYD EVANS 1972

'ALL'S WELL THAT ENDS WELL'

NICHOLAS BROOKE

All's Well exercises a recurrent fascination for criticism, because so many things about it are of striking, and contemporary, interest. Yet despite that fact (or possibly partly because of it, because it can be difficult to correlate 'contemporary' with supposedly 'Elizabethan' interests) the play never quite takes, never quite seems to work. The problem – it's always called a 'problem' play in one sense or another – is just what 'working' should, for this play, consist of. This paper has no more specific title because its aim is simply the play itself, not any single aspect of it; but if it is to have a well-ending, it must respond to G. K. Hunter's challenge that 'criticism of *All's Well* has failed, for it has failed to provide a context within which the genuine virtues of the play can be appreciated'.[1] That is an ambitious aim, and the ambition in my love (of the play) thus plagues itself and must take refuge in the obvious scepticism of Shakespeare's title; a perfectly satisfactory conclusion is hardly probable, however much I believe it to be possible.

Scepticism, at least, will be generally granted to the play (unless 'cynicism' is preferred). Scepticism about *what* is more difficult. Presumably about romance, since in one sense or another it certainly enacts a romance plot. Not merely does girl get boy, but she also achieves a social rise of a kind usually thought of as rags to riches, or servant to princess, on the way; and she uses a pretty potent magic (of obscure kind) to do it – curing the King. But it has to do with the nature of this play that my terms have already become inappro-priate. Helena is socially inferior, but she is a gentlewoman and certainly not in rags. Bertram is a count and a ward of the King, but he is not a prince. The social distinctions are stressed and yet reduced in scale: a folk tale which usually thrives on extremes of contrast is modified into perception of social niceties; and it is when made nice that such distinctions are apt to be most offensive.

The modified social pitch is given at once in the opening prose dialogue between the Countess and Lafew:

> In delivering my son from me, I bury a second husband.　　　　　　　　　　　　(I, i, 1–2)

'Son' and 'husband' mark a domestic pitch, still more remarkable when they discuss the King:

> *Countess.* What hope is there of his majesty's amend-ment?
> *Lafew.* He hath abandon'd his physicians, madam; under whose practices he hath persecuted time with hope, and finds no other advantage in the process but only the losing of hope by time.
> 　　　　　　　　　　　　(ll. 11–15)

This King is a sick *man*, with incompetent doctors. There is respect but no hint of royal glamour in the dialogue, and none ever arises in the play. The plain language does have a suggestion of courtliness in the balanced clauses, but that is its only elevation. It contains at once a touch of sententiousness, of riddling, and of the kind of elegance that

[1] ed. G. K. Hunter: *All's Well That Ends Well*, The Arden Shakespeare (1959), introduction, p. xxix. All quotations are from this edition.

restricts emotion:

Countess. . . . No more of this, Helena; go to, no more; lest it be rather thought you affect a sorrow than to have –
Helena. I do affect a sorrow indeed, but I have it too.
Lafew. Moderate lamentation is the right of the dead; excessive grief the enemy to the living.

(ll. 47–52)

Lafew is courtly; Bertram imitates the manner but misses the tone in his farewells:

The best wishes that can be forg'd in your thoughts be servants to you! [*and then, to Helena*] Be comfortable to my mother, your mistress, and make much of her.   (ll. 71–4)

That is not only cold, it also contrives to stress the social inferiority – or, Bertram's consciousness of it. Lafew's old man's petting is only less insulting:

Farewell, pretty lady; you must hold the credit of your father.   (ll. 75–6)

Both speeches, of course, anticipate the play's development. Helena's soliloquy immediately brings out emotional, sexual, and social undercurrents from this reticent opening:

O, were that all! I think not on my father,
And these great tears grace his remembrance more
Than those I shed for him. What was he like?
I have forgot him; my imagination
Carries no favour in't but Bertram's.
I am undone; there is no living, none,
If Bertram be away . . .   (ll. 77–83)

That is verse, and strikingly so. But of a kind that develops naturally as an intensification of prose speech: it is not romance eloquence; indeed, the opposite. The speech rhythm cuts across the verse, typically creating half-lines of short, singularly bare phrases: 'I think not on my father' – 'What was he like? / I have forgot him' – 'I am undone' – 'There is no living, none, / If Bertram be away'. The terseness is remarkable, and so also is it that in seven lines there is not a single

image of any kind. The one which follows is all the more conspicuous, and it does have a limited eloquence:

'twere all one
That I should love a bright particular star
And think to wed it, he is so above me.
In his bright radiance and collateral light
Must I be comforted, not in his sphere.

(ll. 83–7)

The 'bright particular star' offers a richer possibility, but that is limited by the precision of its reference: Bertram is a star only because she is in love with him, and because he thinks himself one, not (as we have just seen him) in fact; and that is stressed in the neat ambiguity of 'he is so above me' – socially far more than astrally. Further, stars are proverbially cold, and that is emphasized in the expansion '. . . Must I be comforted, not in his sphere' which hints at the warmth of physical embrace. Those last two lines are the largest rhythmic unit the speech allows.

Behind the love there is an implicit recognition of sexuality which gets nearer to direct utterance on Parolles's entry:

I love him for his sake,
And yet I know him a notorious liar,
Think him a great way fool, solely a coward;
Yet these fix'd evils sit so fit in him
That they take place when virtue's steely bones
Looks bleak i'th'cold wind . . .   (ll. 97–102)

She turns with relief from virtue's steely bones to bawdy chatter with Parolles. The old objection to this was, of course, merely silly prudery; but more recent explanations that this was all taken for granted in Elizabethan circles are equally false to the play. The Countess's complacent assurance of conventional values has already been jolted by the revelation of Helena's ambitious love. Her stress on 'modesty' is adjusted here in another way: Helena is a great deal more real (and therefore more attractive) than a merely conventional use of the word would allow:

Parolles. Are you meditating on virginity?
Helena. Ay.

(ll. 108–9)

So she is, but she encourages a routine line of banter before at last bringing it round towards her private thoughts:

How might one do, sir, to lose it to her own liking?

(l. 147)

He answers at length, but little to the point, and when he concludes 'Will you anything with it?' it is obvious that her mind has been wandering, in her distrait response

Not my virginity yet:

(l. 161, F punctuation)

and her speech transposes into a meditation on Bertram at court which ends characteristically:

Now shall he –
I know not what he shall. God send him
        well!
The court's a learning-place, and he is
        one –
Parolles. What one, i'faith?
Helena. That I wish well. 'Tis pity –
Parolles. What's pity?
Helena. That wishing well had not a body in't
        Which might be felt...   (ll. 171–8)

The reluctant, and movingly sharp, revelation of feeling repeats the form of utterance which has by now become established as a characteristic of the play. So far I have shown it only in Helena's language, but it is by no means confined to her. Parolles answered her first question – 'Man is enemy to virginity; how may we barricado it against him?' – with rare bluntness:

Keep him out.   (ll. 110–12)

In the next scene, the King responds to a courtier's flattery:

I fill a place, I know't.   (I, ii, 69)

That defines admirably the play's pitch: no

more, and no less. None of Richard II's glamorous royalty, for instance, in this unromantic king. The language of the play never strays very far from this pitch, and its most impressive moments share this striking bareness. Lavatch makes even more explicit than Helena what drives her on:

My poor body, madam, requires it; I am driven on by
the flesh...   (I, iii, 26–7)

Parolles, after he has been exposed in act IV, is equally terse:

                    If my heart were great
'Twould burst at this. Captain I'll be no more,
But I will eat and drink and sleep as soft
As captain shall. Simply the thing I am
Shall make me live.   (IV, iii, 319–23)

What he is – as he knows – is a braggart and a fool.

Hunter – echoing several others – complains that 'There is a general failure in *All's Well* to establish a medium in verse which will convey effectively the whole tone of the play...' (p. lix) That, I think, is wrong. What Hunter had in mind emerges in his admission that 'one cannot pretend that every speech is a failure or that there is no great Shakespearian poetry in the play'. The speeches I have quoted are certainly not failures, and some of them seem to me very impressive poetry; but they are not great in the sense Hunter's phrase implies – that is, they are not eloquent, they do not sprout garlands of imagery. On the contrary, the play's characteristic medium is precisely this uniquely bare language which excludes decoration and so makes all imagery, or any romantic valuation of experience, evidently superfluous. 'Simply the thing I am' is me plain, not dressed up in delusory clothings of romance, magic, or religion.

In that I find it very impressive. Its effect, evidently, is to stress the 'natural' at the expense of the romance, and it therefore governs the unromantic tone in which the romance plot is developed. 'Naturalism' is notoriously an insecure term, or at least a relative one; it is necessary here because the language so insistently relates romance conventions to a more immediate form of experience. It continually delivers the shock of actuality into the context of anticipated fiction. But the naturalism of such speech is not merely bluntness. It has the quality too of the reticence of natural speech. Without eloquence, not much can be said, and not much *is* said (except by implication). Helena's hesitant and limited comment to Parolles is characteristic: he does not understand her (though we do); and he is not meant to. Even her soliloquy, revealing as it is, does not reveal all; Lavatch's 'driven on by the flesh' is the obvious comment which Helena herself does not quite arrive at.

It follows that reticence is as characteristic of the play as bareness of language; is, indeed, a function of it, and equally a condition of naturalism. Helena's soliloquy in I, i is virtually the only such utterance that allows self-revelation. She does have other soliloquies, but they announce the action, not the emotional resources of it. In one sense this is not remarkable: heroines in Shakespearian comedy are not in the habit of profound self-examination; the expectation of more here is generated out of the particular tone I have analysed. It is generated by it, and it is also frustrated by it. To tell the whole truth about ourselves is impossible (because words always falsify); it is also dangerous, and we instinctively avoid it. The point is made very sharply when it emerges that Helena's last speech in I, i (on her plans to get to Paris and to get Bertram) is not protected by the conventions of stage soliloquy, but has been overheard by the Countess's steward. He reports to his mistress, and she proceeds to extract the information from Helena without revealing her sources; first by pressing on Helena's evasion of the term 'mother', and then more directly:

Helena.   Good madam, pardon me.
Countess.
    Do you love my son?
Helena.   Your pardon, noble mistress.
Countess. Love you my son?
Helena.   Do not you love him,
                                                madam?
Countess.
    Go not about; my love hath in't a bond
    Whereof the world takes note. Come, come, disclose
    The state of your affection, for your passions
    Have to the full appeach'd.
Helena.   Then I confess,
    Here on my knee, before high heaven and you,
    That before you, and next unto high heaven,
    I love your son.   (I, iii, 180–9)

The confession has to be forced, and it is forced. The Countess has the perception to force it only because she has the eavesdropper's report. She is sharp, but never very perceptive; as she is affectionate but slightly sentimental. Helena, forced to confess her love, still masks her ambition:

                        I follow him not
    By any token of presumptuous suit,
    Nor would I have him till I do deserve him;
    Yet never know how that desert should be.
                                        (ll. 192–5)

The first statement is simply untrue; the second is quibbling if not meaningless. With that reservation, she goes on to make an eloquent and moving declaration of her feelings:

    Yet in this captious and inteemable sieve
    I still pour in the waters of my love
    And lack not to lose still. Thus, Indian-like,
    Religious in mine error, I adore
    The sun that looks upon his worshipper
    But knows of him no more. . . .
                        but if yourself,
    Whose aged honour cites a virtuous youth,
    Did ever, in so true a flame of liking,
    Wish chastely and love dearly, that your Dian
    Was both herself and love – O then, give pity . . .
                                        (ll. 197–208)

This is fine; but it does rest on deception – and Helena does not know that the Countess knows that:

> Had you not lately an intent – speak truly –
> To go to Paris?
> *Helena.*   Madam, I had.
> *Countess.*   Wherefore? tell true.
>   (ll. 213–14)

So a bit more is squeezed out of her. She can and does easily tell true about her hope to cure the King, but she does not tell the whole truth – that she plans to use that to trap Bertram. And that, the Countess does not extract.

The scene is brilliant in its gradual exposure of reticence; and brilliant too in the final incompleteness of the exposure (it subsequently emerges that the Countess assumes the catching of Bertram; but not here). It establishes a dramatic strategy as distinctive of the play as its characteristic language: of trap, and forced exposure. Bertram is trapped into marriage with Helena and exposes his vulgarity in the unguarded snobbery of his resentment (not in the fact of it). He is trapped by Diana into giving her his ring; she, like the Countess, has information she does not reveal:

> *Diana.*   Give me that ring.
> *Bertram.*
>   I'll lend it thee, my dear, but have no power
>   To give it from me.
> *Diana.*   Will you not, my lord?
> *Bertram.*
>   It is an honour 'longing to our house,
>   Bequeathed down from many ancestors,
>   Which were the greatest obloquy i'th'world
>   In me to lose.
> *Diana.*   Mine honour's such a ring;
>   My chastity's the jewel of our house,
>   Bequeathed down from many ancestors,
>   Which were the greatest obloquy i'th'world
>   In me to lose. Thus your own proper wisdom
>   Brings in the champion Honour on my part
>   Against your vain assault.
> *Bertram.*   Here, take my ring...

Diana.
> When midnight comes, knock at my chamber
> window ...   (IV, ii, 39–54)

He's caught by his lust and her skill; and she is immediately brisk with practical details. It is not wholly surprising that he takes her for a common gamester.

That is followed by the most extended of the trap scenes, the exposure of Parolles, in which Bertram plays his part on the other side. Parolles, made a fool of, becomes a self-acknowledged fool – which is wiser than Bertram. It thus gives him the position to make some apt comments:

> Who cannot be crush'd with a plot?
>   (IV, iii, 314)

and so to the passage I quoted before, concluding

>   Simply the thing I am
> Shall make me live.

and

> Rust, sword; cool, blushes; and Parolles live
> Safest in shame; being fool'd, by fool'ry thrive.
> There's place and means for every man alive.
> I'll after them.   (ll. 319–29)

The control of tone is perfect: out of context 'There's place and means for every man alive' could be a rich affirmation; in its place in this play it is an affirmation still, but deprived of its richness – defined in the sense of delimited.

It shadows perfectly the final exposure – of Bertram and Diana – the brilliant last scene. At the start, Bertram's disclaimer that his ring was ever Helena's is – so far as it goes – honest enough. But, confronted with Diana's claims, his tone changes disastrously:

> My Lord, this is a fond and desp'rate creature
> Whom sometime I have laugh'd with. Let your
>   highness
> Lay a more noble thought upon mine honour
> Than for to think that I would sink it here.
>   (v, iii, 177–80)

The lie is cheap, and the echo of his reaction to Helena in act II is a sharp irony. Further pressed, he becomes nastier and even more transparent:

Diana.   Good my lord,
  Ask him upon his oath if he does think
  He had not my virginity.
King.
  What say'st thou to her?
Bertram.   She's impudent, my lord,
  And was a common gamester to the camp.
Diana.
  He does me wrong, my lord; if I were so
  He might have bought me at a common price.
                                    (ll. 183–9)

She is cool enough to catch him logically, and so – like Helena with the Countess, but far more discreditably – he is gradually forced to yield bit by bit of the truth:

King.   She hath that ring of yours.
Bertram.
  I think she has. Certain it is I lik'd her
  And boarded her i'th'wanton way of youth.
  She knew her distance and did angle for me,
  Madding my eagerness with her restraint,
  As all impediments in fancy's course
  Are motives of more fancy; and in fine
  Her inf'nite cunning with her modern grace
  Subdu'd me to her rate; she got the ring,
  And I had that which any inferior might
  At market-price have bought.   (ll. 208–18)

That is still unpleasant and it is still untrue; but it is now what he may plausibly think (given the blind arrogance of the young male). It does have an effective reflex on the cunning with which Diana is now behaving. Under still further pressure he comes a shade, but only a shade, cleaner:

  My lord, I do confess the ring was hers.

on which the King comments aptly:

  You boggle shrewdly; every feather starts you.
                                    (ll. 230–1)

Bertram is exposed, sharply and precisely,

but he does not reach the acceptance of folly which gave Parolles a kind of inverted dignity, partly because he is not a fool in that sense, and chiefly because the final trap is not yet sprung. That is achieved via the less expected tenting of Diana. She, like Bertram, is caught with a ring she should not have (it is notable that we may probably get confused about which ring is which, but never about the degree of truth in anyone's words). Where he blustered, she takes to riddling:

King.
  This ring you say was yours?
Diana.   Ay, my good lord.
King.
  Where did you buy it? Or who gave it you?
Diana.
  It was not given me, nor I did not buy it.
King.
  Who lent it you?
Diana.   It was not lent me neither.
King.
  Where did you find it then?
Diana.   I found it not.
King.
  If it were yours by none of all these ways
  How could you give it him?
Diana.   I never gave it him.
Lafew.
  This woman's an easy glove, my lord; she goes off
  and on at pleasure.   (ll. 264–72)

and after further exchanges, the King comments:

  I think thee now some common customer.
                                    (l. 280)

Diana is partly protected by our knowledge that she is not a prostitute (as Bertram was condemned by our knowledge that he was a liar), but the mistake does recall the equivocal tone of her first appearance with her mother and friends to watch the soldiers go by and gaze on the handsome French count who is soliciting her:

Widow. Nay, come; for if they do approach the city, we shall lose all the sight.

Diana. They say the French count has done most honourable service.

Widow. It is reported that he has taken their great'st commander, and that with his own hand he slew the duke's brother. [*Tucket*] We have lost our labour; they are gone a contrary way. Hark! You may know by their trumpets.

Mariana. Come, let's return again and suffice ourselves with the report of it. Well, Diana, take heed of this French earl; the honour of a maid is her name, and no legacy is so rich as honesty.

Widow. I have told my neighbour how you have been solicited by a gentleman his companion.

(III, v, 1–15)

This has more to do with the name of honesty than the fact, as Diana remains a virgin more in fact than spirit. The conventional wisdom leaves the chattering ladies more than half inclined to accept the suit. Diana's name alludes to the goddess, but it is not she; just as Helena's name (altered from the source) has ironic reference to the mythical heroine, stressed in Lavatch's bawdy song about Helen of Troy:

> Among nine bad if one be good,
> There's yet one good in ten.
>
> (I, iii, 75–6)

Diana's false position at last precipitates the dénouement, Helena's re-appearance:

King.   Is there no exorcist
Beguiles the truer office of mine eyes?
Is't real that I see?
Helena.   No, my good lord;
'Tis but the shadow of a wife you see;
The name and not the thing.
Bertram.   Both, both. O pardon!

(V, iii, 298–302)

Bertram is finally crush'd with a plot, forced to a plain concession. But he recovers enough for a notorious last couplet:

> If she, my liege, can make me know this clearly
> I'll love her dearly, ever, ever dearly.
>
> (ll. 309–10)

I said 'recovers' advisedly: the flattened affir-

mation restores something of the false confidence with which Bertram began this scene, assuring the King of his love for Lafew's daughter; still more, its double (feminine?) rhymes recall the equally awful couplet in which Bertram declared his faith to Diana:

> Say thou art mine, and ever
> My love as it begins shall so persever.
>
> (IV, ii, 36–7)

That flat last couplet (so obviously not an accident) focuses the double nature of the scene. Helena's re-appearance is in one dimension the fairy tale miracle which it appears to the King; but it does not at all so appear to us who know precisely the trick by which it has been devised; hence in its other dimension it is severely naturalistic, the springing of the final trap. The end of *The Winter's Tale* has similar dimensions – a magical resurrection for which a naturalistic explanation can be perceived – but there the proportions are completely reversed: the miraculous is celebrated, and the naturalistic possibility hardly articulated.

The ending here is therefore right for the dominant tone of the play, the limiting and very precise application of a naturalistic vision to a magical motif. My account so far has concentrated almost exclusively on the linguistic and dramatic means for presenting that, and I need now to look at how the romance is established, and how the two are related; for they used to be regarded as merely incongruous and evidence of different dates of composition, which is surely a mistake.

In a sense, of course, the romance structure does not need so much establishing. Folk-tale motifs were doubtless familiar in ballads and oral tradition, and they had been material for the stage at least since Peele's *Old Wives' Tale* and Greene's plays, to say nothing of Shakespeare's earlier comedies. What *All's Well* does, is to take that familiar material and look at it in a very unfamiliar way. The effect seems to me closely analogous to that of the early religious paintings of Caravaggio; indeed, to one in particular, a fairly small picture of Mary Magdalene in the Doria Gallery in Rome (Plate I). It shows a young servant girl in a nice dress sitting on a kitchen chair in a room that is otherwise totally bare. Her hands are loosely in her lap, her head drooping, perhaps sleepy, pensive, or sad – or all three. There are a few sharply observed objects scattered casually on the floor: a jar of wine, not quite full, two broken gold neck-chains, a torn pearl necklace. At first sight it seems to be a purely naturalistic study of a genre-type more Dutch than Roman. You might even suspect that the title had been added in pious error to a purely secular painting. I did consider that when I first saw it, and found it rather dull. But I was quite wrong. In fact, the nice dress is far too nice; the servant girl appears to be Cinderella after the ball, before her clothes turn back to tatters. And in fact her dress, like her hair, is reddish gold, iconographically traditional for the Magdalene (as are at least some of the objects on the floor).

What Caravaggio has done is to take the familiar iconography and view it with a wholly unfamiliar naturalism, which projects an entirely new image. His Mary is neither crude whore nor glorious saint, but a quiet and plausible girl, very much alone. Once that is seen the painting becomes extraordinarily interesting; and its interest is generated, not by the naturalism alone, but by the juxtaposition of that with the traditional mythology. That is almost exactly the achievement I am attributing to Shakespeare in *All's Well*: not a simple naturalism, but a consistently naturalistic presentation of traditional romance magic. Caravaggio's paintings were frequently rejected by ecclesiastical patrons; they shocked then and, interestingly, they are still startling now. So is *All's Well*.

The equivalent, I suppose, of Caravaggio's iconographic detail, is the romance plot of *All's Well*; it is that which is treated natural-

istically. The 'story' is both anticipated and expounded with exceptional clarity and skill, and some of the ways in which that is done have been well analysed by Joseph Price in *The Unfortunate Comedy*;[1] they have been implicit in most of what I have said. But the problem is not what story, but what kind of story, is to be anticipated. Naturalistic language proposes a naturalistic story, and since it is not that at all, it needs another form to mark the difference and to sustain the possibility of non-naturalistic developments. This is done by the couplets into which Helena moves at the end of I, i, and which she uses generally (not exclusively) through her progress to Paris, Florence, and back to Rosillion. They used to be the chief evidence of early composition though it has been recognized that they are not 'early' in form or language. That is certainly true. The language is necessarily slightly less close to speech, but only slightly: it remains generally plain, and the sentence structure most often cuts. across the verse structure, resisting its rhythm as much as it does that of the blank verse.

> Our remedies oft in ourselves do lie,
> Which we ascribe to heaven; the fated sky
> Gives us free scope; only doth backward pull
> Our slow designs when we ourselves are dull.
>
> (I, i, 212–15)

It does incline more towards balanced antithesis,

> What power is it which mounts my love so high,
> That makes me see, and cannot feed mine eye?
> The mightiest space in fortune nature brings
> To join like likes, and kiss like native things.
>
> (ll. 216–19)

but in that it only intensifies one characteristic of the prose I discussed in the opening dialogue between Lafew and the Countess.

That prose should be seen, therefore, as

[1] Toronto and Liverpool, 1968.

17

setting a common ground from which the languages of the play can develop: extend it in one direction and you arrive at 'What was he like? I have forgot him', and beyond that Lavatch's cynical bluntness; in another direction you reach riddles, Helena's couplets, or Parolles's affected prose. Either way the development is not very far: the sense of tight control, of modified contrast, of language always related to a common ground, is singularly strong in this play. The restraint is felt in any of the forms of development. Parolles, as people often remark, is not Falstaff; nor is Lavatch quite Touchstone – nor Thersites neither. Though like Thersites, his cynicism expresses a view we might adopt if it were not that it is *he* who expresses it: from that we rebound to a more exact appreciation. Both fools, Lavatch and Parolles, are held within the play's governing tone, just as the blank verse does not soar nor the couplets resonate. In each case the possibilities are glimpsed but restricted. The naturalism imposes a calculated frustration on responses we would like to indulge.

Nonetheless the opposed developments make a sufficiently marked contrast, most conspicuously between Helena's two soliloquies in I, i. The first, in blank verse, I have already discussed: it seems, briefly, to take us inside her, to reveal what makes her tick. The revelation is shown to be incomplete, but it is still revelation, and almost unique in the play; only Parolles's few lines after his exposure come near it; Bertram never reveals himself directly at all – he gives himself away, which is another thing; what he is, or could learn to be, is necessarily enigmatic. Helena's second soliloquy is the couplet speech I have quoted, and it is quite different in effect from her first. It shuts us out, and firmly resists another indulgence we are given to expecting, of sharing the secrets of a character's soul. Helena gives away much (not all) to the Countess; a little to the King, and after that virtually nothing at all. The play depends on exposure, and therefore not on self-revelation. The reticence has another aspect here, insisting on impenetrable surfaces, and the couplets function primarily as barrier. They make the plot develop almost independently of the personalities enacting it.

They are therefore supremely important in what I take to be the play's most difficult achievement, relating naturalism to 'romance'. The form that should take is already recognizable in blank verse in the star image, offering an expansion immediately restricted by its social reference. The fullest development comes with the court scenes of the sickness and cure of the King.

He is said to have a fistula,[1] but of what kind, where, and what its effects are is left vague. When Bertram first arrives at court he is welcomed with reminiscences of his father:

> Would I were with him! He would always say –
> Methinks I hear him now; his plausive words
> He scatter'd not in ears, but grafted them
> To grow there and to bear – 'Let me not live',
> (This his good melancholy oft began
> On the catastrophe and heel of pastime,
> When it was out) 'Let me not live', quoth he,
> 'After my flame lacks oil, to be the snuff
> Of younger spirits . . .'   (I, ii, 52–60)

in other words, with a hangover he was afraid of old age and impotence. That seems to be Lafew's diagnosis of the King in II, i:

> But, my good lord, 'tis thus: will you be cur'd
> Of your infirmity?
> *King*.   No.
> *Lafew*.   O, will you eat
> No grapes, my royal fox? Yes, but you will
> My noble grapes, and if my royal fox
> Could reach them. I have seen a medicine
> That's able to breathe life into a stone,

[1] Hunter quotes Bucknill to the effect that the word was not so specific then as now, though a rectal abscess would fit well enough.

Quicken a rock, and make you dance canary
With sprightly fire and motion; whose simple
  touch
Is powerful to araise King Pippen, nay,
To give great Charlemain a pen in's hand
And write to her a love-line.

> (II, i, 67–77)

Exactly what the point of King Pippen is the notes don't tell us, but a bawdy sense is fairly obvious. So is Lafew's excited hope that Helena's sexual attractions – 'Doctor she' – will revive the King's spirits.

When he does consent to see her, she offers first her father's medical knowledge; then, as couplets take over from blank verse, she can hint at other powers. The first is divine:

> He that of greatest works is finisher
> Oft does them by the weakest minister.

> (ll. 135–6)

She expands on that and then proceeds to another kind of power:

> The greatest Grace lending grace,
> Ere twice the horses of the sun shall bring
> Their fiery coacher his diurnal ring,
> Ere twice in murk and occidental damp
> Moist Hesperus hath quench'd her sleepy lamp,
> Or four and twenty times the pilot's glass
> Hath told the thievish minutes how they pass,
> What is infirm from your sound parts shall fly,
> Health shall live free and sickness freely die.

> (ll. 159–67)

The invocation is now a pagan incantation, and suggests the form of a magic spell, which the couplets can readily do.

The King is persuaded to try, what by he does not say – and what she actually does we do not know, since it is offstage. Total ambiguity is thus set up and maintained. In scene iii Lafew opens (in prose) with the obvious comment:

> They say miracles are past.

> (II, iii, 1)

In this play they probably are; yet the King is cured; and his entry is greeted by Lafew's excited cry:

> Lustique, as the Dutchman says. I'll like a maid the better whilst I have a tooth in my head. Why, he's able to lead her a coranto.

> (ll. 41–3)

The last, as the first, suggestion is of sexual arousal, and the scene moves coherently into Helena's choosing of a mate, at once suggestive of Cressida kissing the Greek generals, and yet characteristically less explicit. Whatever cured the King, Bertram's resistance to the enforced marriage and the King's anger at him make no reference to Divine intervention.

So we are left with hints at four different explanations; hints rather than affirmations precisely as the couplets are couplets but not fully resonant. It may be drugs, or miracle, or magic – or it may simply be sexual response (miracle or magic in nature). And in that ambiguity, and in the use of verse, the necessary relationship between naturalism and romance potential is very subtly established. It could not be done without couplets; yet they are not allowed to over-ride the dominance of naturalism.

That may seem to be baffling: I think it does depend on familiarity with the forms of romance thus insinuated but not developed. It would be easy to claim the Elizabethans had such a familiarity and that we have not. But in truth we still have. Fairy stories of various kinds are still common to the vast majority of children; and if the quantity has been reduced as well as the quality become less grim, the appetite emerges in adult cults for the dubiously adult fantasies of Tolkien or C. S. Lewis. No doubt we have not such an exact equivalent for the experience Shakespeare invokes as his own audience would have understood; but a similar point can be made about all his plays. It is, I think, entirely sufficient for this play, as it is for others. Agnostic viewers bred in a Christian tradition, however ignorant of the

Bible, can still be startled by Caravaggio's paintings. So can we be startled by *All's Well*. Conventional contemporaries mistook Caravaggio for an atheist; more perceptive minds (cardinals, as well as painters like Rubens) understood otherwise. It is a narrow criticism which understands *All's Well* as a mere negation of romance. Caravaggio only indicates the religious values he assumes behind his naturalistic treatment; Shakespeare only indicates the values of fiction, which are also those of imagination, which he assumes behind *his* naturalistic treatment. In fact, he indicates rather more fully than Caravaggio, but only as a play has more need to than a painting. In the cure of the King he does it explicitly, however guardedly; there are hints too of another mythology in the names of Helena and Diana; later in the play, it is always implicit in the use of couplets (especially between Helena and the Florentine ladies). It is implicit too in the bed-trick which is teasingly pitched between a folk-tale game and a naturalistic joke. And it is implicit still for nearly the whole of the final scene, which is in motif the testing of the hero, the virtue of the maiden, and the restoration to life of the heroine; but is seen as the exposure of Bertram, the equivocation of Diana, and the stage-management of Helena. The final lines enunciate the romance potential directly, but necessarily minimally, and the apt comment is left to Lafew:

> Mine eyes smell onions; I shall weep anon.
> Good Tom Drum, lend me a handkercher.
>
> (v, iii, 314-15)

I have already claimed for this play a distinctive and very distinguished language. I also think that, so far from being a play that falls apart, it has a controlled unity of a kind rare even in Shakespeare. Its unity is conditioned by its tone; by the refusal ever to let it move beyond the limits which that defines.

In that too it resembles Caravaggio: after nearly a century of mannerist variety, his paintings were a shock not only in their naturalism but also in their insistent singularity of vision. Shakespeare started as a mannerist writer: *The Two Gentlemen of Verona* is a gallimaufry with an altogether surprising last act; *Love's Labour's Lost* is explicit about its disrupted dénouement; even *As You Like It*, though it has its own unity, contrives it out of a series of 'turns', like a controlled variety show. *All's Well*, by contrast with these, has on its surface (and it is very much concerned with surfaces) an insistent singularity of vision that is unique.

I can only guess how it might work on the stage. I believe it could, but I have only seen it once,[1] and then it was tricked out in late seventeenth-century style like an odd version of *The Three Musketeers*. Tyrone Guthrie's productions sound as though he deployed all his skills to turn it into the play Shaw wished he'd written. It needs, no doubt, more trust than treatment; its language would surely guide sensitive actresses and actors into a satisfactory number of interesting roles, though they are as severely disciplined as the play itself. But although I believe it could work and be very sharply interesting as well as uncomfortably amusing, I do not suppose it would be exactly 'popular'. Its vision resists too consistently our will to indulgence, whether in sentiment, magic, or psychological identification. Caravaggio, I think, faced the problem that he could not expand on the religious themes to which his paintings allude, and in his last works he explored some curious ways of overcoming that. So did Shakespeare. *All's Well* I take to be a superb achievement in its own terms; but also to be limited by them. It is often said to be a twin play with *Measure for Measure*, but they are certainly not identical

[1] At Stratford, England, in 1955.

twins. The later play is more articulate about its themes because it is not committed to the linguistic unity of *All's Well*: it employs varied and strongly contrasted forms of language. So it does not depend on traps for exposure so much as confrontations, both of people and their several languages. Thus it arrives at Isabella's 'Man proud man, dressed in a little brief authority', or the Duke's 'Be absolute for death,' or Claudio's 'Ay, but to die and go we know not where,/To lie in cold obstruction and to rot' – all of them forms of eloquence impossible in *All's Well*. Technically, they are very different plays. The last plays are more remote still, for they invert the relations of naturalism and romance, obtruding extreme improbability, and giving it surprising local possibility. So, for instance, the motif of the bed-trick reaches its final variation in *Cymbeline*: not with Jachimo's visit where (almost as an in-joke?) it does not take place, but with Cloten's decapitated body dressed in Posthumus's clothes and (as Cloten had claimed) so resembling Posthumus that Imogen feels it and faints upon it. That is marvellously grotesque and therefore the opposite of *All's Well* whose naturalism precludes anything of the kind.

I make these comparisons primarily to identify the uniqueness of *All's Well*, secondarily to place its peculiar achievement and the limitation inherent in that. I do not expect to convince anyone of all my claims, and that is why I made my title out of the scepticism of the play's: for better and for worse, all's well that ends well.

1. *All's Well That Ends Well*, Act I, scene iii. Helena (Zoë Caldwell) tells the Countess (Edith Evans) of her love for Bertram. Directed by Tyrone Guthrie, 1959.

2. *All's Well That Ends Well*, Act II, scene iii. Helena (Joyce Redman) makes her choice among the Lords in the presence of the King of France (Alan Webb). Directed by Noel Willman, 1955.

3. *All's Well That Ends Well*, Act II, scene iii. Lafeu (Brewster Mason) and Parolles (Clive Swift). Directed by John Barton, 1967.

4. *All's Well That Ends Well*, Act III, scene v. Watching the army pass by: above, the Widow (Angela Baddeley), Mariana (Mavis Edwards); below, the Neighbour (Diana Rigg), Helena (Zoë Caldwell) and Diana (Priscilla Morgan). Directed by Tyrone Guthrie, 1959.

5. *All's Well That Ends Well*, Act IV, scene iii. The unmasking of Parolles (Cyril Luckham). Directed by Tyrone Guthrie, 1959.

6. *All's Well That Ends Well*, Act v, scene iii. Bertram (Edward de Souza) kneels before Helena (Zoë Caldwell), with the Countess (Edith Evans), the King of France (Robert Hardy), the Widow (Angela Baddeley) and Diana (Priscilla Morgan). Directed by Tyrone Guthrie, 1959.

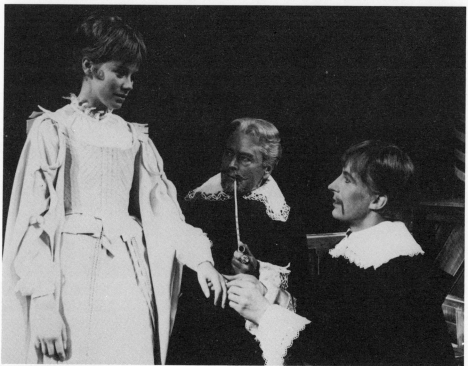

7. *All's Well That Ends Well*, Act v, scene iii. Bertram (Ian Richardson) kneels before Helena (Estelle Kohler), with the King of France (Sebastian Shaw). Directed by John Barton, 1967.

THE DESIGN OF
'ALL'S WELL THAT ENDS WELL'

R. L. SMALLWOOD

All's Well that Ends Well is not an entirely successful work. Its problems have been discussed at length and its shortcomings pointed out, sometimes with little compassion. From Dr Johnson, who could not reconcile his heart to Bertram,[1] to the late Poet Laureate, who found Helena 'a woman who practises a borrowed art, not for art's sake, nor for charity, but, woman fashion, for a selfish end',[2] its principal characters have seemed to critics inadequate or disturbing. Even the first editor of this journal found that the 'kindest thing' he could do with *All's Well that Ends Well* was to suggest that it was 'penned by Shakespeare in a time of illness or mental disturbance'.[3] And yet its two most recent Stratford productions have been surprisingly well received,[4] and it contains, in Helena, what Coleridge called Shakespeare's 'loveliest character',[5] and, in the Countess, Bernard Shaw's idea of 'the most beautiful old woman's part ever written'.[6] This mixture of undoubted success and apparent failure is familiar, of course, in that play with which *All's Well that Ends Well* is often linked, *Measure for Measure*. But while the problems of *Measure for Measure* seem, to some extent at least, to be imposed by Shakespeare himself – he it is who makes Isabella a novice, adds Mariana to the characters he inherited from Whetstone, and imports the bed-trick – those which remain in *All's Well that Ends Well* are fundamental to the story Shakespeare has chosen to dramatise.

All's Well that Ends Well has only one known source, the story of Giletta of Narbonne, the ninth story of the third day of Boccaccio's *Decameron* which Shakespeare found translated in William Painter's *The Palace of Pleasure* (1566 and 1575).[7] This short and sharply-focused tale concentrates exclusively on the ingenuity and determination of the heroine, Giletta, in her securing of the marriage to Beltramo which she desires, and then on her

[1] *The Yale Edition of the Works of Samuel Johnson*, vols. VII and VIII, *Johnson on Shakespeare*, edited by Arthur Sherbo (New Haven, Connecticut, 1968), VII, 404.

[2] John Masefield, *William Shakespeare* (London, 1911), p. 148.

[3] Allardyce Nicoll, *Shakespeare* (London, 1952), p. 116.

[4] It was produced at Stratford in 1959 by Sir Tyrone Guthrie, and in 1967 by John Barton. Joseph Price, the most comprehensive and sensitive critic of *All's Well that Ends Well*, records that the audience 'reacted with ... delight' to Guthrie's production, though admittedly the play was extensively cut (Lavatch disappeared altogether) and much comic business was added (*The Unfortunate Comedy: A Study of 'All's Well that Ends Well' and its Critics* (Liverpool, 1968), pp. 57ff.). I am indebted to Mr Price's excellent book at many points in this essay. He wrote too soon to deal with the Barton production; this offered a much fuller text (though one or two scenes were rearranged) and a more inclusive response to the play's varieties of mood. It was enthusiastically received throughout the season, and later televised.

[5] *Coleridge's Shakespeare Criticism*, edited by T. M. Raysor, 2 vols. (London, 1930), II, 113.

[6] *Shaw on Shakespeare*, edited by Edwin Wilson (London, 1961), p. 10.

[7] My quotations and references are from the text in *Narrative and Dramatic Sources of Shakespeare*, edited by Geoffrey Bullough, vol. II (London, 1958), pp. 389–96.

winning, through further resourcefulness and cunning, his recognition and acceptance of her as his wife. Its narrative speed and attack make it an amusing ten-minute read. But the details of its plot are responsible for many of Shakespeare's difficulties in the play. Indeed it is fair to say that some of the critics' complaints about *All's Well that Ends Well* are above all objections to the narrative material with which Shakespeare is working: Beltramo deserves Dr Johnson's censure for being noble without generosity more than Bertram does, and the vigorously determined selfishness of Giletta is throughout more worthy of the late Mr Masefield's rebukes than ever Helena is. A comparison of the play with its source reveals at every turn the dramatist's care to present the story and its principal characters in as mellow and engaging a light as possible, to give them a dramatic plausibility and a dignity which are entirely absent from the source, and, finally, to bring the story to a conclusion infinitely more moving and more human than that of Boccaccio's simple, vigorous tale. To these ends Shakespeare invents new characters, makes several telling modifications to the plot, greatly develops the hero and heroine, and turns the ending almost upside down. I want to examine these four general aspects of the play and their relationship to the source story, and to suggest some of the ways in which Shakespeare has wrested his successes from what may be rather intractable material for drama. The bones of the source remain at times perhaps too discernible, notably in some of the scenes in Florence in acts III and IV, and, it is sometimes suggested, in the rather abrupt dismissal from our contemplation at the end of the play of the newly reconciled hero and heroine. But Shakespeare's economy in these scenes is also based, I think, on the care he has taken with the adaptation of his source: the strength of characterisation and the dramatic impetus he has achieved in the surrounding parts of the play may be enough,

in performance, to enable the audience to accept scenes that provide little more than the essential development of the plot, but provide it rapidly and succinctly.

The new characters Shakespeare adds or develops in dramatising the story of Giletta of Narbonne form two groups: the older generation and the comics. There is no older generation in Boccaccio's story, except for some rather shadowy 'kinsfolk' of Giletta, and the King of France, whose function in the plot is simply mechanical – he exists to be cured of his fistula and to force Beltramo to marry Giletta. The patient, wise, and gentle trio of the Countess, Lafeu, and the King are entirely Shakespeare's invention. The context of mellow understanding and support which they provide for the awkwardness and sorrows of the youthful characters is a significant element in the overall effect. And their poignant reflectiveness creates also that feeling of autumnal calm which is so precious a part of the mood of *All's Well that Ends Well*. But more immediate to the question of Shakespeare's methods in adapting his source is that all these new and sympathetic characters (and I include the King as a 'new' character, for his role is so much fuller than in Painter) voice, movingly, their affection for Helena, support her in her quest, and direct the audience towards approval of her actions. At the same time they comment on the folly of Bertram's behaviour while still showing themselves ready to make allowances for the misdeeds of youth. The older generation provides the background of sympathy and understanding against which the problems and sufferings of youth can be explored and resolved.

The attitude of the older characters to Helena is consistently used by Shakespeare to guide the reactions of the audience. Helena, like Giletta, is the principal agent in the plot; but unlike Giletta, her actions are accompanied by a commentary of approving remarks and explanations from a group of characters which Shakespeare seems to have invented for just this purpose. The King discerns in her language the voice of 'some blessed spirit' and feels that she possesses 'Youth, beauty, wisdom, courage – all / That happiness and prime can happy call' (II, i, 180).[1] Lafeu, from feeling that her looks could 'breathe life into a stone, / Quicken a rock, and make you dance canary' (II, i, 72–3), goes on to warn us, from the evidence of what he sees of Helena, that the age of miracles is not past (II, iii, 1); and he is heard, towards the end of the play, wistfully describing her: ''Twas a good lady; 'twas a good lady. We may pick a thousand sallets ere we light on such another herb' (IV, v, 13–14). Above all through the gentle graciousness of the Countess, Shakespeare guides our sympathy and affection towards Helena. From her early tributes in the first scene – 'she derives her honesty and achieves her goodness' (l. 42) – to her carefully stated 'epitaph' before the denouement – 'the most virtuous gentlewoman that ever nature had praise for creating. If she had partaken of my flesh and cost me the dearest groans of a mother I could not have owed her a more rooted love' (IV, v, 9–12) – the Countess never ceases to focus our approval on Helena.

Shakespeare, then, through this group of older characters not provided by his source, seeks to create sympathy and affection for Helena, and approval of her quest. They have led some critics, however, to see the play in terms of a 'youth versus age' conflict. Clifford Leech, for example, writes that it 'shows us old and young characters juxtaposed, with the old rebuking the young and sighing at the present corruption of manners. On the one side the King, the Countess, Lafeu, the dead fathers of Bertram and Helena; on the other Bertram and Parolles.'[2] It is significant that the names he sets down in the scroll of youth are only two, the comic villain and his dupe. Yet Helena, with all the marks of ardent, hopeful youth upon

her, achieves throughout the play a remarkable harmony with the older characters. In the third scene of act I, her interview with the Countess shows a touching sympathy of thought and purpose between them. 'Even so it was with me when I was young' (l. 123) is a remark from the old lady which suggests considerable understanding of the problems of youth. 'To be young again, if we could' she says to the clown a few scenes later (II, ii, 37), and goes on to demonstrate a delightful capacity to make the effort. In the scene of Bertram's arrival at the French Court (I, ii), one again sees the wholesome possibility of understanding between the generations. He is welcomed to court by the melancholy figure of the diseased King. Bertram is young, awkward, an 'unseason'd courtier', and he reminds the King of his father. The speech of reminiscence, of friendship in youth recollected in age and illness, is poignant and distressing. The King is surrounded by his lords; they begin the scene talking of the Italian war, and it would seem obvious to play these anonymous lords as the same individuals who later head south in search of military glory. Like Bertram they are full of the confidence of youth, but when the King's recollections bring on this melancholy mood, one of them is there with a moving reply. The King expresses the wish, since he brings home 'nor wax nor honey', that he might be 'dissolved from my hive, / To give some labourers room' (ll. 65–6). The anonymous lord's reply does

[1] My quotations and references are from the new Arden edition by G. K. Hunter (London, 1959).

[2] 'The Theme of Ambition in *All's Well that Ends Well*', *ELH*, 21 (1954), 17–29 (p. 20). There is in fact no real textual evidence of Parolles's youthfulness. Indeed his memories, or pretended memories, of previous service in the Italian wars (II, i, 40 ff.) and his presentation of himself to Diana as a man 'to mell with', in contrast to Bertram, a boy 'not to kiss' (IV, iii, 220), suggest that he should be played as visibly older than Bertram. Bertram's immaturity, of course, is crucial to the play's effect, as I suggest below.

not reason with him, or take up the argument in the terms in which he expresses it; it is a quiet statement: 'You're loved, sir.' It is simple but deeply understanding, and it should come, I feel sure, from a young actor.

Later in the play, the group of young French lords are in Florence, having just captured Parolles in order to expose him to Bertram. Shakespeare holds up the development of the plot for an extended dialogue between two of them (I, iii, 1–71) in which they comment on the behaviour of Bertram and Parolles. There is no question of this being the mean-spiritedness of crabbed age condemning the foibles of youth; these are young men, deliberately used by Shakespeare at this point to provide a commentary on the actions of misguided youth. And in so doing, these young men place themselves alongside the Countess, Lafeu, and the King, as well as Helena, in condemning Bertram's misdeeds while at the same time believing in his potential goodness. There is certainly a division of the play's characters into groups on the lines that Professor Leech and others have suggested, but the distinguishing marks of the parties are surely selfishness and generosity, or folly and goodness, rather than youth and age.

As the King leaves the stage at the end of the second scene, he requests the support of Bertram's arm for his old, frail body, worn out 'with several applications' (l. 74), and he welcomes him again: 'My son's no dearer.' The possibility of harmony and peace between the generations is here strongly felt. In the interview between Helena and the Countess in the scene that follows, we see it achieved. As Bertram and the King leave the stage, Bertram supporting his monarch, we may remember the King's earlier admonition as he remarked on Bertram's physical likeness to his father: 'Thy father's moral parts / Mayest thou inherit too!' (I, ii, 21–2). The capacity of Bertram to fulfil this wish takes the whole play to establish. With the hope of its fulfilment provided at the end of the last scene comes the establishment of total harmony between the generations, comically picked up in the reconciliation of Parolles and his most vigorous mocker, Lafeu. The power of the young to give love and re-creation to the old is vividly seen in *All's Well that Ends Well*: the King is cured by Helena, the Countess responds wholeheartedly to the ardour of Helena's love, Lafeu's sympathy is awakened by the plight of Parolles. In his invention and development of this older group of characters Shakespeare has added a depth to the play far removed from anything in Painter's translation of Boccaccio's story.

As well as this group of older characters, Shakespeare has also added two comedians to his source material, Parolles and Lavatch. Parolles, in the years when *All's Well that Ends Well* was being staged in Garrick's version as a broad, farcical comedy, was the secret of the rather short-lived success it enjoyed.[1] King Charles I had earlier made clear his idea of the play's centre of interest by jotting 'Monsieur Parolles' as an alternative to the title in the royal copy of the Second Folio. Some more recent critics have been much sterner about Monsieur Parolles, who is seen as Bertram's wicked angel, as the counterweight to Helena in the morality scheme of the play. There is something of this pattern in the background no doubt, but to exaggerate it is to ignore the fact that Parolles is constantly and consistently funny. Without any of the loading that Garrick's text gave to the part, Clive Swift, in John Barton's 1967 Stratford production, made the audience laugh a great deal: one remembers especially his mimicry of Lafeu at the beginning of act II, scene iii – 'so say I too'; the mock duel that followed this; and, perhaps above all, the comic soliloquy of self-knowledge after his pretended valour has made him venture too far:

[1] See Price, *The Unfortunate Comedy*, pp. 3–22.

What the devil should move me to undertake the recovery of this drum, being not ignorant of the impossibility, and knowing I had no such purpose? I must give myself some hurts, and say I got them in exploit; yet slight ones will not carry it . . . And great ones I dare not give. (IV, i, 34–40)

The interesting technique following this speech, in which the so-called asides of the listening lords are apparently heard by Parolles and used in his soliloquising, which reads rather oddly, worked brilliantly in the theatre.

Parolles, then, is genuinely comic. And Parolles, wicked angel so-called, is also accepted at the end by Lafeu his sternest critic, and takes a full share in the final forgiveness and joy. Shakespeare seems to have invented Parolles to provide a context for Bertram's follies, and a parallel to them on a baser level. He is an alternative to Helena, but not quite on the rigid morality level that has sometimes been urged. The joint plan of Bertram and Parolles to steal away to the Italian war after the King has refused them permission to go openly (II, i, 29–34) seems at first like little more than the escapade of naughty schoolboys. Parolles is certainly the 'tempter' here, though Bertram is quick on the uptake. Shakespeare carefully places the idea well before the enforced marriage to Helena, and before Bertram has any notion of the existence of such a possibility. This is a deliberate and important departure from the source story, in which Beltramo, after the marriage, 'praied licence to retourne to his countrye to consummate the mariage. And when he was on horsebacke hee went not thither but toke his journey into Tuscane' (p. 392). By thus bringing forward Bertram's decision to go to Italy, and making it dependent on his desire for honour and his envy of the freedom of his fellow courtiers, Shakespeare makes Bertram's behaviour less painful, and ultimately more forgivable. One sees him anxious not to lose face here, and Parolles, whose 'face' is of course his sole fortune, care-

fully encourages this attitude. From this partnership in high, if misguided, spirits, they drift into stupidity, unkindness, selfishness, and finally sin in the attempted seduction of Diana. Always Parolles's actions provide a reflection of Bertram's – even to the extent of his comic attempt, behind his master's back, to deflect the Florentine lady's interest towards himself. Parolles, and Bertram's attraction for him, are no more than the symptom of what is wrong with Bertram – his shallowness, his unthinking carelessness, and lack of thought for others. Shakespeare has paralleled their courses most deliberately in the exposure that each undergoes. That Parolles is not the wicked angel responsible for leading Bertram astray is vividly shown in the final scene where, long after he has been made to see his companion for what he is, Bertram goes on to show himself independently capable of his most objectionable behaviour, in that long demonstration of weakness, cowardice, and lying. There is a good deal of surface similarity in the two exposure scenes: both Bertram and Parolles are ruthlessly stripped of their covering of unmerited honour, and in their increasingly frantic efforts to avoid disaster, each shows himself capable of promising anything, however false or impossible. Parolles betrays his comrades to his comrades, Bertram betrays himself to his friends, his family, and above all to himself. Both of these scenes are carefully arranged and stage-managed, the first by the young lords, the second by Helena, working through Diana. There is one important difference between them, however, and it gives an indication of Shakespeare's purposes in his invention of the role of Parolles and the comic subplot. The exposure of Parolles is funny; the exposure of Bertram is painful. The reasons for this are indicated by those enormously useful anonymous lords.[1] Alone, looking for the

[1] Two of them are later (IV, iii, 171 ff.) named as the Dumaine brothers, and the complication of the speech

drum and 'not ignorant of the impossibility' of finding it, Parolles is overheard by his exposers. One of them comments succinctly: 'Is it possible he should know what he is, and be that he is?' (IV, i, 44). The answer of course is yes, as the exposure itself proves. Utterly humiliated in front of those he has sought throughout to impress, Parolles has a self-knowledge that makes him resilient:

> If my heart were great
> 'Twould burst at this. Captain I'll be no more,
> But I will eat and drink and sleep as soft
> As captain shall. Simply the thing I am
> Shall make me live . . .
> There's place and means for every man alive.
> I'll after them.   (IV, iii, 319–29)

And because this is a comedy and not a morality play, there is, as we see in the final reconciliation with Lafeu, 'place and means', 'drink and sleep', for him. During that blindfold scene of his exposure to Bertram, protected from any danger of over-seriousness by the frequent intrusion of the mumbo-jumbo of the 'choughs' language', Parolles piles outrageous disloyalty on to stupendous insult, from the comical precision of the military information he gives away, accompanied by the broad-minded offer to take the sacrament on it 'how and which way you will' (IV, iii, 133), to the vivid observation that Dumaine will steal 'an egg out of a cloister' (l. 241). It is a theatrical performance of great brilliance, one in which he 'hath out-villain'd villainy so far that the rarity redeems him' (l. 264) – which of course it does. Though Parolles *is* a fool and a knave, as Lafeu tells him again in the penultimate scene, we are content that he 'shall eat' and be on hand at the end to provide Lafeu with a 'handkercher', and with the prospect of making sport with him at home. Bertram's exposure, on the other hand, is the exposure of a man not fully knowing what he is, and with a heart capable, finally, of bursting. But I want to say more of this later.

About Shakespeare's other comic addition to his source in *All's Well that Ends Well*, one hardly knows what to think. R. H. Goldsmith finds Lavatch 'unlike Shakespeare's other fools in that his role bears no significant relationship to the theme of *All's Well*'.[1] This is a curious and difficult part certainly, but it is hard to believe that Shakespeare would deliberately invent a character who 'bears no significant relationship' to the rest of the play. Other critics, of course, have seen the bawdy cynicism of Lavatch as the key to Shakespeare's intention. To R. A. Foakes, this is a play in which 'the irrepressible Parolles, and the sardonic clown Lavache, set the tone. Indeed, Lavache has little other function in the play than this'.[2] Lavatch's harshness, his requests that he and 'Isbel the woman' be permitted to 'do as we may', because he is 'driven on by the flesh' (I, iii, 16 ff.), and his suggestion of the impossibility of finding one good woman in ten, immediately precede Helena's revelation to the Countess of her love for Bertram. It has often been suggested that they therefore undercut the scene and make a mockery of it. But the critic who confuses the point of view of Lavatch with that of the dramatist surely reveals, as Joseph Price aptly observes (p. 147), 'his own cynicism, not Shakespeare's'. Price points out other plays in which a cynical or bawdy element is used along with a serious presentation of romantic love without devaluing it: *As You Like It* (Touchstone and Audrey), *Twelfth Night* (Feste), *Measure for Measure* (Lucio – though perhaps the problems

prefixes in the Folio (see Hunter edition, pp. xv ff.) suggests that Shakespeare had particular actors in mind for these parts. But for their essential roles as manipulators of the plot and commentators on the action, anonymity is perfectly adequate.

[1] *Wise Fools in Shakespeare* (East Lansing, Michigan, 1955), p. 60.
[2] *Shakespeare: The Dark Comedies to the Last Plays: From Satire to Celebration* (London, 1971), p. 17.

here are too similar to those of *All's Well that Ends Well* for this to be a wholly convincing example). One might add the Nurse and Mercutio in *Romeo and Juliet* to his list of the comic, cynical 'safety valves', providing a necessary element of realism and worldliness to make a romantic situation credible, and to prevent it from cloying. Most of the characters listed, one also observes, are added, or developed, by Shakespeare to those he found in his source. Some such explanation of Lavatch's presence in the play is necessary, for it seems hard to imagine that anyone can have much hope of his proving worth employment as a potential source of mirth in the Rossillion household, in spite of R. H. Goldsmith's suggestion (p. 59) that his wit is 'modish, and to the very degree that it was stylish and smart in his day it has become flat and somewhat tedious to us'. Perhaps, with Kittredge,[1] we may think of him as a country clown, out of place in a courtly atmosphere. To contemplate Lavatch, though, is likely to create a feeling of sympathy with Lafeu, who remarks, at the end of a conversation with him, 'Go thy ways; I begin to be aweary of thee' (IV, v, 53). 'A shrewd knave and an unhappy' he calls him a few moments later, and on hearing from the Countess that he remains in the household because her dead husband was fond of him ('and indeed he has no pace, but runs where he will'), comments 'I like him well; 'tis not amiss', and changes the subject. The presence of the shrewd and unhappy Lavatch has its effect, certainly, on the general mood of the play, but to suggest, with Professor Foakes (p. 17), that the play is 'never free . . . from the vision of things as seen by Parolles and Lavache' seems to go against the evidence of Shakespeare's care in presenting the main plot to us. He is, of course, as Professor Bullough observes in his introduction to the source (p. 388), 'bringing into his comedy some of the knowledge of the darker sides of human nature which he has already revealed in his Histories. But he is still the romantic dramatist who delights to show how far a good deed shines in a naughty world . . . and the proof of his continued assurance is Helena'. The presence of Lavatch in *All's Well that Ends Well* serves partly at least as a foil to Helena, to reveal her as a 'bright particular star' way above such earthly mortals as the poor clown, as well as to remind us of her common humanity with him. His touching tribute to her near the end of the play – 'she was the sweet-marjoram of the sallet, or, rather, the herb of grace' (IV, v, 15) – is a nice demonstration of the capacity of even the voice of bawdy cynicism to respond to Helena. In spite of R. H. Goldsmith's belief that Lavatch is a 'clever, urbane jester' (p. 59), it seems difficult to see him in the same company as Feste and Touchstone. In many ways he seems to have the simplicity and vulnerability of Lear's fool, though he lacks his capacity to penetrate to the heart of a situation. He is like Lear's fool too in the gentleness and compassion he calls forth in his patron. The Countess's patience and tolerance towards Lavatch, her protection of him within the security of the Rossillion household, allow this harsh and unlikeable knave to have his part in the scheme of forgiveness and tolerance at the end of the play. This bond of trust and understanding, quite superfluous to anything required by the plot, between two characters whom Shakespeare has added to those he found in Boccaccio's tale, is an epitome of the ways in which he has enriched the story from which he worked.

With two groups of new characters, the older generation and the comics, Shakespeare has, then, vastly altered the mood of Boccaccio's

[1] Referred to by Price, *The Unfortunate Comedy*, p. 153. John Barton's production seemed to be suggesting something of the sort when it presented Lavatch playing with a rabbit-skin – and, moreover, one which, to all appearances, had come from a not-long-dead rabbit.

story and provided a context for Helena and Bertram quite different from that against which they are seen in his source. Before examining the use they make of that context, it may be helpful to isolate some of the often telling modifications he makes in the plot of the story. At the beginning of the play, Shakespeare alters the heroine's circumstances. Giletta was 'diligently looked unto by her kinsfolke (because she was riche and fatherlesse)'; she also 'refused manye husbandes with whom her kinsfolke woulde have matched her' (pp. 389–90). Helena is poor, totally dependent on the kindness and generosity of the Countess, and has never been loved by or loved anyone but Bertram. This makes possible Shakespeare's presentation of her as the inexperienced, humble, timid, innocent girl we see in the first scene of the play, in her interview with the Countess, in her first scene with the King, and in her choosing of a husband after the cure of the King's disease. It is a timidity fired into resolve and strength by the power of her love, but it is a characteristic never shown by Giletta. Shakespeare's changes seem designed to make Helena more attractive to an audience. At the same time, however, the reduction of Helena's social status to that of a sort of servant in the Rossillion household makes Bertram's reaction to the idea of marrying her more understandable. His farewell to her in the first scene – 'Be comfortable to my mother, your mistress, and make much of her' (l. 73) – has all the nonchalance a young man might be expected to show to a girl of inferior station brought up in the family.

Helena's social inferiority and her dependence on the Countess are used to most telling effect in act I, scene iii. It is a scene carefully calculated to gain the sympathy of an audience as Helena, bashfully inarticulate after the initial half-comic awkwardness over the name of 'mother', is coaxed towards a moving declaration of her love by the kindness and understanding of the Countess, whose secret awareness of Helena's situation is shared by the audience. The interview between them concludes with the Countess's approval of Helena's project of going to Paris, which we have already learned of in her second soliloquy: 'Why, Helen, thou shalt have my leave and love . . . I'll stay at home / And pray God's blessing into thy attempt' (ll. 246–9). Whether individual critics find it acceptable or not, Shakespeare has obviously tried, through this scene, to protect his heroine from those charges of predatoriness, of husband-hunting, which might legitimately be levelled at Boccaccio's Giletta. He has used our affection for the old lady, a character invented for this purpose, as a means to win our acceptance of Helena's plan. Seen in the light of the Countess's approval, it gains, or is surely supposed to gain, our approval too.

Helena's modesty and timidity are shown again when she reaches Paris. She is ready to withdraw (II, i, 124 ff.) at the King's first rebuff, and only continues when she has withdrawn her personality behind the disguise of her incantatory couplets (ll. 133 ff.). Helena shows the same humility in the great public scene at court, when she is again ready to withdraw at the revelation of Bertram's antipathy to the idea of marrying her: 'That you are well restor'd, my lord, I'm glad. / Let the rest go' (II, iii, 147–8). This is a very precise and deliberate alteration from Painter, and one to which Shakespeare's other changes contribute. When Giletta declared her choice of Beltramo, the King 'was very loth to graunt him unto her' and only did so because 'he had made a promise which he was loth to breake' (p. 391). There is no such reluctance about the King's 'Why, then, young Bertram, take her' (l. 105) in the play. Bertram's refusal comes as a painful jar in a jovial scene, and the King's insistence produces a speech which Professor Bradbrook sees as 'the germ of the play':[1]

[1] M. C. Bradbrook, *Shakespeare and Elizabethan Poetry* (London, 1951), p. 166.

                    If she be
All that is virtuous, save what thou dislik'st –
A poor physician's daughter – thou dislik'st
Of virtue for the name. But do not so . . .
                    Good alone
Is good, without a name; vileness is so:
The property by what it is should go,
Not by the title. She is young, wise, fair;
In these to nature she's immediate heir,
And these breed honour; that is honour's scorn
Which challenges itself as honour's born
And is not like the sire. Honours thrive
When rather from our acts we them derive
Than our foregoers.   (II, iii, 121–37)

There is nothing like this in Boccaccio's story. The initial reduction of Helena's social status makes it possible in Shakespeare – by 1600 an aristocrat is unlikely to have thought marriage to a wealthy commoner as disgraceful as Beltramo appears to. And the King's willingness to ennoble Helena, a possibility of which there is no mention in the source, removes at a stroke the entire ground of Beltramo's objection and the ostensible ground of Bertram's. From this point on, the relationship between Helena and Bertram is forced on to the personal level of love and disdain, the disdain of familiarity and unawareness. Honour too is placed in perspective by the King: 'Honours thrive/When rather from our acts we them derive / Than our foregoers.' To those who can judge it best, Bertram's mother and the King, the poor physician's daughter proves herself worthy in honour of the hereditary nobleman, Bertram. In a sense Shakespeare has here, in act II, reached the point that Boccaccio reaches only at the end of his story: he has shown Helena worthy of her husband. The rest of the play is in fact to be about something with which the source is never concerned – Bertram's need of Helena.

The circumstances in which the hero and heroine go to Italy are also subtly changed by Shakespeare from the account he found in Painter. That Bertram reaches his decision to slip away to the south before he is forced into marriage has already been mentioned. This slight moderation of Beltramo's deliberate brutality goes some way towards softening the effect of Bertram's behaviour in the play. Helena's departure to the south is much more significantly modified. In Boccaccio's story, the constantly efficient Giletta spent some time putting Beltramo's estates into good running order before 'she toke her way, with her maide, and one of her kinsemen, in the habite of a pilgrime, well furnished with silver and precious Jewels: telling no man whither shee wente, and never rested till sheé came to Florence' (p. 393). It is a purposeful and well thought-out step, and the pilgrim's guise is a deliberate attempt to mislead. Helena, on the other hand, leaves Rossillion with that wistful, tender soliloquy of fear for her husband's safety, entirely selfless in its devotion to Bertram and its despair at the danger to which she thinks she has exposed him. She says nothing of any intention to seek Bertram in Florence and in the letter which her mother-in-law receives two scenes later, announcing that she is 'Saint Jaques' pilgrim, thither gone' (III, iv, 4), the same mood of pity and love for Bertram is maintained. The next time we see Helena she is in Florence, 'somewhat out of the road', as Dr Johnson remarked, 'from Roussillon to Compostella'.[1] Though the suggestion has been made that by St Jaques Shakespeare intends not Compostella but San Giacomo d'Altopascio not far from Florence, and that the pilgrims' hostel at 'Saint Francis here beside the port' (III, v, 36) refers to San Francesco dei Vanchetoni in the neighbourhood of the Porta al Prato in Florence,[2] it is difficult to imagine how an audience could be persuaded to think in such precise geographical terms. Yet some critics of

[1] *Works of Samuel Johnson*, VII, 392.
[2] See Mario Praz, 'Shakespeare's Italy', *Shakespeare Survey 7* (Cambridge, 1954), pp. 96–7. The suggestion, which Praz dismisses, is G. Lambin's.

the play and of Helena's motives have examined the geography with remarkable scrupulosity. Bertrand Evans, for example, admits that the widow evinces no surprise at Helena's presence on pilgrimage in Florence, and even tells her (ll. 94–5) that 'There's four or five, to Great Saint Jaques bound, / Already at my house' (a detail, one notes, that Shakespeare has added to give plausibility to Helena's situation). But he goes on to demand, accusingly, 'was it coincidence that she chose a saint the road to whose shrine ran through Bertram's present location? Had she, at first, a real intention of going beyond Florence?'[1] Such an extraordinary search for motives with which Shakespeare does not concern himself seems to show a misunderstanding of the intention which the modification of the source here makes clear. Shakespeare sends Helena out of the play with a soliloquy of tenderness and love; he deliberately leaves her motives vague, relying on the goodwill he has established for her in the audience, through her behaviour and through the comments of characters he has invented for this purpose, to carry her through the necessary complications of the plot which will lead to the fulfilment of her hopes. Almost as soon as she has left the stage he brings on the Countess to reinforce our approval of Helena and to suggest that Bertram 'cannot thrive' unless Helena's prayers, which 'heaven delights to hear / And loves to grant, reprieve him from the wrath / Of greatest justice' (III, iv, 27–9). This is a remark which critics who see the play in terms of Christian allegory have seized on, and it is, indeed, their strongest evidence. More immediately, though, it is an example of Shakespeare's careful use of plot modification and invented characters to direct in advance the audience's reactions to what will be a slightly difficult phase in the development of the plot. The Countess's remark provides the necessary link between Helena's apparently purposeless exit at the end of act III, scene ii, and her appearance in

Florence in the scene that follows. After it we desire and expect that we should next see Helena near Bertram. A moment later (ll. 38–40) the Countess adds:

> Which of them both
> Is dearest to me I have no skill in sense
> To make distinction.

Shakespeare obviously wants the tenderness and love which this deeply sympathetic character feels for these two rather awkward young people to be reflected in the audience. His intention is clearly to put the audience into a frame of mind in which they are more likely to accept that chain of events which is to protect the Countess from any further necessity of making distinctions in her affections.

The plot modifications of the Florentine scenes of the play stem mainly from the fact that Shakespeare has to present a great deal of invented material relative to Parolles and Bertram. I have already said something about the significance of these scenes in relation to Parolles, and I shall return to them in considering Bertram. Their effect on the main plot, of course, is exactly what Shakespeare requires: they keep Helena in the background. If one sees the play dividing roughly into two at the departure of Helena from Rossillion at the end of act III, scene ii, an interesting pattern becomes apparent. Of the ten scenes up to and including III, ii, Helena appears in seven and speaks 320 of their 1,420 lines; of the thirteen scenes after III, ii, Helena appears in only five and speaks only 143 of their 1,375 lines. This is in sharp contrast to the situation in Painter, where Giletta, as the clever wench organising the means by which she is to answer Beltramo's riddle, is vigorous and busy right through this stage of the tale, her conversations with the widow (or her equivalent) reported at a length which seems disproportionate to the rest of the story. Shakespeare's intention is to carry

[1] *Shakespeare's Comedies* (Oxford, 1960), p. 154.

Helena through this second half of the play on the strength of the impression she has made in the first half. His main emphasis in this area goes on to his 'subplot' scenes as they prepare for the final revelation and the return to Rossillion, with the reappearance of Helena in the final scene. The plot-changes from the source are there more extreme than at any point in the play, but as that is the end, I should like to leave it till then.

To consider Helena and Bertram in relation to Giletta and Beltramo in this new setting of invented characters and modified plot reveals a number of interesting points. The basic aspect of the presentation of Helena has already emerged: that in her search for Bertram's love she has the support and sympathy of everyone in the play except Parolles – and even he betrays some little affection for her in his words of parting in the first scene: 'Little Helen, farewell. If I can remember thee I will think of thee at court' (ll. 184–5). Giletta's smooth efficiency and determination have gone, and our first close view of Helena is in that despairing, yearning soliloquy which reveals her consciousness of her own unworthiness, and her naive preoccupation with Bertram's beauty. She is revived from her despair by the strength of her love, by her fear for Bertram as she realises that 'the court's a learning-place' (l. 173), and by her awakening realisation of the power of virginity (to be understood both in spiritual and sensual terms) during the conversation with Parolles. Through the growing hope and resilience of the second soliloquy and the delightful interview with the Countess, she is prepared, and so is the audience, for her performance at Paris. Her modesty and willingness to withdraw at the beginning of the confrontation with the King lead into the strangely stylised couplets. The couplets recall her assertion at the end of the interview with the Countess that her medicine has something in it

'more than my father's skill' and is, in fact, 'sanctified / By th'luckiest stars in heaven' (I, iii, 237 ff.). The King concludes that in her some 'blessed spirit' speaks (II, i, 174), and Lafeu regards her cure as a miracle. The idea is kept vague – the couplets themselves provide a screen of stylisation in the surrounding realism of presentation – and Helena remains throughout too vividly human to be categorised in schematic terms. She arrives at the choosing scene, however, secure in the approval of the Countess, Lafeu, the King, and, indirectly, of heaven – and so, one must also expect, of the audience. The effect of all this, followed by the modesty of her withdrawal at Bertram's unwillingness, and the ardour of the King's assertion of her 'honour', is to make Bertram's refusal of her seem utterly foolish, though not beyond understanding. She has been presented in the first half of the play on two fronts: as the means by which a miraculous cure comes to the King – 'A showing of a heavenly effect in an earthly actor' in the words of Lafeu (II, iii, 24); and as a physically attractive young woman in love – 'powerful to araise King Pippen' or 'give great Charlemain a pen in's hand', as Lafeu, again, somewhat broadly expresses it (II, i, 75). She is established by the middle of the play as sensitive, intelligent, and strong, and she leaves Rossillion with a soliloquy of selfless tenderness reinforced by the Countess's subsequent praise of her, and inability to say whether Helena or Bertram is dearer to her. This, and Helena's parting speech, are of great importance in directing our attitude to Bertram. That he is capable of foolishness and ingratitude we already know; he has recently demonstrated moral cowardice and, in the scene of his parting with Helena, an insensitiveness that amounts almost to cruelty; he is soon to show himself capable of falling more obviously into wickedness. Yet Helena's speech directs our attention to him as the object of her love; the soliloquy should catch us up with her emotions, keep Bertram and Helena together in our minds, and help us share the Countess's willingness to regard them with equal affection. It is on this that Shakespeare relies as he brings them towards the conclusion through the rather difficult intervening period of plot manipulation.

During the second half of the play we see only as much of Helena as is consistent with making the plot comprehensible. One scene in disguise as a pilgrim, two short scenes with the widow, and a brief scene as she is returning to France, are all that Shakespeare risks before Helena reappears thirty lines from the end of the play. For our impressions of her during the intervening period we have to rely on our memories, on the comments of the Countess in act III, scene iv, on the assessment of her by the young French lords as they comment on Bertram's behaviour – 'so good a wife and so sweet a lady' (IV, iii, 6), and on the remarks of Lafeu, the Countess, and even Lavatch as they deliver (IV, v, 9 ff.) what they think of as epitaphs. When Helena does reappear to accept the penitence of Bertram brought about by her *alter ego* Diana, Shakespeare intends, I feel sure, that the portrait of her established during the first three acts should remain untarnished by the necessary plot manipulation of act IV. One of the crucial questions of the play is whether he has succeeded in this rather daring bit of dramatic legerdemain, succeeded in getting through the somewhat awkward tale he inherited from Boccaccio without allowing our attention to focus too sharply on the mechanics of its plot. He has tried to use the realistic and sympathetic characterisation of Helena so strongly built up in the first part of the play to get her across this bridgeless little channel. And he has diverted our attention from the process of crossing by providing entertainment, with serious implications, through the unmasking of Parolles and its dependent scenes. The intention seems to be, as Joseph Price points out (p. 162), that the bed-trick should be a symbol rather than a realistic plot device, a satisfaction of the demands of the story, and of the audience's expectations of happiness for Helena who has been so sympathetically presented to them. Provided that this sympathy for Helena has been strongly enough impressed by the end of act III – and Shakespeare has surely given an actress enough to make this possible – and that therefore during the rest of the play the audience is seeing Bertram through the glass of Helena's love for him, there is every possibility of success. This becomes clearer if one considers Bertram in the new context that Shakespeare has developed from that provided by Boccaccio for Beltramo.

If the essential point about Helena is the affection she inspires in other characters in the play, the essential point about Bertram is his immaturity, and the readiness of everyone to make allowances for it. The plot itself, of course, asserts Bertram's youth: he is a ward of court, too young to be left to manage the properties inherited from his father. In each of the first two scenes, characters whom we respect tell him that he looks like his father and that they hope he will learn to behave like him. The King's greeting on Bertram's arrival at Court has already been quoted; it follows hard upon his mother's farewell: 'Be thou bless'd, Bertram, and succeed thy father / In manners as in shape!' (I, i, 57–8). The hope is ultimately given promise of fulfilment, but it is his initial lack of moral shape that allows Bertram far too much room for manoeuvre. His youth is stressed throughout: it prevents his going to the Italian war with the legitimate permission of the King; to Lafeu he seems a young ass, but only one of that general group of asses who form the 'unbak'd and doughy youth' of the nation (IV, v, 3); even to Parolles Bertram is a 'foolish idle boy', a 'lascivious young boy' (IV, iii, 207, 290). This stress on Bertram's youth is important: none of the older, dependable characters think his behaviour irredeemably vicious, nor do the young lords who comment on it in act IV, scene iii. Even at the end his misdeeds are, to his mother, 'Natural rebellion done i' the blade of youth' (v, iii, 6). Shakespeare presents him to us as a foolish and misled boy, in need of rescue from the dangers of his own folly. His last escapade in Florence reveals the moral danger in which this folly places him.

The affection which Bertram is capable of inspiring in those around him is remarkable: the Countess, even after his rejection of her beloved Helena, cannot measure her love for him; the King welcomes him to Court as his own son; Lafeu is ready to marry his daughter to him; the Duke of Florence appoints him general of his horse; to Diana and the widow he is 'a most gallant fellow' (III, v, 79). And above all of course there is Helena, who keeps Bertram before our eyes as an object of love, finding excuses for him, blaming herself, constantly presenting him to us in the best possible light. The most remarkable example of this is the speech at the end of act III, scene ii, when Helena, after Bertram's rejection of her, talks only of the danger he is in, forcing the audience to view him tolerantly when he appears in the next scene at the height of his military success. Helena's own comments on her social inferiority, particularly in her first soliloquy and in her conversation with the Countess, also prepare the audience for Bertram's rejection of her on grounds of rank. Joseph Price has even suggested that we are to take the replies of the other lords in the choosing scene (II, iii, 52 ff.) as elaborate but insincere courtesy, rightly, *not* mistakenly, interpreted by Lafeu.[1] Whether he is right or not, there is no doubt that we are asked to understand Bertram's unwillingness. His cry 'a poor physician's daughter my wife' (l. 123) would not, says Professor Bradbrook, 'sound so outrageous to an Elizabethan ear as it does today'.[2] It is essential that the audience should acquiesce in the forgiveness of Bertram at the end, and not go away, with Dr Johnson, unable to reconcile their hearts to the fact that he is dismissed to happiness. So the shape of his career is carefully controlled by Shakespeare; his relationship with Helena is suggested at the beginning with economy and precision, so that his horror at the marriage is understandable, and the terms in which he expresses it, though concealing personal reaction in social generalisation, not unexpected. Parolles is invented to take much of the blame (from Lafeu, the Countess, and the young French lords) for Bertram's youthful follies. Bertram is handsome and young; everyone is prepared to like him and give him the benefit of the doubt. He goes to the war and wins glory; and the war exists only to reflect honour on him – its rights and wrongs are kept delightfully vague, with the French King giving his courtiers permission to fight on either side (I, ii, 15). Bertram achieves a rank much higher than the command of 'a certaine number of men' (p. 392) which is all that Beltramo gets in Painter; the Duke of Florence appoints him 'general of our horse' (III, iii, 1). Even in the scene of Bertram's parting from Helena (II, v) Shakespeare has most carefully maintained the balance which makes the final reconciliation possible. A real showdown here would have a disastrous effect on the play. Instead we have Helena's modest request for a kiss, and Bertram's evasive refusal; his dismissal of her protestations of loyalty with the embarrassed 'Come, come; no more of

[1] Price's argument (*The Unfortunate Comedy*, pp. 155–6) is persuasive without, finally, being capable of proof. He rightly points out, however, that Lafeu, Shakespeare's invented commentator, is not wrong elsewhere, and in predicting Bertram's refusal, is right immediately afterwards; moreover, his being wrong here would serve no particular dramatic purpose. But if the lords' over-courteous replies betray reluctance, Lafeu fulfils the useful function of giving expression to, and sustaining, our feelings for Helena.

[2] *Shakespeare and Elizabethan Poetry*, p. 166.

that' (l. 73);[1] and, finally, his petulant shout 'Go thou toward home, where I will never come' (l. 90), carefully placed by Shakespeare *after* her departure from the stage. There is nothing in this, their final meeting on stage before the last scene of the play, to make their reconciliation there implausible.

That Bertram is young, headstrong, and foolish has, then, been made clear by the end of act III. During act IV we observe that his lack of moral shape is going to allow him to cross the boundary into unequivocal sinfulness. It has sometimes been suggested that Bertram's flirtation with Diana should be regarded only as the misdemeanour of a soldier abroad on active service. But that we are asked to see Bertram as here corrupting 'a well-derived nature' there seems little doubt. In the scenes of the attempted seduction, we should also remember that remark of the Countess which immediately precedes them: that Bertram 'cannot thrive' without the love, and guidance, of Helena. I have tried to suggest that the audience must, if the play is to work at all, be prepared to share in the forgiveness of Bertram at the end of the play; they must also be aware, if the last scene is to succeed, that he *needs* Helena. The two French lords, young men, are allowed to hold the stage for a considerable period at the beginning of act IV, scene iii, interrupting the Parolles episode in which the audience is much interested. They comment very pointedly on what Bertram is doing. They speak of his wife, whom they believe dead, 'so good a wife and so sweet a lady', and they describe his behaviour in unequivocal terms: 'He hath perverted a young gentlewoman here in Florence, of a most chaste renown, and this night he fleshes his will in the spoil of her honour; he hath given her his monumental ring, and thinks himself made in the unchaste composition.' And yet the immediacy of Bertram's sin is put into perspective as they go on to moralise, from Bertram's behaviour, about human con-

duct in general: 'As we are ourselves, what things we are ... Merely our own traitors.' Bertram in this action 'contrives against his own nobility' (l. 23), but in so doing he is not untypical of the human species. Some critics have used this idea to suggest a schematised pattern in the play,[2] with Bertram as a *humanum genus* figure, sinning and needing the forgiveness of divine grace, represented by Helena. The pattern is certainly in the background, though there is always such a vivid humanity about Bertram's misguided immaturity that it is difficult to schematise him into a 'symbol' of anything. The inference of the comments of the two young lords on Bertram's behaviour is, however, clear: that in contriving against his own nobility he rebels against his own better nature, and in giving away his monumental ring he epitomises the perversion of his honour as a nobleman, a son, and a husband. And all this is to satisfy what he himself calls his 'sick desires' (IV, ii, 35), his lust, capable, in Helena's words, of making use of 'what it loathes' (IV, iv, 25).

The trick played on Bertram to divert him from the consequences of the sin the young lords here accuse him of has been fully prepared for: in the earlier part of the play by the creation of the audience's affection for Helena; and, in the second half, by the establishment of Bertram's need of her. The revelation of the

[1] John Barton's 1967 production here carried a hint that Bertram was already, perhaps subconsciously, in love with Helena, but unwilling to admit it to Parolles, or himself, for fear of losing face. This did not seem an intrusive idea.

[2] The best essay on these lines is Robert Grams Hunter's chapter in his *Shakespeare and the Comedy of Forgiveness* (New York, 1965), pp. 106–31. Hunter does not push the schematisation too far, admitting at the end of his interesting discussion that the play 'is a secular comedy concerned with this world and with the relationships between men and women in this life' though it was written 'for a Christian audience and it draws naturally upon a Christian view of the world' (p. 131).

trick during the final scene will expose Bertram to himself, will bring home to him his self-treachery. It will, in those closing words of the conversation of the two lords (IV, iii, 68 ff.), prevent his virtues (which are latently there) from being proud, through the metaphoric whipping which the exposure of his faults will give him; and at the same time the presence and the love of Helena, cherishing those virtues, will prevent despair. These young lords, his peers, quite clearly condemn Bertram's behaviour; they are anxious (l. 43) that there should be no suspicion that they are involved with it. Yet they do not despair of him, and they see the exposure of Parolles as the first step on the road to his salvation. Parolles's search after the drum has something akin to Bertram's pursuit of Diana: neither succeeds, and both are brought to trial as a result of it. One of the lords, predicting Parolles's behaviour when caught, has already exactly predicted Bertram's also: he will 'in the highest compulsion of base fear, offer to betray you and deliver all the intelligence in his power against you, and that with the divine forfeit of his soul upon oath' (III, vi, 27–30). (For Parolles substitute Bertram, and for 'you' read 'yourself', and the lord might be predicting Bertram's behaviour in the last scene.) But while condemning Bertram's behaviour, the young lords see that he lacks self-knowledge, and that he must learn from the exposure of Parolles: 'I would gladly have him see his company anatomiz'd, that he might take a measure of his own judgments' (IV, iii, 30–2). While the exposure of Parolles is primarily a funny scene, it leaves Bertram deeply shocked, conscious of the folly and vulnerability of his own judgement, though for the time being still defiant, the 'ill' of his 'mingled yarn' temporarily overwhelming the 'good'. But the scene, the conversation of the lords, and the fate of Parolles, prepare for the end of the play; once more the material Shakespeare

has added to his source clearly reveals his intentions.

The final scene of *All's Well that Ends Well* is enormously expanded, and its orientation much changed, from the last episode of Boccaccio's tale. In the source, Giletta, with the ring she has secured from Beltramo and the twin sons she has borne to him in secret in Florence, reports back to Rossillion to prove that she has successfully fulfilled her tasks. The story ends when Beltramo 'to kepe his promise made, and to please his subjectes, and the Ladies that made sute unto him to accept her . . . imbraced and kissed her, acknowledging her againe for his lawefull wyfe . . . and from that time forth hee loved and honoured her' (p. 396). Giletta has won Beltramo's bet, has proved herself worthy of him. As a favour to her and to his subjects, and, it seems, after a little hesitation, he takes her back. In the play, on the other hand, we have an elaborate stage spectacle which allows Bertram to expose his cowardice, lust, dishonesty, and fear to all those characters whom he most wishes to impress and who have all along been so willing to give him the benefit of the doubt. The curious role of Diana here, with her riddling remarks, works entirely to this end, infinitely more effective than those incredible twins in Boccaccio in shattering Bertram's self-confidence. His behaviour is arranged to allow him the fullest and most painful self-exposure. He enters full of confidence, fresh from his military triumphs in Italy, with an elaborately turned speech (V, iii, 44–55) of compliment to Lafeu's daughter which he also makes serve as an explanation of his own attitude to Helena. Though it may just be possible that Shakespeare is here suggesting a further excuse for Bertram's earlier behaviour, the tone of the speech seems more calculated to establish him in our eyes as a man with a sense of false security, and of self-importance, who needs to be lowered a little in his own estimation. During the remainder of the scene this is just what happens. Through that long series of twisting complications and increasingly frantic lies, we watch the bewildered young man behaving in a desperately human way, allowing fear and panic to push him further and further towards folly, dishonesty, sin. Our attitude is kept from contempt by our recognition of the normality of what Bertram's fear drives him to, by Shakespeare's carefully withheld surprise of the second ring, which helps us to share Bertram's initial bewilderment, and by our knowledge that the means of relief is at hand, waiting only until Diana's agency has created the right situation. When Bertram has been made to see himself as he was made to see Parolles, the process of recovery can begin and the high hopes expressed for him by his mother, the King, Lafeu, and the young French lords seem to have a possibility of fulfilment. Helena at last appears and the proud boy is brought, with the inarticulate half line, 'Both, both. Oh pardon', metaphorically at least, though surely physically also, to his knees. The moment is underwritten, as is the moment at the end of *Measure for Measure* when Isabella yields to Mariana's entreaties to kneel and beg for Angelo's life. But its theatrical potential, its simplicity and its capacity to catch and satisfy the mood of an audience at the end of the play, their hopes for Helena fulfilled, is, of course, enormous. The surface at last is penetrated, and the foolish, arrogant young man collapses before the woman he has spurned. Bertram's ability to collapse is his salvation; Parolles's heart, one remembers, was incapable of bursting. Bertram achieves this moment of exposure, of defencelessness, of self-giving, because his heart, ultimately, is 'great', or at least has the potential for greatness. And his realisation of his own failings, of his sin, comes before he understands, before the cause of the situation can be explained to him. His openness and generosity in begging Helena's forgiveness,

though on a smaller scale, is reminiscent of Isabella's begging for Angelo's life before she learns that Claudio is not dead, or Posthumus's forgiveness of his wife before he realises her innocence. It is in a minor key, certainly, but the spontaneity of Bertram's collapse has something of the same quality of imaginative human response. It produces, or should produce, a moment of high emotional tension in the theatre, reflected, and yet, appropriately at the end of a comedy, relaxed by Lafeu's confession that his 'eyes smell onions' (l. 314) and by his search for a handkerchief. If the scene has worked well, and the audience has been responsive, as happened on occasions at Stratford in 1967, Lafeu's search may already have been anticipated in the auditorium. The relaxation of tension continues with the King's offer to find Diana a husband – not, surely, the final cynical turn that some critics have suggested, but an appropriately light-hearted conclusion, a laughing reminiscence of all that has passed and ended well, not unlike, as Joseph Price suggests (p. 170), the effect of that momentary last confusion of identity in *The Comedy of Errors*.

All's Well that Ends Well concludes in gaiety and in hope for the future, though not in the triumphant joy of more unequivocally romantic comedy. Dr Johnson complained that Bertram is 'dismissed to happiness' after behaving very badly, and other critics have suggested that we see too little of Helena and Bertram after their reunion for their reconciliation to be convincing.[1] To the first objection, one must reply that the play ends, not in justice, but in mercy and forgiveness. Bertram is given another chance to reveal his better qualities, just as

[1] Clifford Leech, for example ('The Theme of Ambition', p. 23), writes that the end of the play is 'perfunctorily handled' and implies a contrast between Shakespeare's successful treatment of Parolles after his exposure, and the absence of any such portrayal of Bertram, whom we leave 'with no affection, no conviction'.

Angelo is in *Measure for Measure*; and even Parolles, though still, irretrievably, 'a fool and a knave', is to be cared for with the same absence of recrimination as the equally desertless Barnadine. To the second objection, one can only answer that the play ends, and is meant to end, not in fully achieved happiness, but in hope. In his reunion with Helena, Bertram has the chance to fulfil the wish expressed for him at the beginning of the play, that he will succeed his father 'in manners as in shape'. Shakespeare's complete reorganisation of the conclusion to Boccaccio's story has created a mood of hope and promise, satisfying our expectations and leaving us with a belief in the possibility of future joy. Here again the similarity to the conclusion of *Measure for Measure* suggests itself. The effect achieved at the end of *All's Well that Ends Well* is the culmination of Shakespeare's infinite care and subtlety in the handling of his narrative material. Given sympathetic theatrical realisation, it may vindicate his choice of a story that throughout has demanded the constant exercise of his dramatic ingenuity and imagination.

© R. L. SMALLWOOD 1972

WHY DOES IT END WELL? HELENA, BERTRAM, AND THE SONNETS

ROGER WARREN

An extreme version of the general modern reaction to *All's Well* occurs in a review of Tyrone Guthrie's 1959 production: 'the tone of the play and its confusion of values...raises a dozen issues, only to drop them all with a cynical, indifferent 'all's well that ends well'. No wonder Shaw liked it so much'.[1] Now I am convinced that whatever else the ending of this play may be called—puzzling, unsatisfactory, even bungled—Shakespeare was by no means 'indifferent' and certainly not 'cynical'. I think that his own personal poetry, in the Sonnets, sheds an interesting light on exactly *why* he thought the play ended well, and accounts, especially, for his uncompromising treatment of Helena and Bertram. G. K. Hunter rightly calls it a 'peculiar' play, but he emphasizes 'the peculiar force' of both the idealism and the satire.[2] Forceful writing does not reflect 'indifference'; and E. M. W. Tillyard, in finding the play 'full of suffering',[3] isolates the most important characteristic of Helena's love and Bertram's reactions, upon which the Sonnets provide an illuminating commentary.

I

First, though, certain general problems require clarification, not least the choice of the story in the first place. What meaning did Shakespeare wish to convey through dramatizing Boccaccio's story of Giletta of Narbonne? M. C. Bradbrook tries to explain it. That the ending is 'neither hypocritical nor cynical, can be granted only if the play is seen as a study of the question of "Wherein lies true honour and nobility?"'[4] But she has to account for the fact that Shakespeare 'found himself saying more, or saying other, than his purely structural purpose could justify' and so in her terms 'all did not end well'.[5] But what if the debate on virtue and nobility is purely subordinate, achieving forcible expression to place the Helena–Bertram story in perspective? For the incontestable fact is surely that the play cannot adequately be called a morality or a debate, because the extraordinarily vivid characterization of both Helena and Bertram force us to share in their fortunes. It is basically a play about them, not about a moral theme: and the ending stands or falls as it relates to them.

The gnomic passages and stiff, odd outbursts of rhyming couplets led G. Wilson Knight into an extravagant mystical interpretation: Helena functions 'almost as Christ...as a medium only'.[6] But surely nothing else in the play suggests that Helena has so symbolic a role. On the contrary, what is so striking about her is the human intensity of her love, and her capacity for all-too-human suffering. Still, I think the formality of the verse in the healing scene *is* meant to suggest some sort of faith healing, in the limited sense that the King must be persuaded that she can cure him. It has the further effect of establishing how Helena's love strengthens her courage and determination. The King explicitly makes the point: she has

> Youth, beauty, wisdom, courage—all
> That happiness and prime can happy call.
> Thou this to hazard needs must intimate
> Skill infinite, or monstrous desperate.   (II, i, 180–3)

In fact, she has both: she can heal the King by her father's prescriptions and has the courage to risk all for her overpowering, and in that sense 'desperate', love. Elsewhere, the formal and gnomic elements, though admittedly odd in what is otherwise so 'realistic' a play, may be explained by Shakespeare's anxiety to underline matters which seemed to him to be important:

> Who ever strove
> To show her merit that did miss her love?   (I, i, 222–3)

and, even more,

> All's well that ends well; still the fine's the crown.
> Whate'er the course, the end is the renown   (IV, iv, 35–6)

seem to be placed at strategic moments to emphasize the story of Helena and her love. The awkward or (to us) worrying aspects of the plot are scarcely glossed over, and in the finale especially they are dwelt upon. This manner of writing, together with the apparently perplexing blackening of Bertram's character, which, as Hunter says, 'a historical understanding of Bertram in an Elizabethan context cannot remove',[7] bring us back to the question, 'What was it in the story that so interested Shakespeare?'

The clear-eyed, merciless presentation of Bertram supports Tillyard's suspicion that Shakespeare's 'personal feelings, unobjectified and untransmuted'[8] have slipped into the writing. Bradbrook, too, notices that not only is 'the figure of Bertram, so radically changed from that of Boccaccio's Beltramo, . . . drawn with a . . . kind of uncynical disillusion',[9] but that Helena 'is a voice of despair breaking into the play'; and although she rightly warns against too 'crude and direct [a] personal equation . . . ; Shakespeare would certainly not wish to unlock his heart on the public stage', she brings us to the heart of the matter:

In *All's Well* the juxtaposition of the social problem of high birth versus native merit and the human problem of unrequited love recalls the story of the Sonnets; the speeches of Helena contain echoes from the Sonnets...The way in which Bertram is condemned recalls also the plain speaking which is so unusual a feature of the Sonnets.[10]

By the standards of ordinary romantic heroes, Bertram is a 'failure', but as a consistent character he is brilliantly successful, so much so that I think we must assume that Shakespeare meant him that way, and that the worrying effect is intentional. Wilson Knight stresses the play's Sonnet affinities which argue a peculiarly 'personal'[11] interest in the story. By developing these suggestions, and noticing the resemblances and verbal echoes between play and poems, I hope to account for much of the 'peculiarity' of *All's Well*, including the effect of its finale, and to suggest the reasons why there is so much intensity and heartbreak—but not 'indifference' or 'cynicism'—and, in the end, perhaps, a curious worrying uncertainty.

44

However the play is interpreted, the centre must surely be Helena's passionate love and the power of its expression. In her speeches there is an extremity of utterance which is so powerful that it goes far beyond conventional compliment in its attempt to express an emotional intensity which is almost inexpressible, as Shakespeare himself so often strives in the Sonnets.

> Better 'twere
> I met the ravin lion when he roar'd
> With sharp constraint of hunger; better 'twere
> That all the miseries which nature owes
> Were mine at once.   (*A.W.*, III, ii, 116–20)

> But in the onset come; so shall I taste
> At first the very worst of fortune's might;
>   And other strains of woe, which now seem woe,
>   Compar'd with loss of thee will not seem so.   (Sonnet 90)

There could be few better mottoes for Helena's love than

> Such is my love, to thee I so belong,
> That for thy right myself will bear all wrong.   (Sonnet 88)

And Wilson Knight[12] notes the same intense suggestion of devotion in Shakespeare's loving his friend 'next my heaven the best' (Sonnet 110) and Helena's loving Bertram 'next unto high heaven' (I, iii, 188). But he takes this as another proof that Shakespeare is examining sainthood in Helena, while I take both as similar attempts to suggest an overwhelming human passion by hyperbolical means—hyperbolical, that is, in the intense, exclusive, serious manner of the tragedies rather than in the witty, half-amused manner of the earlier comedies.

Helena's first soliloquy plunges us into that uncompromising obsession with her beloved that many of the Sonnets show:

> my imagination
> Carries no favour in't but Bertram's.   (I, i, 80–1)

This is paralleled, in a simple way, by the disturbed rest with which the friend's 'shadow' torments Shakespeare:

> my soul's imaginary sight
> Presents thy shadow to my sightless view,
> Which, like a jewel hung in ghastly night,
> Makes black night beauteous and her old face new.   (Sonnet 27)

The preoccupation with Bertram has an intensity, in words like 'plague', which is reflected in the Sonnets by the vivid impression of an overpowering obsession, especially in words like 'surfeit' and 'gluttoning', or

> Sometime all full with feasting on your sight,
> And by and by *clean starved* for a look   (Sonnet 75, italics mine)[13]

The desperate fervour of Helena's

> I am undone; there is no living, none,
> If Bertram be away   (I, i, 82–3)

has a very similar ring to the 'You are my all the world' and

> You are so strongly in my purpose bred
> That all the world beside methinks are dead

of Sonnet 112. When Helena says 'my idolatrous fancy/Must sanctify his relics' (I, i, 95–6) she uses an image which aptly describes both her love and Shakespeare's own. Shakespeare's denial, 'Let not my love be call'd idolatry' (Sonnet 105) only serves in fact to stress that element of 'religious adoration' which is so strong in them. Both he and Helena devote the whole of their praises 'To one, of one, still such, and ever so' (105). J. B. Leishman, calling Shakespeare the lover 'indeed a worshipper',[14] says that many of the Sonnets are 'religiously idolatrous'; and though Helena makes only a single comparison, she echoes that particularly Shakespearian idea that the old loves are reincarnated in the friend, as well as the 'holy' tears and image of the beloved.[15] Helena returns to phrases of religion in her next scene:

> Thus, Indian-like,
> Religious in mine error, I adore
> The sun that looks upon his worshipper
> But knows of him no more.   (I, iii, 199–202)

Helena's combination of unhappiness and abject devotion is echoed in the two Sonnets 57 and 58, which perhaps more than any others seem to be very close to Helena's expression of her love:

> Being your slave, what should I do but tend
> Upon the hours and times of your desire?   (Sonnet 57)

Those Sonnets, moreover, in their almost heartbreaking simplicity of statement, remind us that passionate hyperbole is not the only style in the sequence. That simplicity which is so marked a feature of Shakespeare's undeceived lovers in the earlier comedies (the finale of *Love's Labour's Lost*, Beatrice and Benedick in the church, above all Viola's 'sister' speech to Orsino) and which suggests so much emotion and awareness of potential unhappiness makes a powerful impression both here and in Helena's language too. What J. W. Lever calls Shakespeare's 'extreme capacity for self-effacement'[16] in the Sonnets, the simple quietness and lack of self-display, 'painting', or 'ornament' in much of the language, is clearly shown in

> Nor dare I chide the world-without-end hour,
> Whilst I, my sovereign, watch the clock for you,
> Nor think the bitterness of absence sour,
> When you have bid your servant once adieu.   (Sonnet 57)

The same humility which conceals anguish, the same reticence in proclaiming a bond between the beloved and the speaker is evident in all Helena says to Bertram ('I am not worthy of the wealth I owe', 'Sir, I can nothing say But that I am your most obedient servant', 'I shall not break your bidding, good my lord'). There is a marked contrast between the 'ornament' of Parolles's deceitful remarks about Bertram,

> Whose want and whose delay is strew'd with sweets,
> Which they distil now in the curbed time,
> To make the coming hour o'erflow with joy
> And pleasure drown the brim　　　　　　　　　　　(II, iv, 42–5)

and her utter simplicity ('What's his will else?', 'What more commands he?', 'In everything I wait upon his will'). Her fear of being 'refused' is typical of her humble, fearful approach to Bertram, reflected in her actual words to him:

> I dare not say I take you, but I give
> Me and my service, ever whilst I live,
> Into your guiding power.　　　　　　　　　　　　(II, iii, 102–4)

The statements of service here are closely paralleled, again in Sonnets 57 and 58 ('Being your vassal bound to stay your leisure', 'O, let me suffer, being at your beck') and in Sonnet 87 ('My bonds in thee are all determinate').

Against her own simplicity or intensity is Helena's picture of a more superficial kind of love which Bertram may meet at the court, expressed in the conceited language of flattering Elizabethan love poetry such as is also used by the muddled lovers in *A Midsummer Night's Dream* (cf. II, i, 220–6; III, ii, 58–61, 137–44, etc.):

> His humble ambition, proud humility,
> His jarring-concord, and his discord-dulcet,
> His faith, his sweet disaster; with a world
> Of pretty, fond, adoptious christendoms
> That blinking Cupid gossips.　　　　　　　　　　(I, i, 167–71)

The conventional oxymorons and the 'blinking Cupid' are so superficial, so different from Helena's powerful self-expression, that Hunter must be right in taking all this to refer to the courtly lovers: 'Helena's refusal to trade on her virginity leads to the sense that others elsewhere may be less scrupulous, which leads directly to her evocation of the amorous dialect of the court.'[17] And the point of such an evocation is that it leads to a fear about Bertram himself:

> Now shall he—
> I know not what he shall. God send him well!
> The court's a learning-place, and he is one—　　(I, i, 171–3)

Hunter notes that 'What is suppressed must be something like "all too apt to learn courtly ways" '. This realistic fear, even while she adores Bertram, is very similar to Shakespeare's own saddened awareness that his beloved was by no means a paragon:

> But why thy odour matcheth not thy show,
> The soil is this—that thou dost common grow. (Sonnet 69)

And when Bertram actually justifies Helena's fears, he woos Diana in conventional complimentary phrasing like 'Titled goddess; And worth it, with addition' and 'holy-cruel' which have a very different ring from Helena's statements of her love and service: Bertram will love

> By love's own sweet constraint, and will for ever
> Do thee all rights of service...
> *Diana:* 'Tis not the many oaths that makes the truth,
> But the plain single vow that is vow'd true. (IV, ii, 16–22)

Such a vow is Helena's

> I will be gone,
> That pitiful rumour may report my flight
> To consolate thine ear (III, ii, 126–8)

or Shakespeare's own

> I am to wait, though waiting so be hell. (Sonnet 58)

Helena emphasizes that her love depends upon a real concern for desert; it is this which is proper to a servant:

> Nor would I have him till I do deserve him;
> Yet never know how that desert should be. (I, iii, 194–5)

An exactly similar feeling of unworthiness underlines several of the Sonnets, all of them very sad, as when Shakespeare guards 'Against that time when thou shalt strangely pass':

> Against that time do I ensconce me here
> Within the knowledge of mine own desert,
> And this my hand against myself uprear,
> To guard the lawful reasons on thy part. (Sonnet 49)

The final couplet,

> To leave poor me thou hast the strength of laws,
> Since why to love I can allege no cause,

parallels Helena's strikingly sympathetic use of 'poor' elsewhere ('poor lord', 'poor thief').[18] If the similarities between her language and that of the Sonnets indicate anything, it would seem to be that Shakespeare intends Helena's passion to have an all-consuming, overpowering intensity which makes descriptions like 'cynicism' and 'man-hunting' very unsuitable.

III

The most extraordinary feature of *All's Well*, surely, is the curiously unsympathetic portrait of its hero. Tillyard comments:

The irony and the truth of Helena's situation are that with...so firm a mind she can be possessed by so enslaving a passion for an unformed, rather stupid, morally timid, and very self-centred youth.[19]

As well as the irony, though, Tillyard stresses the 'truth' of the situation. For Shakespeare, the source seems to have provided a story of essential truth: and it seems to have been a peculiarly personal response to it which suggested his notorious alterations to Boccaccio's Beltramo, which, as Bradbrook notes, consistently show 'greater dependence, humility, and enslavement on Helena's part and greater weakness and falsehood on Bertram's'.[20] Bertram stands universally criticized, and what is so interesting is that this criticism corresponds with even the details of the suggested 'fault' of the friend of the Sonnets. Though the friend is praised for his outward show, his 'sensual fault' provokes criticism as well: others

> In other accents do this praise confound
> By seeing farther than the eye hath shown.
> They look into the beauty of thy mind,
> And that, in guess, they measure by thy deeds.   (Sonnet 69)

So Bertram's own mother condemns the deeds of this 'rash and unbridled boy', and suggests that his 'well-derived nature' is being corrupted (III, ii, 26–31, 88). Helena herself had feared what Bertram would 'learn' from the court. Bertram is shown sinking lower and lower into unworthiness, and is presented much more harshly than Shakespeare's love will allow him to present his friend. Though the friend lives 'with infection', he *graces* 'impiety' (Sonnet 67).[21]

Far more central to the play is the constantly emphasized contrast in rank between Helena and Bertram. This is the cause of some of the most harsh utterances in the play and it has a strong parallel with some of the most deeply felt and unhappy Sonnets. Helena's feeling of utter social separation from Bertram:

> My master, my dear lord he is; and I
> His servant live, and will his vassal die   (I, iii, 153–4)

is closely paralleled by the 'vassalage' shown to Shakespeare's own 'Lord of my love' (Sonnet 26). The image of the star is used by both:

> 'twere all one
> That I should love a bright particular star
> And think to wed it, he is so above me.   (I, i, 83–5)

The 'comfort' sought by Helena from Bertram's 'bright radiance' is echoed in Shakespeare's personal hope for some 'good conceit' of his friend,

> Till whatsoever star that guides my moving
> Points on me graciously with fair aspect,
> And puts apparel on my *tattered* loving,
> To show me *worthy* of thy sweet respect.   (Sonnet 26, italics mine)

Bertram emphasizes the social gulf in violently humiliating terms:

> But follows it, my lord, to bring me down
> Must answer for your raising? I know her well:
> She had her breeding at my father's charge—
> A poor physician's daughter my wife! Disdain
> Rather corrupt me ever!   (II, iii, 112–16)

In Sonnet 49, Shakespeare feared that time

> When I shall see thee frown on my defects, ...
> ... that time when thou shalt strangely pass,
> And scarcely greet me with that sun, thine eye.

The insulting aspersion cast on the 'physician's daughter' is paralleled in Shakespeare's emphasis of his 'fault' which seems to depend chiefly on his being 'a motley to the view', an actor who depends on

> public means which public manners breeds.
> Thence comes it that my name receives a brand.   (Sonnet 111)

Shakespeare's saddened awareness of the social gulf leads him to the admission that, love or no love, he cannot be acknowledged in public:

> I may not evermore acknowledge thee,
> Lest my bewailed guilt should do thee shame;
> Nor thou with public kindness honour me,
> Unless thou take that honour from thy name.   (Sonnet 36)

But Shakespeare will not put his lover in this position:

> But do not so; I love thee in such sort,
> As, thou being mine, mine is thy good report.

Similarly, Helena, discovering too late that Bertram cannot show 'public kindness' in any way, tries to save him:

> *Bertram:* I cannot love her nor will strive to do't. ...
> *Helena:* That you are well restor'd, my lord, I'm glad.
> Let the rest go.   (II, iii, 145–8)

Shakespeare's Sonnets stress the unhappiness stemming from the friend's public behaviour, and, especially, some kind of rejection of the poet as is suggested in the near-bitter anguish of Sonnet 87:

> Thy self thou gav'st, thy own worth then not knowing,
> Or me, to whom thou gav'st it, else mistaking;
> So thy great gift, upon misprision growing,
> Comes home again, on better judgement making.

Though there is giving as well as taking back here, the actual suggestion of taking back on a question of legal ('patent') worth is chilling, as is the suggestion of utter deception in the conclusion:

> Thus have I had thee, as a dream doth flatter:
> In sleep a king, but waking no such matter.

The implied rejection of the poet seems to have been a shatteringly humiliating one: and something of the same discomfort is surely felt by any audience as it hears Bertram speak of his 'clog' whom he will not 'bed', or, worse:

> Wars is no strife
> To the dark house and the detested wife. (II, iii, 287–8)

And one of the most disturbing scenes in all Shakespeare (disturbing not because it is horrifying or tragically shattering, but because it is so *coldly* formal) is that in which Bertram refuses Helena a kiss. His clipped language reminds us of such sad phrases in the Sonnets as the suggestion that the friend will 'strangely pass', 'frown on my defects' and speak with 'settled gravity'. If ever there was 'settled gravity' it is in Bertram's denial to Helena of

> The *ministration* and *required office*
> On my *particular*. Prepar'd I was not
> For such a *business*; therefore am I found
> So much unsettl'd. (II, v, 60–3, italics mine)

Those abstract nouns have the coldly legal ring suggested in Sonnet 87 by 'the charter of thy worth', 'my bonds', 'my patent', and 'misprision'. That sonnet touches a bitterness which Shakespeare never shows elsewhere in the sequence, and which Helena does not show in her reply. Indeed, she reaffirms her service—'Sir, I can nothing say But that I am your most obedient servant'—in terms which recall the absolute self-effacement of 'Being your slave, what should I do but tend' (Sonnet 57).[22]

The icy unpleasantness of Bertram's curt 'Come, come; no more of that', 'My haste is very great. Farewell. Hie home' and 'What would you have?' is so unavoidable as to suggest something like the 'wakened hate' which Shakespeare so feared from his own beloved (Sonnet 117). But not even this can destroy Helena's love, though the suffering as well as the passion emerges as she begs the kiss:

> I am not worthy of the wealth I owe,
> Nor dare I say 'tis mine—and yet it is;
> But, like a timorous thief, most fain would steal
> What law doth vouch mine own. (II, v, 79–82)

The verbal echoes of Sonnet 40 serve to underline, not an exact parallel, but a similarity of devotion between Helena and Shakespeare himself:

> I do forgive thy robb'ry, gentle thief,
> Although thou steal thee all my poverty.

Her terror of calling Bertram hers echoes the disenchanted 'The cause of this fair gift in me is wanting' (Sonnet 87) and the simple hesitation of

> Something, and scarce so much; nothing indeed.
> I would not tell you what I would, my lord   (II, v, 83–4)

and

> I shall not break your bidding, good my lord   (II, v, 88)

are closely parallel to the utterly simple, unaccusing misery of

> And patience, tame to sufferance, bide each check,
> Without accusing you of injury.   (Sonnet 58)

And Bertram's heartless refusal, 'I pray you, stay not, but in haste to horse' is the kind of remark which seems sufficiently brutal to provoke such a reaction as Sonnet 58. The scene is a masterly one. It is horrifying in human terms, but it is not cynical or indifferent. There seems a confident, open-eyed realism about the portrayal of both characters that suggests that Shakespeare knew exactly what he was doing. The parallel with the Sonnets is intended to suggest no more than that it was a personal awareness of this *kind* of unequal relationship that made him believe that he could convincingly bring Giletta's story to the stage. Whether he in the end succeeded depends on how the final scene is interpreted; but the kiss scene is so unflinchingly presented, that to play it with Bertram almost giving the kiss until recalled by a 'psst' from Parolles, as happened in two recent productions, is a piece of cheap sentimentalism which only serves to remind us how searingly painful the original writing is.

IV

The complex turns of the finale, both here and in *Measure for Measure*, seem intended to twist the tension so that the key moments—Helena's reconciliation and Isabella's plea for Angelo— may be almost unbearably poignant. Neither case is wholly successful. Though Shakespeare attempts to maintain the unyielding realism of Bertram to the end, there is just too much weight of honesty for the romantic situation to carry. There is, indeed, no other description than Hunter's 'cryptic fustian'[23] for Bertram's

> If she, my liege, can make me know this clearly
> I'll love her dearly, ever, ever dearly.   (v, iii, 309–10)

Determined not to falsify, and to maintain Bertram's shallowness to the end, Shakespeare has imperilled the impression of reconciliation he needs at this point. I believe that his determination stemmed from his conviction that, from his own experience, Bertram's story was a meaningful, possible one.

The mature, melancholy poetry with which the King sets the tone of this scene echoes those images in the Sonnets by which Shakespeare conveys his sense of loss and hence of love,[24] and especially the very intense Sonnets 33 and 34. The King's

> I am not a day of season,
> For thou may'st see a sunshine and a hail
> In me at once. But to the brightest beams
> Distracted clouds give way
>
> (V, iii, 32–5)

strongly recalls the imagery of those two Sonnets of disappointment at—and forgiveness of—the friend's fault: after the glorious sun has flattered the mountain tops, and kissed the meadows, he will

> Anon permit the basest clouds to ride
> With ugly rack on his celestial face
>
> (Sonnet 33)

but then, in the next Sonnet, the 'rotten smoke' of the 'base clouds', as in the King's image, gives way:

> through the cloud thou break
> To dry the rain on my storm-beaten face.
>
> (Sonnet 34)

At first, this is 'not enough' to Shakespeare 'to dry the rain'. In this impressively honest Sonnet, Shakespeare gives his disappointment rein:

> For no man well of such a salve can speak
> That heals the wound, and cures not the disgrace.
> Nor can thy shame give physic to my grief;
> Though thou repent, yet I have still the loss.

Helena never reminds Bertram of her earlier humiliation before the court; but as Bradbrook notes, 'her devotion (is) tinged for the first time with bitterness'[25]:

> O my good lord, when I was like this maid
> I found you wondrous kind.
>
> (V, iii, 303–4)

When she says

> 'Tis but a shadow of a wife you see;
> The name and not the thing
>
> (V, iii, 301–2)

one is reminded of the constant recurrence of the word 'shadow' in Shakespeare's presentation of his relationship with his friend; of the suggestion of deception and uncertainty in 'Thus have I had thee, as a dream doth flatter'; and of implied sexual betrayal:

> For thee watch I, whilst thou doth wake elsewhere,
> From me far off, with others all too near.
>
> (Sonnet 61)

Helena surely refers back to that remarkable speech made after sleeping with Bertram:

> But, O strange men!
> That can such sweet use make of what they hate,
> When saucy trusting of the cozen'd thoughts
> Defiles the pitchy night.
>
> (IV, iv, 21–4)

It is an extraordinary statement of her awareness that this act, 'strange' and 'defiling' the darkness

53

of night in a 'saucy', not a 'tragic' way, is oddly insignificant. It is dismissed ('But more of this hereafter') to give place to her confidence in the future:

> But with the word: 'the time will bring on summer'—
> When briars shall have leaves as well as thorns,
> And be as sweet as sharp.   (IV, iv, 31-3)

The freshness of this speech has to be set against the 'pitchy', defiling night: that is over, and in itself has not been intensely important. What Helena relies upon is the power of her own love. In this play, love is a matter *both* of 'pitchy' night and 'sweet' leaves; both thorns and flowers are used to evoke the complex experience of love:

> this thorn
> Doth to our rose of youth rightly belong.   (I, iii, 124-5)[26]

Yet, however much his vices may be stressed, it is made clear that Bertram is not wholly beyond redemption,[27] and it is *because* Helena is aware by the end of his *whole* personality that she may redeem him. So, to return to Sonnet 34, after Shakespeare has given full vent to his 'wound', as Helena does less sharply, he concludes on a totally forgiving note:

> Ah! but those tears are pearl which thy love sheds,
> And they are rich, and ransom all ill deeds.

So Bertram's direct 'Both, both. O pardon!' gives hope. That, at least, is not 'cryptic fustian': yet perhaps it is even more convincing because *combined* with the fustian, suggesting that the direct outburst is real because he speaks like his former self as well. If Helena had a speech at this point like her Rossillion one in III, ii, we might be fully convinced that her love is enough to make the marriage work; but the problem is that in front of the court this just cannot be said. M. C. Bradbrook is quite right: the emotional situation does require 'another mode of expression than the last dozen lines allow',[28] something like that final couplet of Sonnet 34. But such intensely personal feeling *cannot* be spoken in public. What we long for her to say she cannot say—but not because Shakespeare did not know how to say it; the Rossillion soliloquy expressed her love perfectly. But in this formal finale the situation is too intense for Helena's (as opposed to Bertram's) emotion to be made clear. To this extent, the King's cautious, slightly uneasy 'All yet *seems* well' and his wistful epilogue have to close the play, and leave us dissatisfied. We have to refer back to Helena's earlier speeches, and though this does not excuse flawed stagecraft, it explains, I think, why Shakespeare felt that it ended well. Sonnet 34, because it states grievance as well as passion, convinces in its reconciling couplet. If the Sonnets in general state anything, it is surely Shakespeare's conviction that to love, and to forgive, is what is important, not necessarily to receive. For, as Leishman says,

nowhere...is there unmistakable evidence that Shakespeare really believed that his friend, in any deep and meaningful sense of the word, loved him at all. At most, perhaps, his friend 'quite liked him'. Saddest of all...are those sonnets where Shakespeare speaks of their difference in rank...as an insuperable barrier between them, for they suggest that he may actually have had to endure (and to forgive)...slights and insults.[29]

And the poignant unhappiness of such a relationship is the basic situation Shakespeare found in the story of Giletta of Narbonne.

Shakespeare's problem was to transform Boccaccio's wit into serious emotion, presumably because he did not want to tell Helena's story wittily, since it contained emotions he understood and could express in powerful poetic terms. Helena, in the end, survives her humiliations, not through resilient, witty gaiety, but through a completely clear-eyed view of herself and Bertram. Shakespeare invests her with a near-desperate fervour to communicate unmistakably that her love is sufficiently powerful to enable her to overcome all humiliations: and the key is the 'Rossillion' soliloquy. The most impressive writing occurs at the most crucial moment of the play when the strength of Helena's love must be made unforgettable. And unforgettable it is. The tone of mingled sadness and tenderness in

> *Poor* lord, is't I
> That chase thee from thy country, and expose
> Those *tender* limbs of thine to the event
> Of the none-sparing war?   (III, ii, 102–5, italics mine)

recalls the self-effacement of

> That god forbid that made me first your slave
> I should in thought control your times of pleasure.   (Sonnet 58)

Helena's sad, simply-expressed resolve,

> I will be gone,
> That pitiful rumour may report my flight
> To consolate thine ear. Come, night; end, day;
> For with the dark, poor thief, I'll steal away   (III, ii, 126–9)

has the same immensely quiet but immensely unhappy note as

> I'll myself disgrace, knowing thy will...
> Be absent from thy walks.   (Sonnet 89)

The whole speech is crowned by the memorably intense hyperbole of

> Shall I stay here to do't? No, no, although
> The air of paradise did fan the house
> And angels offic'd all   (III, ii, 124–6)

which has an eloquent grandeur similar to Shakespeare's great manifesto of what he understood by 'love':

> Love is not love
> Which alters when it alteration finds,
> Or bends with the remover to remove.
> O, no! it is an ever-fixed mark,
> That looks on tempests and is never shaken.   (Sonnet 116)

Helena's love is sorely tried; her suffering and her hint of reproach, though it is barely per-ceptible, in the finale, do not however destroy it. Shakespeare's love in the Sonnets seems to have undergone similar trials and overcome them. He seems to convey both Bertram's cruelty and Helena's ecstasy and anguish in the kind of language which he had used to express his own passion and his friend's behaviour. If in the finale he failed to provide a powerful and reassuring speech for her, he may have felt that it was not necessary; that what he had already given her to say would convince his audience that despite—maybe because of—everything, her single-minded love would ensure that all ended well.

All's Well, it must be admitted, is not a complete success; if it were, it would not have worried so many, nor have taken so many words here. But since so much of it is very impressively written, it can tease the mind. The uncompromising power with which Bertram is drawn and the memorable intensity of Helena compel attention and, because of the last scene, explanation. In suggesting that the Sonnets cast a revealing light on Shakespeare's attitude to Helena and her story, I have tried not to excuse dramatic weaknesses. The play remains a 'peculiar' one; but Helena's passion, which always emerges as the centre-piece in performance, has so much in common with the Sonnets that this may indicate why Shakespeare chose the story. I think that he made Helena so intense, and presented her beloved with such relentless honesty, because he had something especially personal to say about the power of love to prevail over all 'alteration' and humiliation, even if it proved less easy to show matters ending well in dramatic than in non-dramatic terms.

NOTES

1. *Leamington Spa Courier*, 24 April 1959.
2. *All's Well That Ends Well*, The Arden Shakespeare (1959), pp. xxix, liii. All quotations from *All's Well* are from this edition; those from the Sonnets are from Peter Alexander's 1951 edition of the *Complete Works*.
3. *Shakespeare's Problem Plays* (1951), p. 104.
4. 'Virtue Is the True Nobility', *R.E.S.*, XXVI (1950), p. 301.
5. *Ibid*. p. 290.
6. *The Sovereign Flower* (1958), pp. 146, 154.
7. Hunter, *op. cit.* p. xlvii.
8. Tillyard, *op. cit.* p. 106.
9. *Shakespeare and Elizabethan Poetry* (1951), pp. 169–70.
10. *R.E.S.*, XXVI (1950), p. 290.
11. Wilson Knight, *op. cit.* p. 132.
12. Wilson Knight, *op. cit.* p. 136. Cf. also *A.W.*, I, i, 89–90, and Sonnet 92, lines 2–4.
13. Cf. *A.W.*, I, i, 93–4, and Sonnet 113, lines 9–12.
14. *Themes and Variations in Shakespeare's Sonnets*, 2nd edn. (1963), p. 133.
15. Cf. *A.W.*, I, i, 77–81, and Sonnet 31, lines 5–8.
16. *The Elizabethan Love Sonnet* (1956), p. 185.
17. Hunter, *op. cit.* pp. 13–14.
18. Cf. also *A.W.*, I, iii, 196–9, and Sonnet 87, lines 4–8.
19. Tillyard, *op. cit.* p. 112.
20. *R.E.S.*, XXVI (1950), p. 291.
21. But cf. *A.W.*, I, i, 97–103.
22. Cf. also *A.W.*, II, v, 73–6, and Sonnet 58, lines 9–12.
23. Hunter, *op. cit.* p. lv.
24. Cf. *A.W.*, V, iii, 38–42, and Sonnets 77, line 8, and 65, lines 11–12.
25. *R.E.S.*, XXVI (1950), p. 301.
26. Cf. Sonnet 35, lines 1–4.
27. Cf. *A.W.*, IV, iii, 68–71, and Sonnet 35, line 5.
28. *R.E.S.*, XXVI (1950), p. 301.
29. Leishman, *op. cit.* p. 226.

THE RENAISSANCE BACKGROUND OF
MEASURE FOR MEASURE

ELIZABETH MARIE POPE

When critics of *Measure for Measure* [1] are not staggered or repelled by the ethical presuppositions upon which the characters act, they usually try to justify and explain the work on the ground that its morality is specifically Christian. But while such scholars as Roy Battenhouse, C. J. Sisson and R. W. Chambers have thus defended Shakespeare's treatment of law, authority, justice, and mercy, they have not inquired what exact meaning was attached to these terms in the Renaissance, apparently because they assume that he thought of them very much as we do. [2] But did he? What doctrines of equity and forgiveness were actually taught to the Elizabethan layman? Would the first audience that saw *Measure for Measure* find them in the play? Can they explain anything in Shakespeare's presentation of the subject that we might otherwise overlook or misunderstand? And for the answers to these questions we must turn to the popular religious text-books of Shakespeare's own day—not to the Church Fathers or the Latin works of the great contemporary Reformers and Counter-Reformers, but to the annotated Bibles, the translations, the English commentaries, the sermons, and the tracts through which the teaching of the Church reached the individual without special training or interest in theology.

The first point to be noted is that *Measure for Measure*, unlike some of Shakespeare's comedies, has a highly significant title, a phrase which not only sums up the basic theme of the play, but is brought out and emphasized at the crisis in the last act, when the Duke condemns his deputy:

> 'An Angelo for Claudio, death for death.'
> Haste still pays haste, and leisure answers leisure;
> Like doth quit like, and Measure still for Measure.   (v, i, 414–6)

Shakespeare is of course thinking of a verse from the Sermon on the Mount: "With what measure ye mete it shall be measured to you again." In both Matthew and Luke, however, the text is not isolated, but forms an integral part of a short passage which in Luke immediately follows—and is linked with—Christ's great pronouncement on Christian forgiveness:

27 ...Love your enemies: do well to them which hate you....

31 And as ye would that men should do to you, so do ye to them likewise.

32 For if ye love them which love you, what thank shall ye have: for even the sinners love those that love them. [The Matthew, Bishops, and Great Bibles read: "for sinners also love their lovers."]

33 And if ye do good for them which do good for you, what thank shall ye have? for even the sinners do the same....

35 Wherefore love ye your enemies, and do good, and lend, looking for nothing again, and your reward shall be great, and ye shall be the children of the most High: for he is kind unto the unkind, and to the evil.

36 Be ye therefore merciful, as your Father also is merciful.

37 Judge not, and ye shall not be judged: condemn not, and ye shall not be condemned: forgive, and ye shall be forgiven.

38 Give, and it shall be given unto you: a good measure, pressed down, shaken together, and running over shall men give into your bosom: for with what measure ye mete, with the same shall men mete to you again.

39 And he spake a parable unto them, Can the blind lead the blind? Shall they not both fall into the ditch?

40 The disciple is not above his master: but whosoever will be a perfect disciple, shall be as his master.

41 And why seest thou a mote in thy brother's eye, and considerest not the beam that is in thine own eye?

42 Either how canst thou say to thy brother, Brother, let me pull out the mote that is in thine eye, when thou seest not the beam that is in thine own eye? Hypocrite, cast the beam out of thine own eye first, and then shalt thou see perfectly to pull out the mote that is in thy brother's eye.[3]

Matt. vii, 1–5 corresponds to Luke vi, 36–42, but does not include verses 36, 39 or 40, and does not follow or refer to the command to forgive. Luke vi, 36–42 was evidently considered the more authoritative rendering of the passage: it was the one chosen by the Anglican Church as the gospel for the fourth Sunday after Trinity; as such, it was also the one analysed in the postils (or formal collections of sermons on the assigned readings for the year); and the most famous and popular of the annotated Bibles, the Geneva version, assigns it five explanatory notes as against one to the equivalent texts in Matthew. Doctrinal teaching on the Luke passage, however, differs only slightly from that on the Matthew; and it is this teaching which is of primary importance, since it covers most—if not all—of the major ethical issues that appear in *Measure for Measure*.

To begin with, the authorities argue, the passage shows that it is intolerable when a man "narrowly examineth his brother's manners, and is desirous to bewray his brother's fault", especially if at the same time he neither recognizes nor regrets his own.[4] Critics who are themselves vicious can no more correct others than the blind can lead the blind. The little allegory of the mote and the beam is meant to drive home and reinforce the same lesson. "O how uncomely", cries the author of the *Brief Postil*,

how wicked, how hypocrite like, how uncharitable a thing it is, to judge our neighbours of light matters, whereas we be an hundred time worse ourselves! Why do we not rather gently bear, dissemble, and interpret well the small error and fault of our brethren? Why do we not rather go down to the entrails of our own heart, and see our own stuff?[5]

The forbearance recommended must not of course be carried to the point of condoning or refusing to censure open and serious wrong. As Calvin puts it:

He which judgeth by the rule of charity, always first examining himself, he, I say, keepeth the true and right order of judging. Nevertheless it is not only lawful for us to condemn all sins, but also it is necessary, except we will abrogate the laws of God and overthrow his judgement. For he would have us to be proclaimers of his sentences which he pronounceth as concerning the deeds of men.[6]

William Perkins, in his *Treatise of Christian Equity and Moderation* (Cambridge, 1604), is even more emphatic: courtesy and tolerance, he insists, are proper only so long as

> they whom we forbear...do not exceed, nor break out into any outrage, or extremity: for then they are not to be forborne, but to be told, and reproved for them, and man's duty is not to wink at them, but to take notice of them, and to show open dislike of them [p. 41].

But otherwise we are strictly forbidden to judge, condemn, or refuse to forgive our fellows. In the first place, we ought to be merciful, even as God also is merciful:

> Because that he hath pardoned and forgiven all our offences and trespasses, of his mere grace, without any deserving, and that through his only son Jesus Christ...according to this example, our heavenly father requireth the same thing of us.[7]

This argument is, as one might expect, used chiefly by writers on Luke, who so pointedly links his version of the passage with the doctrine of Christian forgiveness. Secondly—and on this tenet all the authorities agree—we ought to remember that whatever we do invites retaliation in kind. The good will receive their own back with interest, and "so in like manner", says Martin Bucer,

> they which are malicious against others, seekers of revengement, mindful of wrongs past, straight examiners and judgers of other men's faults, shall find also, by God's justice, such as shall handle them after the like fashion.[8]

The continual use of the passive voice in the Gospels—"ye shall be judged", "ye shall be condemned"—makes it uncertain just who is to exact this reckoning. Becon and Corvinus assume that it is God, but the general consensus seems to be rather that it is other men, for, as Calvin explains, "though this be done by the just vengeance of God, that they should again be punished, which have judged others: yet the Lord doth execute this punishment by men" (p. 210). To back this hypothesis, there is the fact that in Luke (though not in Matthew), Christ declares that "a good measure...shall *men* give into your bosom"; and we must also remember that according to the four English translations most widely used in the sixteenth century—the Matthew, the Great Bible, the Geneva, and the Bishops—the sentence immediately following ought to read: "For with what measure ye mete, with the same shall *men* mete to you again." Here or elsewhere Shakespeare evidently picked up the idea that the verse was to be taken in this sense: Richard of Gloucester uses it in *3 Henry VI* to justify the most savage and literal sort of retaliation in kind:

> From off the gates of York fetch down the head,
> Your father's head, which Clifford placed there;
> Instead whereof let this supply the room.
> Measure for measure must be answered.
>
> (II, vi, 52–5)

But however natural and authorized such an interpretation of the text might have been, it was not quite a satisfactory one when the passage was considered as a whole, especially in the Luke version. For who actually is to return rash judgment for rash judgment, condemnation for condemnation, like for like? Men? The same men who have just been explicitly commanded to forbear judgment and forgive injuries?[9] God, then? The same God whom His Son has just described as "kind to the unkind, and to the evil", the Father according to Whose example we are urged to be merciful? At least one Renaissance theologian, William Perkins, seems to have been so distressed by these alternatives that he feels obliged to explain in his *Exposition* (p. 417) that though God does not will men to return evil for evil, and those who indulge in the practice are miserable sinners, God nevertheless uses their wickedness to punish the other miserable sinners who have done evil in the first place. But the rest of the commentators I have seen hardly appear to recognize the problem at all. It is almost as if they approve of mercy at one level of consciousness, and of retaliation in kind at another: separate concepts which do not interact and remain essentially unfused, like the responsibilities Pooh-Bah attaches to his various offices in *The Mikado*. One is certainly aware of a logical incoherence, a failure to think through the question clearly or completely. We may of course argue that if the professional exponents of the Scriptures did not perceive these difficulties, they would scarcely be likely to worry the Elizabethan layman; but it is at least conceivable that a sensitive reader of the passage, even in the sixteenth century, might have observed them—and been troubled.

One more point of doctrine still remains to be discussed. Since extreme sects like the Anabaptists habitually used Scriptural authority to support their arguments for a community of goods, the abolition of civil government, and the like, Protestant theologians took particular pains to qualify or explain away texts capable of any such dangerous interpretation; and as a result we find Becon, Corvinus, Heminge, Perkins, and the author of the *Brief Postil* going out of their way to make it clear that the commands to be merciful, to forgive, and to abstain from judging are meant to bind only the private individual, not to restrict or abolish the authority of the State. Even the Geneva Bible devotes part of its limited and precious marginal space to a note on Luke, vi, 37, warning the reader that Christ "speaketh not here of civil judgments, and therefore by the words, forgive, is meant that good nature which the Christians use in suffering and pardoning wrongs". "Mark, my friends", says the author of the *Brief Postil*,

that this is only spoken of private judgment and private condemnation, that is to say, I may not be mine own judge, I may not revenge mine own quarrel....It is lawful for rulers, to judge and to condemn, because they do it not in their own name, but as God's ministers and vicars. To this do all the ancient expositors and doctors agree, as Saint Austin, Jerome, Ambrose, Chrysostom, and the rest. Wherefore the wicked Anabaptists are to be banished which condemn temporal or civil judgments.[10]

On the other hand, the civil magistrate was evidently not considered entirely exempt from all the rules Christ lays down in this passage, especially the stipulation that a man should not try to pull the mote from his brother's eye before casting the beam out of his own. "Consider", writes William Perkins in his *Exposition*,

how Christ would have all those which are to give judgment of the offences of others to be themselves without reproof or blame: else they are no fit persons to give censure of those that be under them. And therefore the Magistrate in the town and commonwealth...and every superior in his place must labour to be unblameable [p. 424].

But when the theologians begin arguing in this vein, they are drawing into the discussion the whole question of the rights and obligations of the temporal authority; and it is to the special studies made of this particular subject that we must turn for further light on our problem.

Sermons and treatises defining the status, privileges, and responsibilities of the Christian governor are plentiful enough during the sixteenth century—Antony Guevara's *Dial of Princes*, translated by North in 1557; Geoffrey Fenton's *Forme of Christian Pollicie* (1574); Henry Bullinger's *Fiftie Godlie and Learned Sermons* (1587); James I's *Basilicon Doron* (1599), to name only a few. But in 1603 and 1604, public interest in the question seems to have been especially keen. In those years, King James's *True Lawe of Free Monarchies* was reprinted twice and his *Basilicon Doron* seven times—nine if we count the Welsh translation and William Willymat's digest in Latin and English verse. There also appeared a number of works dealing wholly or in part with the office and duties of the Christian ruler—such as six sermons preached before King James at various times by Thomas Bilson, Richard Eedes, Henry Hooke, Thomas Blague, and Richard Field; reprints of Henry Smith's *Magistrates Scripture* and *Memento for Magistrates*; Andrew Willet's *Ecclesia Triumphans*, a tract showing how James met all the requirements of an ideal ruler; *A Loyal Subiect's Looking-Glasse*, by William Willymat; Ben Jonson's *Panegyre* on the King's first entrance into Parliament; and William Perkins' posthumous *Treatise of Christian Equity and Moderation*. This outburst of concern with the theory of government seems to have been inspired primarily by the accession of James. A certain amount of such preaching and writing would probably have occurred on the arrival of any new monarch, but in this particular case, it must have been greatly stimulated by the fact that the new monarch was himself an authority on the subject, whose work was being eagerly discussed by the public and whose favour the court clergy and *literati* were naturally anxious to gain. It is noticeable how much of the material listed above was originally composed to be delivered before James himself, and how many of the authors manage to include flattering tributes to their royal master and his work in the field, as Thomas Bilson did:

In the Prince's duty I may be shorter, because I speak before a religious and learned King, who both by pen and practice hath witnessed to the world these many years, how well acquainted he is with Christian and godly government.[11]

Now *Measure for Measure* is very largely concerned with the "Prince's duty", particularly in regard to the administration of justice. At no time, perhaps, could Shakespeare have presented such a subject without reckoning to some extent on what his audience would be predisposed to think of his characters and their behaviour. But if he *did* write the play about 1603–4, he had unusually good reason to believe the subject would be popular and to consider it in terms of the contemporary doctrine of rule—even if we do not assume that he, like so many others, was seriously concerned over the problems of Christian and godly government and deliberately trying to catch the eye of the King, at whose court it was acted and to whose well-known dislike of crowds two passages apparently allude (I, i, 67–73; II, iv, 26–9).

According to Renaissance theory, the authority of all civil rulers is derived from God. Hence, they may be called 'gods', as they are in Psalm lxxxii, 6, because they act as God's substitutes, "Ruling, Judging, and Punishing in God's stead, and so deserving God's name here on earth", as Bilson put it in the sermon he preached at King James's coronation.[12] "The Prince", says Henry Smith in his *Magistrates Scripture* (pp. 339–40), "is like a great Image of God, the Magistrates are like little Images of God", though he is careful to point out that they are not indeed divine: the name is given them only to remind them that they are appointed by the Lord "to rule as he would rule, judge as he would judge, correct as he would correct, reward as he would reward". This doctrine may very well explain why the Duke moves through so much of the action of *Measure for Measure* like an embodied Providence; why his character has such curiously allegorical overtones, yet never quite slips over the edge into actual allegory; and finally, why Roy Battenhouse's theory that Shakespeare subconsciously thought of him as the Incarnate Lord is at once so convincing and so unsatisfactory. Any Renaissance audience would have taken it for granted that the Duke did indeed "stand for" God, but only as any good ruler "stood for" Him; and if he behaved "like power divine", it was because that was the way a good ruler was expected to conduct himself.

Furthermore, since the ruler's authority was considered an extension of the same kind of power God delegates to parents, teachers, ministers, masters, shepherds, and husbands, all these terms were frequently used to describe him, especially 'father' and 'shepherd'.[13] So when the Duke compares himself to a fond father who has not disciplined his children for so long that they have run wild (I, iii, 23–8), the image probably meant rather more to a Renaissance audience than it would mean to a modern one. When later, after his discussion with the Provost, he rises at dawn to go about his work with the remark: "Look, th'unfolding star calls up the shepherd" (IV, ii, 219), one wonders if he may not be thinking of himself and his office. God was, moreover, supposed to endow rulers with what was called "sufficiency of spirit" to carry out their duties, though He might withdraw this gift if they disobeyed Him, as He withdrew it from Saul.[14] It is possible that this doctrine has some bearing on the treatment of Angelo in *Measure for Measure*, though there is no reason why Shakespeare should not have been thinking of something much more elementary when he showed him failing to pray successfully after his fall, or lamenting:

> Alack, when once our grace we have forgot,
> Nothing goes right—we would, and we would not.   (IV, iv, 31–2)

In their capacity as God's substitutes, rulers have four privileges. The first is sanctity of person, especially in the case of an anointed prince. No man may raise his hand against him, or even disparage him in speech or thought.[15] To abuse a ruler, according to William Willymat, by "evil speaking, mocking, scorning, scoffing, deriding, reviling, cursing", is a thing "most unhonourable, yea worthy of death" (p. 32)—a belief which must have made Lucio's malicious gossip about the Duke appear a much more serious offence than it seems to a modern audience. Secondly, the ruler has sovereignty of power: all men must obey him without question, except when his commands directly contradict God's ordinances. Even then, disobedience must be entirely passive, and any retaliation from the authorities endured with patience—although Roman Catholics held that open rebellion was sometimes permissible when the ruler was a heretic.[16] As the authorities in *Measure for Measure* are not heretics, this particular question does not arise: there is no doubt that the characters are legally bound to reverence and obey them. But this raised a problem which required—and received—very delicate handling. Since to yield to Angelo would mean breaking a law of God, Isabella is fully entitled to resist him; but the measures taken to circumvent him are by no means passive and might even have been considered to savour dangerously of conspiracy against a lawful magistrate if Shakespeare did not slip neatly away from the whole difficulty by making the chief conspirator the highest officer of the State himself. And as if to ensure that no one should miss the point, he brings it out clearly and carefully in IV, ii, where the excellent Provost refuses to join the plot to save Claudio until he is convinced by the Duke's letter that the friar has the necessary secular power to override the deputy.

The third privilege of rulers is the right to enforce the law. In civil matters, the avenging of evil, which God has strictly forbidden to private individuals, is the office and duty of the ruler and his subordinates,[17] to whom the Duke bids Isabella turn when, in her agony at Claudio's supposed death, she momentarily thinks of punishing Angelo herself. The further question of the ruler's title to authority in ecclesiastical as well as civil matters (since, as King James puts it in the *Basilicon Doron*, p. 110, "a King is not *mere laicus*, as both the Papists and Anabaptists would have him; to the which error the Puritans also incline over-far") is not brought up in *Measure for Measure*.

Finally, the ruler has the privilege of using extraordinary means. As Gentillet points out, this certainly does not imply that he is entitled to deceive, betray, and commit perjury in the manner recommended by Machiavelli, but only, in the words of William Willymat, that

Kings, Princes, and governors do use oftentimes to use diverse causes to disguise their purposes with pretences and colours of other matters, so that the end of their drifts and secret purposes are not right seen into nor understood at the first, this to be lawful the word of God doth not deny.

He then cites the examples of Solomon ordering the child divided; Jehu pretending he would serve Baal, when by this subtlety he really intended to destroy the servants of Baal (II Kings x); and the Emperor Constantius threatening to persecute the Christians when all he actually meant to do was by this stratagem to separate the sheep from the goats.[18] Hence, the Duke in *Measure for Measure* is quite justified in using disguise, applying "craft against vice" (III, ii, 291), and secretly watching Angelo much as King James advises his son in the *Basilicon Doron* to watch his own subordinates: "Delight to haunt your Session, and spy carefully their proceedings...to take a sharp account of every man in his office" (pp. 90–2). There would have been no need to apologize for these practices to a Renaissance audience; they would have shrugged them off with the equivalent of Willymat's conclusion to his argument: "Had it not been great lack of wisdom to have interrupted these Christian princes' pretences and commandments tending as afterward proved to so good an end?"

But in the eyes of the Renaissance, the Christian prince had not only authority and privileges, but a clearly defined and inescapable set of duties to perform as well. The first is to remember that he is not really God, but man "dressed in a little brief authority", as Isabella reminds Angelo—mere man, whom his God will in the end call strictly to account, although his subjects may not.[19] He cannot make a single decision at which the Lord is not invisibly present and which He does not weigh and record, as He is said to do in Psalm lxxxii, 1, where, according to Henry Hooke,

the Prophet David reproving the judges and magistrates of his time...rippeth up the secret cause of such supine defect in matter of justice: They understand nothing, saith he, they know not that God standeth as a judge in the middest of their assemblies; therefore, they walk in darkness, the eye of their conscience being hoodwinked, that they could not see to do equity and judgement.[20]

It is to this text (with all its associations) that Angelo is almost certainly referring when he cries at his exposure:

I perceive your grace, like pow'r divine,
Hath look'd upon my passes.

(V, i, 374–5)

As ever in his great Taskmaster's eye, therefore, the ruler must labour to be what God would have him. To begin with, he must be sincerely religious [21]—or, as the Duke puts it in his soliloquy at the end of Act III,

> He who the sword of heaven will bear
> Should be as holy as severe. (III, ii, 275–6)

Furthermore, he must know and be able to govern himself; for, says Guevara, "when they asked [Thales] what a prince should do to govern others, he answered: he ought first to govern himself, and then afterwards to govern others"[22]—a principle we have already encountered in the commentaries on the mote and the beam and find again in *Measure for Measure*, where it is most clearly stated when the Duke declares in his soliloquy that the ruler must be a man

> More nor less to others paying
> Than by self-offences weighing.
> Shame to him whose cruel striking
> Kills for faults of his own liking! (III, ii, 279–82)

He should also cultivate all the virtues to the best of his ability, but according to the *Basilicon Doron,*

make one of them, which is Temperance, Queen of all the rest within you. I mean not by the vulgar interpretation of Temperance, which only consists in *gustu & tactu,* by the moderation of these two senses: but I mean of that wise moderation, that first commanding your self, shall as Queen, command all the affections and passions of your mind [p. 84].

Therefore, when Escalus describes the Duke as "one that above all other strifes, contended especially to know himself", and "a gentleman of all temperance" (III, ii, 246–7, 251), what may seem rather faint praise to a modern reader would have been regarded as a very high tribute indeed during the Renaissance. Finally, in all he does, the ruler must remember that his life is the pattern for his subjects, and that, as Richard Eedes explains, "neither are the hearts of the people so easily turned and carried with the dead letter of a written law, as with that life of law, *Justice* living in the life of the prince".[23]

> Pattern in himself to know
> Grace to stand and virtue go, (III, ii, 277–8)

is the way the Duke puts it in his soliloquy.

The more practical and specific duties of the ruler are to get a good education, especially in political theory; to love his subjects and be thoroughly acquainted with them—"O how necessary it is", exclaims Guevara, "for a prince to know and understand all things in his Realm, to the end no man might deceive him, as they do nowadays!" (I, 55ʳ); to levy no undue taxes, or waste them when collected—the reciprocal duty of the subject being to pay up cheerfully; to keep peace with all nations if possible, but to protect his own against foreign injury or aggression; to make his laws clear and plain; to choose wise subordinates, control them carefully, and according to Gentillet, let them execute any measures so rigorous that the ruler may be suspected of a purely arbitrary use of his power: "to shun that suspicion and blame, it is good that the prince delegate and set over such matters to Judges, which are good men, not suspected or passionate"

(p. 350). It should be noted that this is just what the Duke does in *Measure for Measure*. As he confides to Friar Thomas,

> I have on Angelo impos'd the office,
> Who may in th' ambush of my name strike home,
> And yet my nature never in the fight
> To do it slander.
>
> (I, iii, 40–3)

He also conforms to the Renaissance ideal in loving his subjects and taking steps "to know and understand all things in his Realm, to the end no man might deceive him". His accomplishments in education, taxation, legislation, war, and peace, however, have little bearing on the major issue of the play, and are huddled away under the general statement that "let him be but testimonied in his own bringings-forth, and he shall appear to the envious a scholar, a statesman, and a soldier" (III, ii, 152–5).

But the highest and most important of the ruler's specific duties is to see well to the administration of justice. Here more than anywhere else he and his deputies must act consciously as the substitutes of God; or, in Fenton's words: "the Judges raised by [God] to dispense justice in his place, ought always to have the Majesty of him in their minds, and his judgments in imitation."[24] "They should think", adds Henry Smith, in his *Magistrates Scripture*, "how Christ would judge, before they judge, because God's Law is appointed for their Law" (p. 342). They must not, of course, play favourites, put off decisions, allow their passions to carry them away, accept bribes, give in to fear, be ignorant, listen to slander, or refuse to hear the complaints of the oppressed. But above all, both the chief and the inferior magistrates must cherish the innocent and punish the wicked with all due severity. Bad judges, according to William Perkins' *Treatise on Christian Equity and Moderation*, are of two kinds: the first are

such men, as by a certain foolish kind of pity are so carried away, that would have nothing but *mercy, mercy*, and would...have the extremity of the law executed on no man. This is the high way to abolish laws, and consequently to pull down authority, and so in the end to open a door to all confusion, disorder, and to all licentiousness of life. But I need not say much herein, for there are but few that offend in this kind, man's nature being generally inclined rather to cruelty than to mercy.

The second kind are

such men as have nothing in their mouths, but the *law*, the *law*: and *Justice, Justice*: in the meantime forgetting that Justice always shakes hands with her sister mercy, and that all laws allow a mitigation.... These men, therefore, strike so precisely on their points, and the very tricks and trifles of the law, as (so the law be kept, and that in the very extremity of it) they care not, though equity were trodden under foot: and that law may reign on earth, and they by it: they care not, though mercy take her to her wings, and fly to heaven. These men (for all their goodly shews) are the decayers of our estate, and enemies of all good government.

Mercy and justice, he goes on to say,

are the two pillars, that uphold the throne of the Prince: as you cannot hold mercy, where Justice is banished, so cannot you keep Justice where mercy is exiled: and as mercy without Justice, is foolish pity, so Justice, without mercy, is cruelty [pp. 15–18].

65

The same contrast and conclusions drawn by Perkins can be found in many other authorities;[25] and nobody, as far as I know, quarrels with the general principle that mercy should temper justice. The authorities tend, however, to apply it rather narrowly, and only to cases where, as Gentillet cautiously insists, it can "have a good foundation upon reason and equity" (p. 217), as when a man accidentally kills his friend— the example given by Bullinger (p. 188); or a young boy steals food because of hunger—the one given by Perkins in his *Treatise* (pp. 13–14). No one advocates showing leniency to more serious or hardened criminals. Since, as we know, Christian forgiveness was looked on as something apart from public and civil judgment, it is perhaps hardly surprising to find judicial clemency thus limited in practice to considerations of ordinary common sense and a reasonable regard for the circumstance of a case. But when we remember that ideal rulers were also by definition deeply religious men, who were supposed to "think how Christ would judge, before they judge", we cannot help feeling that the theorists have raised a problem to which they do not give all the attention it deserves. To a lesser degree, this holds true even when they turn to the private individual. He may, they argue, appeal to the law for the redress of injury, since God ordained the civil order for that purpose, though as a Christian he must forgive the malice which accompanied the injury.[26] But as was probably only natural in an age when personal revenge still enjoyed a certain amount of social (though not religious) prestige, the great majority of writers are concerned simply with establishing the tenet that punishment is the proper business of the civil authorities, to whom the private individual must leave it. Whether he has any further practical responsibility for his enemies beyond letting the law take its course is a question they do not go into. Again, however, when we remember how eloquently Erasmus Sarcerius, for instance, can argue (fol. xciv^v) that charity must be extended without reservation to "friends or enemies, Christians or not Christians...according to the example of the heavenly father, as before is said (Math. v, Luc. vi)", we are aware of a certain failure to pull the concepts of mercy and retaliation together—a failure not clearly intentional or obvious, but present, as it is in the commentaries on the measure-for-measure passage we have already discussed.

Allusions to the measure-for-measure passage occasionally crop up in the studies of rule, just as references to the doctrine of rule keep recurring in discussions of the measure-for-measure passage. Guevara, for example, writes that wicked rulers are like the blind leading the blind (I, 50^v), and Fenton, that they are like men with motes or beams in their eyes which prevent them from seeing anything justly (p. 64). Willymat orders the slanderers of princes to stop judging, "lest (as Christ Jesus said) you yourselves be judged" (p. 64), while King James in the *Basilicon Doron* urges his son to give measure for measure, warns him that he must expect to receive it, and advises him to be faultless because what would be "a mote in another's eye, is a beam in yours" (pp. 152, 32, 2). Evidently the passage was one which writers often recalled when working on the doctrine of rule, and frequently brought to the attention of their readers. But Shakespeare would have had special reason to take note of it. The heroine of his play is a private individual wrestling with the very issues raised by the passage: judgment, tolerance, mercy, retaliation in kind, and Christian forgiveness. His hero and his villain are primarily concerned with the same issues as they appear on a different level—to the holder of public office. His villain has, in addition, just those deficiencies of character which form the clearest and most commonly observed link between the doctrine of rule and the commentaries on the passage.

And so, centred as *Measure for Measure* is on the very points at which the two are either parallel or interlocked, it is hardly surprising to find that Shakespeare was apparently influenced to some extent by both.

His treatment of the initial situation seems to have been based in part on the crude but picturesque contrast which the Renaissance theorists so often drew between the two types of bad magistrate. The Duke, at the beginning of the play, would be recognized at once as the type who has failed because he was too merciful to enforce the laws properly. Shakespeare is certainly no Anabaptist—he sees, as clearly as William Perkins himself, the necessity of civil authority, and the terrible picture he paints of Vienna society in decay fully supports Perkins' contention that sentimental pity in a governor merely "opens a door to all confusion, disorder, and to all licentiousness of life". The Duke is essentially a wise and noble man who has erred from an excess of good will; he has put an end to his foolishness before the action proper begins, and so can step gracefully into the role of hero and good ruler; but Shakespeare does not disguise the fact that he has been wrong: he himself frankly describes his laxity as a 'vice' (III, ii, 284), and as such any Renaissance audience would certainly consider it.

Angelo, on the other hand, is a perfect case-study in the opposite weakness. Whatever he afterwards becomes, he is not from the first the ordinary venal judge, who is ignorant or cowardly, refuses to hear complaints (for he listens to Isabella), or takes bribes (for his indignation when she unfortunately uses the word sounds quite real); and as she pleads on his behalf at the end of the play:

> A due sincerity governed his deeds,
> Till he did look on me.
>
> (v, i, 451–2)

But he is the epitome of all the men who "have nothing in their mouths but the *law*, the *law*: and *Justice, Justice*, in the meantime forgetting that Justice always shakes hands with her sister mercy". This harshness Shakespeare traces to the personal flaw described in the measure-for-measure passage: the bitter and uncharitable narrowness in judging others that springs from a refusal to recognize or deal with one's own faults. Unlike the Duke, Angelo has not contended especially to know himself; he has no real conception of the potentialities of his own character. As a result, he thinks so well of himself that he neither has any defence against sudden overwhelming temptation nor possesses the humility and comprehension necessary to deal properly with Claudio.

His treatment of Claudio is from the first inexcusable, even by the strict standards of the Renaissance. For clemency in this particular case would certainly have had "a good foundation upon reason and equity": Claudio and Juliet are betrothed; they fully intend to marry; they are penitent; and the law was drowsy and neglected when they broke it. Furthermore, Claudio comes of a good family; and his fault is, after all, a very natural one. Shakespeare wisely leaves these last points to be made by Escalus and the Provost, both kind, sensible men who represent the normal point of view and whose support of Claudio is therefore significant. But Isabella cannot treat the offence lightly without weakening both the dignity of her calling and the force of her horror at Angelo's proposal. So in the first scene where she implores him for her brother's life, she bases her plea chiefly on modulations and variations of the two great Christian arguments we have already encountered in discussions of the measure-for-measure passage, interwoven with appropriate material from the doctrine of rule. The first is most clearly stated when, after pointing out that clemency is considered a virtue in the ruler, she begs him to remember that we must be merciful, as the Father was also merciful in redeeming us:

> Why, all the souls that were were forfeit once,
> And he that might the vantage best have took
> Found out the remedy. How would you be
> If he which is the top of judgement should
> But judge you as you are? O, think on that!
> And mercy then will breathe within your lips
> Like man new-made.   (II, ii, 73–9)

And then, after reminding him that a ruler is only a man dressed in a little brief authority, she urges him to think of his own faults before he condemns Claudio's:

> Go to your bosom,
> Knock there and ask your heart what it doth know
> That's like my brother's fault. If it confess
> A natural guiltiness such as is his,
> Let it not sound a thought upon your tongue
> Against my brother's life.   (II, ii, 136–41)

But it should be noted that she does not threaten him with retaliation in kind for his cruelty. Indeed, in her eagerness to show him that it *is* cruelty and to convince him that he ought to do as he would be done by, she argues rather that she in his place would not be so severe:

> I would to heaven I had your potency
> And you were Isabel! Should it then be thus?
> No! I would tell what 'twere to be a judge,
> And what a prisoner.   (II, ii, 66–9)

Her problem is not, however, to be quite such a simple one. Angelo's next move is not to throw himself on her kindness, but attempt to take advantage of it. If she is truly so merciful, he implies, she should be willing to rescue Claudio even at the expense of breaking what the Renaissance regarded as a most sacred law of God, and one doubly binding upon her because she is not only a virgin but a novice: if she refuses,

> Were you not then as cruel as the sentence
> That you have slandered so?   (II, iv, 109–10)

The modern reader may find it difficult not to echo this question, particularly when Claudio himself breaks down and adds the weight of his own desperate pleading to Angelo's arguments. Why, after all her talk of charity and forbearance, should Isabella not only decline to save her brother's life by an act of generosity, but condemn him so unsparingly for begging her to do so? When, however, we remember the limitations which Renaissance doctrine set on both charity and forbearance, we have no right to assume that Shakespeare is deliberately and cynically implying that his heroine is, in her own way, as narrow and cold as his villain. He seems rather to be trying to emphasize and illustrate the familiar tenet that neither charity nor forbearance must be carried to the point of permitting or condoning outrage. Like the Duke on the public level, Isabella is not entitled to let Angelo and Claudio use her mercy as their bawd; and, as the commentators on the measure-for-measure passage had made clear, her "duty is not to wink at them, but to take notice of them, and to show open dislike of them". Claudio is such a pathetic figure, and his horror of death so dreadfully comprehensible, that it may be fair to wonder if Shakespeare, when writing the prison scene, was not momentarily caught in what Tucker Brooke would call one of his conflicts of "intuitive sympathy with predetermined form"; [27] but there is no evidence that he or his audience would not have felt Isabella's conduct was both demanded and justified by the ethical pattern of the play as he had consciously established it.

The conspiracy which follows also has its place in that pattern. It takes the form of a deliberate infliction upon Angelo of like for like, as the Duke is at pains to inform the audience in his soliloquy:

> So disguise shall, by th' disguised
> Pay with falsehood false exacting (III, ii, 294–5)

—offence punishing offence just as it is said to do in the measure-for-measure passage and the commentaries upon it. It should be noted, however, that the responsibility for devising and managing the whole plot rests on the shoulders of the Duke, who has a ruler's right to see to retaliation in kind and a ruler's privilege of using extraordinary means to ensure the success of a worthy cause. The part which Isabella necessarily plays in the conspiracy is as far as possible minimized: we are not allowed actually to see her persuading Mariana, reporting to Angelo, or doing anything but simply agreeing to the scheme because it is presented to her as the only sure way to save Claudio, protect herself, right Mariana, and secure any real evidence against the deputy. Unlike the Duke, she acts from no special desire to pay Angelo back in his own coin; it is only afterwards, when she hears the news of Claudio's death by his treachery, that she breaks down and very understandably cries for personal and immediate revenge: "O, I will to him and pluck out his eyes!" (IV, iii, 124). The calmer Duke then very properly persuades her that she ought instead to turn her cause over to the civil authorities:

> And you shall have your bosom on this wretch,
> Grace of the Duke, revenges to your heart,
> And general honour. (IV, iii, 139–41)

The audience at the first performance of the play probably took this promise at its face-value, as a prediction that Angelo was to suffer full legal punishment for his offences in the trial to come. Nor would they have disapproved. His case is very different from Claudio's. His judge, the Duke, is not, as he was, unfit for his task; and he cannot plead for mercy "with a good foundation upon reason and equity", as Claudio could. Although he has not actually succeeded in doing the worst he intended to do, there is still a heavy count against him: attempted seduction, abuse of his authority, deception of his prince, and treachery of the meanest kind; while if he *had* done what he himself and every character on the stage except the Duke believes that he has, there was nothing to be said against the Duke's sentence:

> The very mercy of the law cries out
> Most audible, even from his proper tongue,

'An Angelo for Claudio, death for death.'
Haste still pays haste, and leisure answers leisure;
Like doth quit like, and Measure still for Measure....
We do condemn thee to the very block
Where Claudio stooped to death, and with like haste.   (v, i, 412–20)

The audience, knowing what they knew, probably did not expect that the execution would really take place; but they can hardly have been prepared for what actually follows. First, Mariana, still pathetically devoted to her husband, begs the Duke for his life; and then, failing, she turns to Isabella—who is not in love with Angelo, who has every good reason to loathe him, who might plead with justice that his punishment is now entirely a matter for the civil authorities —and begs for her help.

The cruelty of the appeal is obvious; and the natural, the instinctive, and (we must remember) the allowed reply to it is implicit in the shocked exclamation of the Duke:

Against all sense you do importune her.
Should she kneel down, in mercy of this fact,
Her brother's ghost his paved bed would break,
And take her hence in horror.   (v, i, 438–41)

Then Mariana cries out to Isabella again—and she kneels, not in silence, which is all Mariana dares to ask for, but generously to make the best case she can for Angelo. Her act is not natural; it is not (as the Duke has carefully pointed out) even reasonable: it is sheer, reckless forgiveness of the kind Christ advocates in the Sermon on the Mount—the great pronouncement which in Luke immediately precedes and forms part of the measure-for-measure passage. And like Christ, Shakespeare contrasts this sort of forgiveness with another. Mariana is certainly more praiseworthy than the 'sinners' described by the Lord, for Angelo has treated her very badly; but her mercy to him resembles theirs in that it springs primarily from preference and affection: she loves her lover (to quote the common sixteenth-century translation of Luke vi, 32) and she hopes for something again—the renewal of his devotion and a happy marriage with him. Hence, however gracious and commendable her conduct may be, it differs markedly from that of Isabella, who has nothing to sustain her but the conviction that she *must* be merciful and the memory of what she had promised Angelo on the strength of it. And then, almost before the audience at the first performance had time to catch its breath, the Duke, having summoned Claudio and revealed the truth, proceeds not only to pardon him, but to let off Angelo, Lucio, and Barnardine as well, with penalties entirely disproportionate to what their conduct deserved by ordinary Renaissance standards.

We may, if we please, argue that Shakespeare suddenly remembered he was writing a comedy and decided he had better botch up some sort of happy ending to send the audience home contented, regardless of probability and doctrine alike. But all the evidence goes to show that the audience would have left for home equally contented—perhaps even more contented—if Angelo, Lucio, and Barnardine had been punished, like Shylock, or remanded for judgment at some future date, like Don John in *Much Ado about Nothing*. And when we recall the special difficulties and defects of Renaissance doctrine, it seems at least possible that the conclusion of

Measure for Measure may rather represent a deliberate effort—perhaps a little clumsy, certainly romantic—to "do something" about that disturbing discrepancy between the concepts of religious mercy and secular justice which we find in the commentaries on the measure-for-measure passage and again in the studies of rule. Like the theorists, Shakespeare was apparently prepared to concede that the private Christian should not (in the name of mercy) weakly condone every form of injustice and oppression, and may, if necessary, invoke secular authority to defend what he knows to be right. But it is not enough merely to wash his hands of personal revenge, and—let the secular authority do the dirty work for him. Nor should the secular authority himself forget that "judging as Christ would judge" means something more than weighing each case according to common sense and ordinary good will. He need not make a scarecrow of the law: he must be vigilant to suppress or prevent disorder and evil; and he should see to it that the innocent are properly protected—that Isabella's name is cleared by her traducer; that Barnardine is committed to the friar instead of being turned loose on society; that Claudio makes amends to Juliet, Angelo to Mariana, Lucio to the girl he has wronged. He may even, to a certain extent, use retaliation in kind, or the threat of retaliation in kind, to bring malefactors to their senses: it is no accident that Angelo is paid with falsehood false exacting, or finds himself sentenced to the very block where Claudio stooped to death, and with like haste. But his primary duty is, like God, to show mercy whenever he possibly can, even when the fault is disgusting and the criminal despicable: to remember that Lucio's slanders hurt chiefly the Duke's own personal feelings; that Barnardine is a mere animal,

> A creature unprepared, unmeet for death;
> And to transport him in the mind he is
> Were damnable;   (IV, iii, 71–3)

that Angelo has been blasted and shamed out of his appalling complacency, and may, as Mariana pleads: "become much more the better / For being a little bad" (V, i, 445–6). It is the difference between the "Like doth quit like" with which the Duke begins his sentence on his deputy and the "Well, Angelo, your evil quits you well", with which he concludes it.

In all this, Shakespeare is not so much rejecting the ordinary Christian doctrine of the Renaissance as clarifying it, strengthening it, and holding it true to its own deepest implications. Just how or when he formed his own opinions on the question there is no telling. We do not know what books he read or what sermons he attended, although we should note that he could have picked up practically all the necessary doctrinal instruction from reading two books or hearing two sermons that interested him, while the agreement between the various authorities makes it certain that the theories he was taught would not differ drastically from the ones we have already summed up and discussed. The investigation, however, sheds no light on his own denominational preferences; he touches in this play only on such elements of traditional theology as were shared by Anglican, Puritan, and Roman Catholic alike. Nor, since to dramatize a doctrine is not necessarily to believe in it, are we entitled to use *Measure for Measure* as evidence that he himself was even a Christian. All that can be said with safety is that when he put his mind to it, he could produce a more coherent, a more independent, and in the last analysis, a more Christian piece of thinking on the subject than nine out of ten professional Renaissance theologians.

NOTES

1. This article is based on material gathered when the writer was holder of a research fellowship at the Folger Shakespeare Library.

2. R. W. Battenhouse, "*Measure for Measure* and Christian Doctrine of the Atonement", *P.M.L.A.* LXI (1946), 1029–59; C. J. Sisson, *The Mythical Sorrows of Shakespeare* (Annual Shakespeare Lecture of the British Academy, 1934), p. 17; R. W. Chambers, *The Jacobean Shakespeare and 'Measure for Measure'* (Annual Shakespeare Lecture of the British Academy, 1937), p. 54.

3. Luke vi, 27–42. Geneva version (London, 1599). The spelling of this and all subsequent citations from Renaissance sources has been modernized for the convenience of the reader.

4. John Calvin, quoted by Augustine Marlorate, in his *Catholike and Ecclesiasticall Exposition of...S. Mathewe*, trans. Thomas Tymme (London, 1570), p. 136. See also J. Calvin, *A Harmonie vpon...Matthewe, Marke, and Luke*, trans. E. P. (London, 1584), p. 209; *The Epistles and Gospelles with a Brief Postil* [ed. R. Taverner], (n.p., 1540), sig. Bb. 1ʳ; Desiderius Erasmus, *The First Tome...of the Paraphrase...vpon the Newe Testament* (London, 1548), fol. lxxviiᵛ; [Antonius Corvinus], *A Postill...vpon Euery Gospell through the Yeare* (n.p., 1550), sigs. Piiᵛ–Piiiiᵛ; Nicholas Heminge [Niel Hemmingsen], *A Postill or Exposition of the Gospels*, trans. Arthur Golding (London, 1569), fol. 208ʳ; William Perkins, *Exposition of Christs Sermon in the Mount* (Cambridge, 1608), pp. 408–13; the Rheims note on Matt. vii, 1 in William Fulke's *Text of the Newe Testament...translated out of the vulgar Latine by the Papists of the Traiterous Seminarie at Rhemes* (London, 1589), sig. F1ᵛ.

5. *Brief Postil*, sig. Bb. 1ʳ. See also Calvin, p. 211; Musculus and Bullinger, quoted by Marlorate, *Exposition of Matthew*, p. 137; Thomas Becon, *A New Postil* (London, 1566), sigs. Eeiʳ–Eeiiᵛ; note on Luke vi, 42 in Geneva Bible; Perkins, *Exposition*, pp. 419–31; Corvinus, sig. Piiiiᵛ; Erasmus, fol. lxxviiiʳ; Heminge, fol. 210ᵛ.

6. Calvin, p. 209. See also Marlorate, *Exposition of Matthew*, p. 136; *Brief Postil*, sig. Bb. 1ʳ; Rheims note on Matt. vii, 1; Geneva note on Luke vi, 37; Perkins, *Exposition*, pp. 408, 424–5; Erasmus, fol. lxxviiᵛ.

7. Corvinus, sig. Piiiiᵛ. See also Becon, sigs. Ddiʳ–Ddiiiʳ; Ddvʳ–Ddviʳ; *Brief Postil*, sigs. Aa. iijʳ–Aa. iijᵛ; Erasmus, fol. lxxviiʳ; Heminge, fols. 208ᵛ and 209ᵛ.

8. Quoted by Marlorate in *A Catholike and Ecclesiastical Exposition of...S. Mark and S. Luke*, trans. Thomas Tymme (London, 1583), p. 160. See also Calvin, pp. 209–10; Perkins, *Exposition*, p. 415; *Brief Postil*, sig. Aa. ivᵛ; Corvinus, sigs. Pvʳ–Pvᵛ; Becon, sig. Eeiʳ; Erasmus, fol. lxxviiᵛ; Heminge, fol. 210ʳ.

9. It should also be noted that in Matt. v, 38 ff., the passage which corresponds to the pronouncement on Christian forgiveness in Luke (vi, 27–35) begins with a specific repudiation of the *lex talionis*.

10. *Brief Postil*, sigs. Aa. iijᵛ–Aa. ivʳ. See also Becon, sigs. Ddiiiʳ–Ddiiiᵛ; Corvinus, sig. Piiiiʳ; Heminge, fols. 207ᵛ, 208ʳ, 209ʳ; Perkins, *Exposition*, pp. 407–8.

11. Thomas Bilson, *A Sermon Preached at Westminister before the King and Queenes Maiesties, at their Coronations* (London, 1603), sigs. C3ʳ–C3ᵛ. See also Andrew Willet, *Ecclesia Triumphans* [1603], (Cambridge, 1614), p. 33 and sigs. A3ʳ–A4ʳ, A4ᵛ–A5ʳ; William Willymat, *A Loyal Subiects Looking-Glasse* (London, [1604]), sig. A1ʳ, pp. 10, 39, 46; Richard Eedes, "The Dutie of a King", two sermons preached before James (9 and 30 August, 1603), printed in *Six Learned and Godly Sermons* (London, 1604), sigs. Fijᵛ–Fiijʳ.

12. Bilson, sigs. A6ᵛ–A7ᵛ. See also Perkins, *Treatise*, p. 6; Willymat, pp. 3–4, 5–6; Willet, p. 3; Richard Field, *A Learned Sermon Preached Before the King* (London, 1604), sigs. A3ᵛ–A4ʳ; Henry Smith, *The Magistrates Scripture* [1590], printed in *Sermons* (London, 1631), p. 344; Ben Jonson, *King James His Royall and Magnificent Entertainment* (London, 1604), sig. A4ᵛ; Erasmus Sarcerius, *Commonplaces of Scripture*, trans. R. Taverner (n.p., 1538), fol. lxxi; H. Bullinger, *Fiftie Godlie and Learned Sermons*, trans. H. I. (London, 1587), pp. 152, 219; Geoffrey Fenton, *A Forme of Christian Pollicie* (London, 1574), p. 61; G. Gifford, *A Dialogue Betweene a Papist and Protestant* (London, 1599), pp. 101–2; James I, *True Lawe of Free Monarchies* (London, 1604), sig. B3ʳ.

13. The reason for applying such terms to rulers is given by Bilson, sigs. B5ʳ–B5ᵛ, C3ʳ; [Homilies] *Certaine Sermons Appointed by the Queens Maiestie* (London, 1595), sig. 13ʳ; Bullinger, pp. 145–6; J. Dod and R. Cleaver, *Exposition of the Ten Commandments* (London, 1604), p. 181; R. Bellarmine, *An Ample Declaration of the Christian Doctrine* (Roane, n.d.), p. 182; Henry Smith, *A Memento for Magistrates*, printed in *Sermons* (London, 1604), pp. 534–5. The ruler is also called, or compared to, a 'parent', or 'shepherd', or 'teacher', etc. by Willet, sig. A2ʳ;

Jonson, *Panegyre*, in *Entertainment*, sig. F1ʳ; Fenton, p. 310; Antony Guevara, *The Dial of Princes*, trans. T. North (n.p., 1568), I, 53ᵛ; Laurentius Grimaldus Goslicius, *The Counsellor*, trans. anon. (London, 1598), p. 74; James I, *True Lawe*, sigs. B4ʳ, B4ᵛ–B5ʳ, D2ᵛ–D3ᵛ, and *Basilicon Doron* (London, 1603), p. 25. See also commentaries on measure-for-measure passage: Becon, sig. Ddiiiʳ; Perkins, *Exposition*, p. 424.

14. Bilson sigs. A7ᵛ–A8ʳ; Eedes, sigs. Eᵛ–Eviʳ; Smith, *Magistrates Scripture*, pp. 341–3, 337, and *Memento for Magistrates*, p. 530.

15. Bilson, sigs. B1ʳ–B1ᵛ; *Homilies*, sigs. I8ᵛ–K2ʳ; Mm4ᵛ–Nn1ᵛ; Nn7ʳ–Nn7ᵛ; Bullinger, p. 219; Dod and Cleaver, pp. 235–6.

16. Bilson, sigs. B6ʳ–B6ᵛ; Willymat, pp. 4–5, 26–7, 44–5; *Homilies*, sigs. I5ᵛ–I8ᵛ; Bullinger, pp. 173–5; Dod and Cleaver, p. 236; Nicholas Gibbens, *Questions and Disputations Concerning the Holy Scriptures* (n.p., 1601), p. 377; James I, *True Lawe*, sigs. B7ᵛ–C5ᵛff.; Gifford, pp. 145–51.

17. Bilson, sigs. B3ᵛ–B4ᵛ; Perkins, *Treatise*, pp. 6–7; *Two Guides to a Good Life* (London, 1604), sig. G2ᵛ; Willymat, pp. 48–9; Sarcerius, fols. lxxiiᵛ, ccvʳ, ccviiiʳ; Innocent Gentillet, *A Discovrse vpon the Meanes of Wel Governing*, trans. Simon Patericke (London, 1602), pp. 109–10; *Homilies*, sigs. F2ᵛ–F3ᵛ, I4ʳ–I5ᵛ; Bullinger, pp. 168, 196–8; Fenton, pp. 75–6; Gibbens, pp. 376–7; Bellarmine, pp. 153–4; James I, *True Lawe*, sigs. D5ᵛ–D6ʳ. See also commentaries on the measure-for-measure passage: listed under note 10, above.

18. Willymat, pp. 58–9. For other arguments in favour of the ruler's right to use extraordinary means, see Bilson, sig. B4ᵛ; Gentillet, pp. 246–51; Goslicius, pp. 90, 119–20; James I, *True Lawe*, sigs. D1ᵛ–D2ʳ.

19. Bilson, sigs. C3ᵛ–C4ʳ; James Godskall, *The Kings Medicine for this Present Yeere* (London, 1604), sig. K1ʳ; Smith, *Magistrates Scripture*, pp. 336–7; Jonson, *Panegyre*, sigs. E4ʳ and F1ᵛ; Bullinger, p. 172; Fenton, pp. 57–8, 65–8; James I, *Basilicon Doron*, pp. 17, 95, and *True Lawe*, sigs. B4ʳ, E3ᵛ.

20. Henry Hooke, *Sermon Preached Before the King* (London, 1604), sig. Bviʳ. See also Bilson, sig. C7ʳ; Perkins, *Treatise*, pp. 86–7; Bullinger, p. 172; Smith, *Memento for Magistrates*, p. 532; Fenton, pp. 66–7; Goslicius, p. 105.

21. Bilson, sigs. C3ᵛ–C4ʳ; Willet, sig. A4ʳ; Godskall, sigs. N2ᵛ–N3ʳ, G7ᵛ–G8ʳ, K1ʳ; Eedes, sigs. D1ᵛ–Diiʳ; Smith, *Magistrates Scripture*, pp. 339–41, 337, and *Memento for Magistrates*, p. 527; Jonson, *Entertainment*, sig. A3ʳ; Sarcerius, fol. ccviᵛ; Gentillet, pp. 97, 357; *Homilies*, sigs. I4ʳ, I5ʳ–I5ᵛ, Pp5ᵛ; Bullinger, pp. 175–6, 184, 187–8; Fenton, pp. 7, 69–71; Goslicius, pp. 100, 104, 107; James I, *Basilicon Doron*, pp. 1–21. See also commentaries on the measure-for-measure passage: Becon, sig. Ddiiiᵛ; Perkins, *Exposition*, p. 424.

22. Guevara, I, 51ᵛ. See also *ibid.* 52ʳ; James I, *Basilicon Doron*, pp. 1–2; Goslicius, p. 106. See also commentaries on the measure-for-measure passage: Erasmus, fol. lxxviiiʳ; Perkins, *Exposition*, p. 424.

23. Eedes, sigs. Dviiiʳ–Dviiiᵛ. See also Willet, sig. A3ᵛ; Godskall, sig. K1ʳ; Jonson, *Panegyre*, sig. F1ʳ; Gentillet, pp. 99, 279; Smith, *Memento for Magistrates*, p. 532; Fenton, p. 13; Guevara, I, 50ᵛ; Goslicius, p. 104; James I, *Basilicon Doron*, pp. 3, 23–4, 60–61, and *True Lawe*, sigs. D1ᵛ–D2ʳ.

24. Fenton, p. 64. See also *ibid.* pp. 58–9; Bilson, sig. C7ʳ; Smith, *Magistrates Scripture*, pp. 337, 339–40; Jonson, *Panegyre*, sig. E4ʳ; Bullinger, pp. 152, 194; Guevara, I, 4ʳ–4ᵛ; James I, *Basilicon Doron*, pp. 35, 91, and *True Lawe*, sigs. B3ʳ–B3ᵛ.

25. Eedes, sigs. Eijʳ–Eiiijʳ, Eiᵛ–Eiiʳ; Guevara, III, 3ᵛ; Goslicius, pp. 106–10; James I, *Basilicon Doron*, pp. 29–31; Thomas Blague, *A Sermon...Before the Kings Maiestie* (London, 1603), sig. B4ᵛ. The following writers condemn the over-merciful judge, but not the over-severe one: Gentillet, p. 189; *Homilies*, sig. F3ᵛ; Bullinger, pp. 168, 197–8; Fenton, pp. 81–2; and in the commentaries on the measure-for-measure passage: Becon, sigs. Ddiiiᵛ–Ddvʳ. The following writers condemn the over-severe judge, but not the over-merciful one: *Two Guides*, sigs. K2ʳ–K3ᵛ; Bellarmine, pp. 234–5. The general principle that mercy should temper justice is approved by Bilson, sigs. C2ʳ–C2ᵛ; Gentillet, p. 276; Bullinger, pp. 118, 199; Bellarmine, p. 234; Willet, p. 22; Jonson, *Panegyre*, sig. F1ʳ; Hooke, sigs. Diiiᵛ–Divʳ; and in the commentaries on the measure-for-measure passage: Becon, sig. Ddiiiᵛ.

26. Perkins, *Treatise*, pp. 55–6; Fenton, p. 355; Godskall, sig. K7ʳ.

27. Tucker Brooke, "The Renaissance", in *A Literary History of England*, ed. A. C. Baugh (New York, 1948), p. 527.

9. *Measure for Measure*, Act I, scene ii. Mistress Overdone (Eileen Beldon), with Lucio (John Kane), reads the proclamation that brothels must be closed. Directed by John Barton.

8. *Measure for Measure*, Act I, scene ii. Lucio (Barry Stanton) learns from Mistress Overdone (Dan Meaden) of Claudio's imprisonment. Directed by Keith Hack, 1974.

74

10. *Measure for Measure*, Act II, scene ii. Angelo (Ian Richardson) assumes the Duke's authority.
Directed by John Barton, 1970.

11. *Measure for Measure*, Act II, scene iv. Isabella (Estelle Kohler) hears Angelo's declaration.
Directed by John Barton, 1970.

12. *Measure for Measure*. The Duke (Harry Andrews) with prisoners. Directed by Peter Brook, 1950.

13. *Measure for Measure*, Act III, scene i. Isabella (Judi Dench) begs Claudio (Ian Holm) to save her chastity. Directed by John Blatchley, 1962.

14. *Measure for Measure*, Act v, scene i. 'Justice, O royal Duke!': Isabella (Barbara Jefford) kneels before the Duke; Angelo (John Gielgud) looks on. Directed by Peter Brook, 1950.

THE UNFOLDING OF
'MEASURE FOR MEASURE'

JAMES BLACK

The 'bed-trick' in *Measure for Measure* has always caused embarrassment of one sort or another. 'This thing of darkness' must be acknowledged, but no critic has managed to assimilate the device fully into his view of the play or quite been able to come to terms with what has seemed to be an 'incompatibility of the intrigues of comedy with the tone of what has gone before'.[1] Schucking was offended by its employment: 'It is astonishing to see with how little self-esteem [Shakespeare credits a woman] here';[2] so was Brander Matthews: 'The artifice itself is unlovely, and it cannot be made acceptable';[3] and so was Quiller-Couch: '[Isabella] is all for saving her own soul...by turning...into a bare procuress.'[4] Apologists claim that in adding this detail to what he carried over from his source and using it to preserve the heroine's chastity Shakespeare thereby made more gentle 'one of the quite horrible situations of the [older] drama'[5] and prevented a forced marriage between Isabella and Angelo.[6] W. W. Lawrence, going outside the play for a justification, asserts that Shakespeare's audiences would have seen nothing wrong with this kind of marriage-device,[7] and G. K. Hunter has adduced an example from real life.[8] But to his impressive marshalling of sources and analogues incorporating bed-tricks Lawrence still adds a slightly uneasy rhetorical flourish: 'Would Shakespeare...have made the ensky'd and sainted Isabella, the gentle forsaken Mariana, and the benevolent Duke use [this] stratagem if he had felt it repugnant

to modesty?'[9] And Hunter's observation on *All's Well* has equal application to *Measure for Measure*: 'the Christian and gnomic overtones of the play...seem to raise issues which cannot easily be resolved by plot-manipulation'.[10] The Arden editor of *Measure for Measure*, though he draws on Hunter's *All's Well* essay, seems to have turned away from these issues: in justifying the bed-trick as strictly within the bounds of legality he disposes of a case, not of the human situation.[11]

Thus the explanations of the bed-trick have mainly been negative ones – Mariana and her accomplices and Shakespeare have done nothing unusual or strictly wrong. Although 'we are meant to approve not only of the Duke's stratagem, but of Mariana's, and even Isabel's,

[1] Philip Edwards, *Shakespeare and the Confines of Art* (London, 1968), p. 118.
[2] L. L. Schücking, *Character Problems in Shakespeare's Plays* (London, 1922), p. 197.
[3] *Shakespeare as a Playwright* (New York, 1913), p. 227.
[4] The New Cambridge Shakespeare *Measure for Measure* (Cambridge, 1922), p. xxx.
[5] R. W. Chambers, 'Measure for Measure', in Anne Ridler (ed.), *Shakespeare Criticism 1935–60* (London, 1963), p. 4.
[6] Ernest Schanzer, *The Problem Plays of Shakespeare* (London, 1963), p. 109.
[7] *Shakespeare's Problem Comedies* (New York, 1960), pp. 38, 83.
[8] The Arden Shakespeare *All's Well that Ends Well* (London, 1959), p. xliv.
[9] *Shakespeare's Problem Comedies*, p. 51.
[10] The Arden *All's Well*, p. xliv.
[11] The Arden Shakespeare *Measure for Measure* (London, 1965), pp. li–lv.

77

part in it', says Mary Lascelles, the employment of this convention, if it is not justified, can leave us with 'a deep and corroding discontent'. She believes that Shakespeare probably intended, before the end of the play, to offer more justification, but 'considerable items are overlooked and forgotten as he presses on to his consummation. There is, for example, Isabel's behaviour in furthering . . . Mariana's unpropitious marriage . . . There is the Duke's behaviour in promoting the affair . . . These anomalies remain.'[1]

My own approach to *Measure for Measure* is going to be from the point of view that Shakespeare did not simply forget to justify his use of the bed-trick device, nor did he adopt in this play a policy of 'never apologise, never explain'. I believe that he intended the play as it stands (textual corruptions aside) to convey the sense that Mariana in sleeping with Angelo has done something right, and that the play turns upon the positive virtue of her action.

Measure for Measure is set largely in a series of places of confinement or retreat. Claudio is under the strict restraint of prison, as are Barnardine and, to a lesser extent, Pompey. Julietta also is in prison and the late stages of pregnancy, and much of the action takes place in the gaol, where, as A. P. Rossiter has observed, 'the worlds of Mrs. Overdone and Pompey, of Claudio and Julietta, and of Isabella and Angelo all meet'.[2] Escalus and Angelo try Pompey, and Isabella and Angelo face one another, in antechambers to this prison. There also is the St Clare nunnery, on whose threshold we first encounter Isabella. The ethos of this place is conveyed only through the quoting of a single rule, but it is a curious either-or prescription whose terms compel notice:

When you have vow'd, you must not speak with men
But in the presence of the prioress;
Then, if you speak, you must not show your face;
Or if you show your face, you must not speak.
(I, iv, 10–13)

Though Isabella never completes this vow there is no doubt that she has prescribed for herself an ideal kind of nunnery whose rules transcend in strictness those of the actual sisterhood. These rules she wishes for herself, and it appears she would extend them to others as well:

I speak not as desiring more [privileges],
But rather wishing a more strict restraint
Upon the sisterhood, the votarists of St. Clare.
(I, iv, 3–5)

Isabella is not alone in wishing to impose her self-restraints upon others. Angelo would do this as well through his application of the law, of which he is not just a representative but the actual embodiment, for 'Mortality and mercy in Vienna Live in [his] tongue, and heart' (I, i, 44–5). His self-restraint is famous, and of choice, and he soon reveals an awareness that it is something he has imposed upon his nature. He uses the disguise words 'case', 'habit' and 'seeming' for the formality he wears (II, iv, 12–15), appears to affect gravity as energetically as Lucio claims to affect flippancy, and indeed at a moment of intense self-awareness conveys that he might just as easily exchange his austereness for Lucio's kind of demeanour:

Angelo.   Yea, my gravity,
Wherein – let no man hear me – I take pride,
Could I with boot change for an idle plume
Which the air beats for vain   (II, iv, 9–12)

Lucio.   'Tis my familiar sin,
With maids to seem the lapwing, and to jest
Tongue far from heart.   (I, iv, 31–3)

Angelo has adopted gravity as his role, and over the years has carefully built a *persona*, persuading the world – and himself – of 'a kind of character in [his] life' (I, i, 27). His reading of the law has been and is closely tied up with his creation of this character, as is suggested in his reference to 'the state whereon

[1] *Shakespeare's 'Measure for Measure'* (London, 1953). See pp. 121, 137 and 163.
[2] *Angel With Horns* (London, 1961), p. 156.

I studied' (II, iv, 7). The setting through which he moves – we may as well call it the courtroom – is dominated by this *persona*, for, as the play never lets us forget, the law exists as it is applied and as it begins to be applied to Vienna it takes on the peculiar stamp of Angelo's repressive character. Thus his courtroom and his very presence stand, like the nunnery of Isabella's ideal, for 'a more strict restraint'.

Within his carapace of legal interpretation Angelo feels protected by the abstract generality of law from having to make difficult personal or human decisions. 'Pretending in [Mariana] discoveries of dishonour', he has been able to make himself 'a marble to her tears, [be] washed with them, but [relent] not' (III, i, 226–30); and thereby has dismissed Mariana to her unique place of confinement, the moated grange. With Isabella he soon adopts a Pilate-like dissociation of himself from the law's supposedly necessary course:

> Your brother is a forfeit of the law...
> It is the law, not I, condemn your brother...
> The law hath not been dead, though it hath slept.
> (II, ii, 71, 80, 91)

This self-preserving technique might be allowable if adopted only here, in the difficult situation of a sister's pleading for her condemned brother. But Angelo also uses it in much less pressing circumstances, telling Escalus that no exception may be made for Claudio:

> What's open made to justice
> That justice seizes. (II, i, 21–2)

In considering this case, both with Escalus and Isabella, Angelo heads unerringly for the safe ground of abstract theory. Asked by Escalus to reflect whether he himself might not have erred like Claudio given Claudio's opportunity, he swiftly renders the idea merely academic:

> I not deny
> The jury passing on the prisoner's life
> May in the sworn twelve have a thief, or two,
> Guiltier than him they try. (II, i, 18–21)

And there is a debater's relish in his parrying of Isabella's opening move, which is itself academic:

> *Isabella.*
> I have a brother is condemn'd to die;
> I do beseech you, let it be his fault,
> And not my brother...
> *Angelo.*
> Condemn the fault, and not the actor of it?
> Why, every fault's condemn'd ere it be done
> (II, ii, 34ff.)

These exchanges make clear Angelo's steadfast refusal to be lured out of the narrowest interpretation of the law, which he will consider only in the letter or theory and not as it personally affects others or himself. His answer to Escalus, 'Tis one thing to be tempted...another thing to fall' (II, i, 17–18) is an academic disposition of an hypothesis, as he has not yet been tempted to his own limits. He is embarrassed and impatient when Isabella insists upon his personal response in Claudio's case:

> *Angelo.*
> I will not [pardon him].
> *Isabella.*
> But can you if you would?
> *Angelo.*
> Look, what I will not, that I cannot do.
> (II, ii, 51–2)

Clearly, in his use of the law he does not *want* room for manoeuvre. The inflexible statute, the irreversible sequence of procedure ('He's sentenc'd, 'tis too late' II, ii, 55), the judge's anonymity (Escalus never addresses him by name while discussing this case, and Isabella calls him Angelo for the first time only when his carnal intentions are clear to her, II, iv, 150) – all of these conventions shield him from the necessity of taking decisions on individual circumstances. In sum, he is as circumscribed and secure in the law as Isabella in her ideal nunnery. And we scarcely need Angelo's admission that he takes pride in his gravity to make us see that these two people, each bounded in his or her chosen nutshell, count themselves kings of infinite space.

But there is no suppressing what is for them the bad dream of sexuality.[1] It breaks through just where Angelo has every expectation of security: a courtroom, a legal debate, the appellant a religious novice. All that passes between them is words, which Angelo always has been able to use to bind with or hide in. While words hold to the meanings their users intend, so long as Angelo can positively label and anathematise 'these filthy vices' in others, and so long as 'be tempted' keeps its proper distance from 'to fall', his legalistic enclosure is secure. Very early in the play, however, it is shown that words are very shaky foundations upon which to build a system of absolute law. The trial of Pompey in II, i degenerates into farce because of the way language lends itself to misuse. The continual malapropisms of Elbow, the prosecuting officer, undermine the dignity of these proceedings from the beginning; and no sooner have the judges Escalus and Angelo attuned their ears to his 'misplacings' than Pompey offers his side of the case in a run of bawdy equivocations, giving hilariously suggestive connotations to the most innocent-seeming words.[2] Escalus eventually begins rather to enjoy the travesty, but Angelo sharply tries to direct the proceedings back on the rails. He impatiently shrugs off Escalus' tolerant bemusement, grills Elbow, and rounds fiercely on Pompey:

Escalus. [to Angelo] This comes off well: here's a
  wise officer.
Angelo. Go to. What quality are they of? Elbow is
  your name? Why dost thou not speak,
  Elbow?
Pompey. He cannot, sir: he's out at elbow.
Angelo. What are you, sir?   (II, i, 57–61)

Escalus hereafter tries to keep the quibbling Pompey to strict meanings, but in vain, and Angelo at last loses patience and departs. Escalus eventually lets Pompey off with a warning: in the fog of equivocation he scarcely can do otherwise.

It is difficult to credit Ernest Schanzer's explanation of this scene as having 'been introduced mainly to show the ideal judge at work',[3] for the scene demonstrates the sheer impossibility of judging when neither prosecutor nor defendant can or will stay within the logical bounds of words where law can work. 'As their testimonies unfold through a haze of "misplacings" and irrelevancies', says J. W. Lever, 'time, place and all ethical distinctions lose their contours. "Justice" represented by Elbow, and "Iniquity" by Pompey, seem interchangeable and equally meaningless.'[4] The scene suggests that it is impossible to apply – or to take refuge in – the letter of the law when letters themselves will not yield to organisation or discipline.

In this trial of Pompey the tone also is set for the scene which follows, where in an antechamber to the courtroom Angelo hears Isabella appeal on Claudio's behalf and where despite the terrible gravity of the occasion words soon again begin to veer into equivocation and suggestiveness. Isabella 'speaks, and 'tis such sense That [Angelo's] sense breeds with it' (II, ii, 142–3). He has just come from a courtroom where double-entendre reigned, and now, approached by a beautiful girl whose intellect itself stimulates him, and who directs his attention to his own human frailty –

> Go to your bosom,
> Knock there, and ask your heart what it doth know
> That's like my brother's fault –   (II, ii, 137–9)

he finds his legal world of words unbalanced and betraying, his security threatened. Misconstruction follows misconstruction in a run of the kind in which one verbal slip is compounded by another as the speaker continues

[1] Claudio 'hath but as offended in a dream', II, ii, 4. And see Hamlet, II, ii, 260–2.
[2] See J. W. Lever's Arden Edition notes on II, i, 88–112.
[3] The Problem Plays of Shakespeare, p. 116.
[4] The Arden Measure for Measure, pp. lxvi–lxvii.

unaware or even as he tries to correct the impression – as when Samuel Johnson, having unwittingly caused mirth by the solemn pronouncement that a woman had 'a bottom of good sense', tried to retrieve the situation by adding that he meant she was 'fundamentally sound'.[1] 'O perilous mouths, . . . Hooking both right and wrong to th'appetite' (II, iv, 171–6), Isabella will cry in dismay when she fully understands Angelo's drift. Meantime, ignorant of any sensual coloration in her words, or of his alertness thereto, she says 'Heaven keep your honour safe' and 'save your honour' ('From thee', responds Angelo under his breath, II, ii, 162), and tells him 'I am come to know your pleasure'. The terms of her offer to bribe Angelo with prayers (II, ii, 150–6) are curiously suggestive,[2] and her strenuous avowal of willingness to die is charged with a 'sensuality of martyrdom':

> Were I under the terms of death,
> Th' impression of keen whips I'd wear as rubies,
> And strip myself to death as to a bed
> That longing have been sick for, ere I'd yield
> My body up to shame.   (II, iv, 100–4)

Words are associated with the law and with rank: condemnation and reprieve live in Angelo's tongue, and Isabella says 'That in the captain's but a choleric word / Which in the soldier is flat blasphemy' (II, ii, 131–2). The play began with the Duke's test to see 'If power change purpose, what our seemers be', and now as Angelo goes further into temptation both power *and* words change purpose. In this moral whirligig, which exemplifies Lear's 'change places, and, handy-dandy, which is the justice, which is the thief?' (*King Lear*, IV, vi, 157–8), Angelo changes from judge to ravisher, Pompey from bawd to hangman – 'a feather will turn the scale', says the Provost (IV, ii, 28). Angelo may well ask, 'The tempter, or the tempted, who sins most?' (II, ii, 164), and Abhorson expatiate upon how 'every true man's apparel fits your thief' (IV, ii, 41–5).

Indeed, a key to the non-absoluteness of words in moral contexts is provided by the executioner's portmanteau name. He is by his trade 'abhorrent', and as a 'whoreson' seems a lively embodiment of what as the law's instrument he punishes. His name also incorporates and perhaps gives ambivalence to the word which Isabella uses more than any other to express her hatred of vice: 'There is a vice that most I do abhor' (II, ii, 29); 'such abhorr'd pollution' (II, iv, 182); 'That I should do what I abhor to name' (III, i, 101).

It is little wonder that in a world of such shifting possibilities the prison has no lack of inmates, or that Isabella and Angelo should seek refuge in the nunnery and the self-constructed enclosure of reputation and legal absoluteness. Despite these precautions, however, Isabella finds herself eventually in the confine of a terrible dilemma which delimits movement as effectively as any actual chain. When she and Claudio come together for the first time, in III, i, they are like the claustrophobe of Angelo's fancy (II, iv, 19–26), struggling in ever-growing panic against the press of dreadful alternatives.

The philosophy which will free all from their confinements is never far to seek in the play. It is stated at the outset:

> If our virtues
> Did not go forth of us, 'twere all alike
> As if we had them not. Spirits are not finely touch'd
> But to fine issues.   (I, i, 33–6)

There is repeated insistence that not only must the professors of virtue 'issue' their talents, but also they must stand-in for others and do so in such a way as wholly to be the person sub-

---

[1] *Boswell's 'Life of Johnson'*, ed. Sydney Roberts (London, 1960), II, 384.

[2] Connoisseurs of the so-called Freudian slip might note how the words 'sickles' and 'tested' may be combined, especially as they associate in this speech with 'stones' and 'up...and enter'. F. R. Leavis coined the phrase 'sensuality of martyrdom' ('The Greatness of *Measure for Measure*', *Scrutiny*, X (1942), 234).

stituted for. 'In our remove, be thou at full ourself', says the Duke (I, i, 43) when commissioning Angelo to 'supply [his] absence' (I, i, 18). Two scenes later he tells Friar Thomas that he has delivered to Angelo 'My absolute power and place' (I, iii, 13). The meaning is not restricted to that of office-bearing: Angelo soon is invited by Escalus to put himself in Claudio's shoes and to ask himself whether, if he had been given the opportunity, he 'had not sometime in [his] life / Erred in this point...' (II, i, 8–16). The invitation is swiftly turned aside, but returns later when Isabella says to Angelo:

> Go to your bosom,
> Knock there, and ask your heart what it doth know
> That's like my brother's fault... (II, ii, 137–9)

This is intensified to

> If [Claudio] had been as you, and you as he,
> You would have slipp'd like him, but he like you
> Would not have been so stern; (II, ii, 64–6)

and then more passionately and prophetically to

> I would to heaven I had your potency,
> And you were Isabel! Should it then be thus!
> No; I would tell what 'twere to be a judge,
> And what a prisoner. (II, ii, 67–70)

By these graded steps, as it were, the dialogue comes to the greatest of all examples of substitution for others:

> Why, all the souls that were, were forfeit once,
> And He that might the vantage best have took
> Found out the remedy... (II, ii, 73–5)

It is all splendid talk of the necessity of loving and feeling for one's neighbour as oneself. But fired as it may be by desperation and danger, it is still – it seems we may say *only* – talk. To Isabella's evangelistic fervour Angelo returns 'Why do you put these sayings upon me?' (II, ii, 134). Shortly after citing Christ's supreme example of substituting Himself for others – finding 'the remedy' – Isabella can say 'We cannot weigh our brother with ourself' (II, ii, 127); and realising she

cannot dictate the terms of her martyrdom will stand on 'More than our brother is our chastity' (II, iv, 184). She is being challenged to go beyond words when Angelo asks 'What would you do?' (II, iv, 98). As they do in the Gospels, words must find enactment, else

> Heaven in my mouth,
> As if I did but only chew his name.
> (II, iv, 4–5)

As Angelo has put the letter of the old law into effect, so Mariana sets the letter of forgiveness and love in act. This she does through the bed-trick. In its simplest terms this is a liberating action for her: it initiates her release from the moated grange, where for five years she has hidden herself away, grieving not only for a dead brother but also for Angelo's broken promise (III, i, 225–9), and feeding her melancholy with songs which 'please her woe'. In sleeping with Angelo she acts as a substitute, literally giving her body in place of someone else's. She is more than a convenient body, however, for in Angelo's apprehension she *is* Isabella. Hers is the first act of wholehearted substitution: although Angelo was enjoined to be 'at full' the Duke he has not exercised power as the Duke would do, nor can Isabella substitute for her brother in the manner which Angelo has proposed. Putting herself so fully in another's place, Mariana makes good the moral dicta that till now have been not much more than splendid pronouncements, and makes of the bed-trick – to quote Isabella talking theory – 'no sin at all, but charity' (II, iv, 66).

If Shakespeare needed the bed-trick to resolve his plot, he has made a virtue of necessity. We also should note that this action of Mariana's takes place in the most confined of settings. Angelo

> hath a garden circummured with brick,
> Whose western side is with a vineyard back'd;
> And to that vineyard is a planched gate,
> That makes his opening with this bigger key.
> This other doth command a little door
> Which from the vineyard to the garden leads;

> There have I made my promise
> Upon the heavy middle of the night
> To call upon him.   (IV, i, 28–36)

This setting – the bed within the garden-house (V, i, 211) within the walled and locked garden within the gated and locked vineyard – would seem to pattern out the labyrinth of dilemma into which Isabella, Claudio and Angelo have wound. It answers also, keys and all, to the confines and wards of Claudio's prison; while the very arrangements for Angelo's deception – the 'repair in the dark' which will have 'all shadow and silence in it' (III, i, 245) – also suggest restrictions which go beyond even the nunnery's.

> If you speak, you must not show your face;
> Or if you show your face, you must not speak.

It is as if Mariana, encountering darkness like a bride, has reached into all those confines where the others are enthralled: from this bedroom of darkness and silence events turn back toward light and freedom. The 'repair' in the dark is a remedy as well as an assignation.

Tensions wound up by fearful debate in the first half of the play find partial release through activity in the second half. Isabella has to go over the assignation route twice with Angelo and then acquaint Mariana with the whole matter (IV, i, 36–59). Maidenhead-for-maidenhead inspires head-for-head as a substitute for Claudio – and Barnardine – is found in Ragozine. The purpose is once again to deceive, and save, Angelo and thus buy time for Claudio. But Isabella is told by the Duke that her brother has been executed. She must make her own repair 'in the dark' – that is, be tested on her forgiveness of Angelo's trespass while still ignorant of Claudio's preservation.

The public setting of the final scene is heavily stressed (IV, iii, 95–6; IV, iv, 4–5, 9; IV, v, 9; IV, vi, 15). From the pent-up atmosphere of court, prison, and grange the action is removed to the open and public space by the city gates, where under the Duke's stage-management (cf. IV, vi, 1–8) each character in turn is made to play out actions of self-enfranchisement. Mariana is first: after Isabella has, on the Duke's prior instructions, accused Angelo and then been 'arrested' for slander, Mariana enters heavily veiled. The Duke's command both echoes and overrides the nunnery's rule:

> First, let her show her face, and after, speak.
>   (V, i, 170)

Mariana fulfils this command both literally and symbolically, showing her face and declaring herself in public for the first time in five years. The Duke also 'shows his face' when, after leaving and returning in his Friar's habit, he is unhooded by Lucio. These two dramatic enactments of 'coming out' lead of course to the unmasking of Angelo.

But an even more dramatic issuing-forth has yet to be undertaken by Isabella. Still with every reason to hate Angelo, believing her brother to be dead, and with Angelo's own ordainment of his penalty and the Duke's legalistic explication of the case fresh in her ears – 'An Angelo for Claudio; death for death' – Isabella is begged by Mariana to take Angelo's part. The play suddenly compresses into two brief speeches the opposites that have warred throughout:

Mariana.   Sweet Isabel, take my part;
>   Lend me your knees, and all my life to come
>   I'll lend you all my life to do you service.
Duke.
>   Against all sense you do importune her.
>   Should she kneel down in mercy of this fact,
>   Her brother's ghost his paved bed would
>   break,
>   And take her hence in horror.   (V, i, 428–34)

The Duke invokes the 'sense' of the law, the 'fact' of an unjustly dead brother and natural as well as legal revenge, family honour (which counted much with Isabella before, II, iv, 178 and III, i, 71), and even the superstition of a certain kind of morbid religiosity. Mariana appeals as Isabella formerly pleaded with

Angelo, in the terms of redemptive substitution and self-sacrifice: 'take my part' and 'all my life to come I'll lend you all my life' – offering her own life in place of what Isabella may in justice demand, Angelo's death. Mariana, 'craving no other nor no better man' than Angelo and offering herself thus, is spiritually at one with Juliet, who earlier in prison answered the Duke's question so affirmatively: 'Love you the man that wrong'd you? Yes, as I love the woman that wrong'd him' (II, iii, 24–5). It is now Isabella's turn to join their company; and she who talked so much about mercy is again being asked to *do* something, indeed something physical. For the whole scope of Mariana's plea should be noticed: she asks only a silent gesture:

> Sweet Isabel, do yet but kneel by me;
> Hold up your hands, say nothing; I'll speak all.
> (v, i, 435–6)

This to Isabella, whom we remember to have been not only morally but also physically unyielding:

> Had [Claudio] twenty heads to tender down
> On twenty bloody blocks, he'd yield them up
> Before his sister should her body stoop
> To such abhorr'd pollution,

she has said (II, iv, 179–82), and to Claudio's face,

> Die, perish! Might but my bending down
> Reprieve thee from thy fate, it should proceed.
> I'll pray a thousand prayers for thy death;
> No word to save thee.   (III, i, 143–6)

Therefore it is an act of self-conquest (and a great stage gesture) when Isabella falls on her knees.

She does more than kneel, however. Mariana asked only for a silent appeal – 'Say nothing; I'll speak all' – but Isabella goes the second mile to speak on Angelo's behalf:

> Look, if it please you, on this man condemn'd
> As if my brother lived.   (v, i, 442–3)

The legalism of her plea for Angelo has been strongly denounced: Ernest Schanzer, for example, says 'One's spirit recoils at hearing this girl, who had not a word to say in excuse of her brother but rather admitted the justice of his doom, now plead, with all the finesse of a seasoned attorney, on the most purely legalistic grounds for her would-be ravisher and the judicial murderer of her brother'.[1] But such a response overlooks at least three factors. First, so far as Isabella knows she is addressing in the Duke a judge who up to now has invoked the strict letter of the law, and so she must plead the letter if Angelo is to have any chance. Second, it is in itself a striking reversal that the letter is being cited, not to kill as in Claudio's situation, but to save. And third, it ought to be recognized that the real force of this plea lies not so much in its terms as in the fact that Isabella is interceding for Angelo at all. The stubborn Barnardine is rightly admired for his determined refusal to co-operate with his executioners: he is 'absolute for life'.[2] But the formerly stubborn Isabella has now surpassed Barnardine in that she is absolute for someone else's life, and that life her enemy's. Perhaps Barnardine and Isabella together illustrate the Duke's distinction between a grace that 'stands' and a virtue that 'goes' (III, ii, 257); this is the distinction between the 'old' and 'new' Isabellas as well.

So Isabella's own enfranchisement from the exactness of 'measure still for measure' is being enacted when she pleads for Angelo. The reciprocal virtue of her action is expressed in Romeo's joyful realisation that in loving Juliet, his 'enemy': 'My intercession likewise steads my foe' (*Romeo and Juliet*, II, iii, 54). Kneeling in public with Mariana, Isabella has 'shown her face', and she has spoken as well. Thus she has come fully out of the nunnery, where

> If you speak, you must not show your face;
> Or if you show your face, you must not speak.

[1] *The Problem Plays of Shakespeare*, p. 101.
[2] J. W. Lever has anticipated my use of this phrase: Arden *Measure for Measure*, p. lxxxviii.

84

She sees the narrowness and irreversible nature of justice. Having formerly cried out for 'Justice! Justice! Justice!' (v, i, 26), she now can say 'My brother had but justice.' The 'but' contains a whole statute of limitations.

Just as Isabella shows her face so too has Angelo's been shown, and what he knows about himself painfully revealed to the world. No-one who feels that Angelo is treated too leniently has fully taken into account the city-gate setting and the public humiliation there endured (to Shakespeare's contemporaries it was a recognised factor in punishment). The exposure of so essentially withdrawn a man and the breaking through of his *persona* is in itself a punishment which if it does not exactly fit the crime certainly fits the offender. To Angelo execution would be preferable, entailing as it does the concealment of prison and the oblivion of death: it is the public session he wants curtailed:

> No longer session hold upon my shame.
> But let my trial be mine own confession.
> Immediate sentence, then, and sequent death
> Is all the grace I beg.   (v, i, 369–72)

The soul-searching Angelo underwent before sinning, his remorse and fear when his villainy has, as he thinks, succeeded (IV, v, 18–32), and the penitence he expresses when caught (v, i, 472–5) – all these cannot be left out of the reckoning; and as his public humiliation is prolonged the audience may sum up, with the Duke, 'Your evil quits you well.'

The theme of releasing is formally enacted once more when Claudio is brought on 'muffled'; then revealed and pardoned. This unwrapping, Mariana's unveiling, and the Duke's being unhooded, together with the more metaphorical uncovering of Angelo, have all been foreshadowed in a word of the Duke's – 'unfold'. He uses this word at his very first appearance to mean 'explicate' or 'reveal'; and in greeting this day of revelation for so many of his subjects suggests releasing with 'Look, th'

unfolding star calls up the shepherd' (IV, ii, 202). With these implications of the truth making free, the word comprehends both the range of the play's events and the Duke's part in them.

But although the Duke 'like power divine, Hath looked upon [Angelo's] passes', it does not follow that he should be seen as God.[1] It is not so much divine power as resourcefulness and good luck which enable him to counter Angelo's attempted double-cross (IV, ii, 113f.). In becoming the Friar he undergoes, like others, his own process of self-removal: though he does this voluntarily, some sort of drastic action obviously has been dictated by Vienna's condition. The Duke has been a secretive man – 'I love the people', he says, 'But do not like to stage me to their eyes' (I, i, 67ff.) – and only Escalus seems to know him well. Retiredness encourages rumour, and even Friar Thomas seems to think that his ruler's disguise may have a nefarious motive (I, iii, 1–6). It is therefore salutary that the Duke–Friar must perforce listen to Lucio's slanders, as well as see his prison. At the play's end he indicates that he is not God (or even a Friar) by making himself one partner in the marriage-pairings which have the earthy membership of Lucio and his paramour. The emphasis, in this final scene, upon action and gesture makes it fairly clear that although Isabella is silent after the Duke's proposal she may not necessarily be equivocal in accepting. 'Give me your hand and say you will be mine' is followed directly and conclusively by 'He [Claudio] is my brother too' (v, i, 490–1), a firm indication that the Duke has received the sign he asked for. In the marriage-pairings he is associated with men and women: wedlock qualifies the 'too much

[1] Lever (*ibid.*, pp. lvii-lviii) discusses the theory of the play as allegory of the Divine Atonement with the Duke symbolising the Incarnate Lord, outlined in studies by G. Wilson Knight, Roy W. Battenhouse and Nevill Coghill.

liberty' which formerly turned to restraint (I, ii, 117–20), and is the best assurance that none of them will any longer 'forswear the full stream of the world and...live in a nook, merely monastic' (*As You Like It*, III, ii, 440–1).

Measure for Measure, as I see it, is about human beings who in an uncertain world are shut up against themselves and from one another. They find release and fulfilment in 'going forth' through self-abnegation and forgiveness. The play illustrates that a fugitive and cloistered virtue is of equal uselessness with a buried talent, and that noble ideals are supposed to be put into action. In making Mariana's trick an important part of the ethical fabric of *Measure for Measure* Shakespeare has wedded a traditional comic device to a serious moral intention. They are not at all strange bedfellows.

'THE DEVIL'S PARTY': VIRTUES AND VICES IN 'MEASURE FOR MEASURE'

HARRIETT HAWKINS

Where God hath a temple, the Devil will have
a chapel.
      (Burton, *The Anatomy of Melancholy*)
Utter my thoughts? Why, say they are vile
and false;
As where's that palace whereinto foul things
Sometimes intrude not? Who has that breast
so pure
But some uncleanly apprehensions
Keep leets and law-days and in sessions sit
With meditations lawful?   (Iago)

Writing about 'the Integrity of *Measure for Measure*' (*Shakespeare Survey 28* (1975), pp. 89–106), Arthur C. Kirsch severely reprimands Dr Johnson, Coleridge, and numerous modern critics, including myself, for our failure to 'take the play's Christian ideas seriously'. We are guilty of a 'fatal' misunderstanding of the tragicomedy, because we have been either unable or unwilling to place ourselves 'in the position of the play's first audience'. According to Professor Kirsch, we show an absolutely unforgiving and specifically un-Christian refusal to accept the ending and pardon Angelo, whose libidinousness was miraculously transformed by the bed-trick. Indeed, in the course of his essay, Kirsch goes on to conclude that most of the problems which, over the centuries, have vexed so many commentators, can now be 'explained'. All difficulties will be made comparatively 'easy' by an 'apprehension of certain fundamental Scriptural texts', and by Kirsch's own scholarly consideration of how those texts 'might have been understood and have affected Shakespeare's contemporary audience' (quotations are from pp. 89–91). Happily, however, this is simply not true. In spite of all Kirsch's arguments, the fact remains that any number of (quite rightly) unanswered questions and unsolved problems seem, whether deliberately or unconsciously, to have been built in to the text of *Measure for Measure* by Shakespeare himself, and these problems and questions are immeasurably more interesting than the solutions to them that have been propounded by modern scholars. For after all, the duty of the artist (as opposed to the scientist) is not to provide us with solutions, but, rather, to make certain that the problems under consideration are accurately posed: 'Not a single problem is solved in *Anna Karenina* and in *Eugene Onegin*,' wrote Chekhov to his publisher–critic, 'but you find these works quite satisfactory... because all the questions in them are correctly posed.'[1]

Surely no one would deny that serious questions about certain religious values are raised by the action of *Measure for Measure*, as well as its title. But underlying many discussions of its religious references is the facile assumption that the human problems posed here are, theologically at least, soluble, as well as the equally facile (and fallacious) assumption that, back in the good old days of William Shakespeare, there was general agreement about what did, or did not, constitute proper Christian conduct. There was no such agreement.

[1] See the *Letters of Anton Chekhov*, ed. Avrahm Yarmolinsky (1974), p. 86.

Different people, different denominations, held diametrically opposite views. Confusing 'benefactors' with 'malefactors' in a series of malapropisms pointed at people like Angelo, poor Elbow reflects a general state of confusion concerning good Christian behaviour:

I know not well what they are. But precise villains they are, that I am sure of, and void of all profanation in the world, that good Christians ought to have.

(II, i, 53–5)[1]

Indeed, so far as Christian doctrines are concerned, *Measure for Measure* may itself reflect a kind of dramatic, theological, social, and emotional civil war between dialectically opposed ideologies, and this possibility will get further discussion later on. But first it seems necessary to mention several historical, dramatic, and all-too-human problems in this play that cannot be solved by scholarly appeals to contemporary orthodoxies.

Here are several questions that Shakespeare chose to raise, not to answer, in this particular tragicomedy, and no formalist, thematic, or theological interpretation can answer them for him. How important is physical purity? Given a conflict between Christian virtues, like chastity and charity, which should take precedence? Should, or should not, a brother willingly die for the sake of his sister's chastity? Should, or should not, the sister yield up her chastity to save her brother's life? What if the laws set down in heaven or on earth clash with the biological and psychological laws of human nature? What *about* shot-gun weddings (Shakespeare may have had good personal reasons to feel extremely ambivalent about them)? Is not the mutual and free consent of both parties as important in marriage as it is in sex? If it is better to marry than to burn, what constitutes a true marriage? How binding is a legal certificate when there is no marriage of true minds?[2]

And do not the confrontation scenes between Angelo and Isabella establish mysterious and powerful psychological and sexual affinities between them that make incredible the incongruously banal futures assigned them by the Duke? For that matter, what help are pious guidelines from contemporary sermons in those darker realms of human sexuality and psychology so boldly ventured upon, by Shakespeare himself, in this strange course of dramatic events?

Everyone (ask anyone) who knows *Measure for Measure* will surely remember Isabella's

[1] Quotations are from the Arden text of *Measure for Measure*, ed. J. W. Lever (1966). Other citations from Shakespeare are from *The Complete Plays and Poems*, ed. William Allan Neilson and Charles Jarvis Hill (Cambridge, Mass., 1942). So far as an easy religious orthodoxy is concerned, K. V. Thomas, A. L. Morton, and Christopher Hill (among other historians) have knocked the bottom out of the idea that the common people in the sixteenth and seventeenth centuries accepted the religious orthodoxies of their betters. See (for instance) Christopher Hill, *Irreligion in the 'Puritan' Revolution* (1974), p. 25: 'When the lid is taken off, what bubbles out must have been there all the time. Was active – as opposed to passive – irreligion there all the time? English experience suggests that this was indeed the case . . . the formal Christianity of the established churches never had so complete a monopoly as appears.'

[2] Kirsch argues that 'Marriage always in Shakespeare has sacramental value' (p. 100). But see also A. D. Nuttall's argument that 'Elizabethan marriage held at its centre a high mystery, but at the same time it seems plain that the ease with which it could be contracted had trivialized it . . . on the one hand we see old Capulet . . . arranging a marriage for his daughter with a casual celerity which shocks us, and on the other marriage itself is so absolute' ('*Measure for Measure*: The Bed Trick', *Shakespeare Survey 28* (Cambridge, 1975), p. 56). And what about all the things that, as Shakespeare himself reminds us, could cause serious difficulties for love and marriage alike – most notably the lack of 'sympathy in choice'?

Hermia.   O cross! too high to be enthrall'd to
             low.
Lysander. Or else misgraffed in respect of years –
Hermia.   O spite! too old to be engaged to young.
Lysander. Or else it stood upon the choice of
             friends, –
Hermia.   O hell! to choose love by another's eyes.
Lysander. Or, if there were a sympathy in choice,
             War, death, or sickness did lay siege to it.

searing, shocking, provocative and disturbing refusal to lay down the treasure of her body to the Lord Angelo:

> Were I under the terms of death,
> Th' impression of keen whips I'd wear as rubies,
> And strip myself to death as to a bed
> That longing have been sick for, ere I'd yield
> My body up to shame.   (II, iv, 100–5)

In its dramatic context, this speech is peculiarly powerful. Everything in it is associated with death, yet Isabella's references to whips and rubies of blood, to stripping herself as to a bed that she had longed for, are charged with an erotic power that might well evoke a gleam in the eye of the most depraved marquis in the audience, to say nothing of a saint-turned-sensualist like Angelo. In its psychological implications, Isabella's speech is like nothing else in Elizabethan drama. Other characters (like Claudio and Antony) associate death with sex; and other threatened heroines of the time (like Whetstone's Cassandra and Jonson's Celia) would prefer torture or death to dishonour. But here and only here – or so a lurid play-bill might put it – are fused the red and black extremes of passion and pain, the whips and longings of martyrdom and desire, of repression and sensuality. Obviously, no commercially-minded producer would dream of cutting this speech.

Yet perhaps partly *because* of their provocative power, these lines of fire and ice have (so to speak) been given a critical X-rating and effectively banned from many scholarly discussions of the text. If they are cited at all, and they usually are not, they tend to be considered 'out of character' or dismissed in a sentence or two: 'Isabella expresses her readiness to die in erotic terms.' Certainly their darker overtones, to say nothing of their obviously sado-masochistic undertones, are either utterly disregarded or summarily bowdlerized in representative scholarly commentaries like these:

There is . . . the note of strenuousness, of a kind of moral athleticism which appears in this – as in so many of Isabella's utterances.

To suppose that Shakespeare gave these burning words to Isabel so that we should perceive her to be selfish and cold is to suppose that he didn't know his job.

What this speech conveys . . . is that Isabella is afraid not only of Angelo's desires, but of her own.[1]

In effect at least, these dismissive, low-key, reductively easy, or beside-the-point interpretations of Shakespeare's lines would seem ingeniously contrived to de-fuse a dramatic bombshell that, in spite of all such efforts, will explode in any theatre, in any classroom discussion of the play. They certainly would seem to disregard important evidence concerning the dramatic nature of the confrontations between Angelo and Isabella. So, for the purposes of further argument, here is a discussion emphasizing the perversely fascinating sexual and psychological issues involved.

As Shakespeare reminds us elsewhere, 'Lilies that fester smell far worse than weeds'. It is, however, when Angelo crosses it that Shakespeare most dramatically erases the fine line between virtuous and vicious forms of human psychology and sexuality that may elevate men (and women) or degrade them. As all the world well knows, Angelo, a man who never feels the 'wanton stings' of sensuality, but 'doth rebate and blunt his natural edge / With profits of the mind, study and fast' (I, iv, 60–1) is brought in by the Duke of Vienna to

[1] Quotations are from Ernest Schanzer, *The Problem Plays of Shakespeare* (1963), p. 99; R. W. Chambers, 'The Jacobean Shakespeare', *Proceedings of the British Academy*, 23 (1937), and Kirsch (cited above), p. 97. By the way, I, too, daintily skirted the sexual and psychological issues involved here in two discussions of *Measure for Measure* – see *Likenesses of Truth in Elizabethan and Restoration Drama* (Oxford, 1972), and ' "What Kind of Pre-Contract had Angelo?" A Note on some Non-problems in Elizabethan Drama', *College English*, 36 (1974), 173–9.

bring back the birch of law. He soon goes beyond all measure in punishing sexual offences, and his self-righteousness immediately begins to manifest itself in sadism: '[I hope] you'll find good cause to whip them all' (II, i, 136). '*Punish them unto your height of pleasure*', says the Duke, much later on (V, i, 239 – italics mine) when Angelo asks to have his 'way' with Isabella and Mariana, thus significantly implying that the bed-trick certainly failed to effect any miraculous transformation so far as Angelo's gratuitous sadism is concerned.

Anyway, from the beginning of the play, the punishment of vice itself turns vicious, misapplied. Furthermore, *virtue* itself enkindles vice when the purity of a young novice ignites Angelo's desire to defile it. 'Love in thousand monstrous forms doth oft appear', wrote Spenser, and this is one of them:

> Shall we desire to raze the sanctuary
> And pitch our evils there? O fie, fie fie!

> Th' impression of *keen* whips I'd wear as rubies,
> And *strip myself*... as to a bed
> *That longing have been sick for*, ere I'd *yield*
> *My body up* ...

Angelo seems to be recalling, and either deliberately or unconsciously echoing, Isabella's memory-searing lines. She must fit her consent to his 'sharp appetite' (his sexual equivalent of 'keen whips'?). She must 'lay by' (strip herself of) all blushes 'That banish what they sue for'. In short, she must come to his bed as to a bed 'That longing have been sick for' (there is surely a pointed echo in the parallel phrases here). Otherwise, he will have Claudio subjected to prolonged torture before he has him killed. Angelo's lines are far more explicitly

> What doest thou, or what art thou, Angelo?
> Dost thou desire her foully for those things
> That make her good? ...
> O cunning enemy, that, to catch a saint,
> With saints doth bait thy hook! Most dangerous
> Is that temptation that doth goad us on
> To sin in loving virtue.   (II, ii, 171–83)

There is a vicious circle here: the saintlier Isabella is, the more Angelo desires her. So perhaps any sincere refusal from her might arouse him still further. Yet her fiery lines, with images of passionate sexuality underlying a prayer for martyrdom, for torture or death, for anything but sexual violation, would seem deliberately designed by Shakespeare to arouse Angelo as saint, as sensualist, and as a sadist. And so, of course, they do. Here is Angelo's response, his answer, his ultimatum to Isabella (for obvious reasons, parallel passages from her speech, which comes less than five minutes before his, are also cited):

Angelo.   I have begun
And now I give my sensual race the rein:
Fit thy consent to my *sharp* appetite;
Lay by all nicety and prolixious blushes
That banish what they sue for. Redeem thy brother
By *yielding up thy body* to my will;
Or else he must not only die the death,
But thy unkindness shall his death draw out
To ling'ring sufferance.

                      (II, iv, 158–66 – italics mine)

---

sexual, his threats more sadistic, than earlier propositions urging Isabella to ransom her brother with the treasure of her body. They are also far more demanding: he insists upon a completely uninhibited response.

Indeed, one might infer from this ultimatum that Angelo sees in Isabella the feminine counterpart of himself. As he was, so she is; as he is, so she might become. As 'black masks / Proclaim an enciel'd beauty', so the saintly asceticism of her life, precisely like his own, may mask a keen appetite that could

90

indeed give full and fit consent to his desire. As he will give the 'sensual race the rein', so must she. He will allow her no modesty, no nicety, no blushes to banish what he now believes they sue for. He will have a response equivalent to his own sexual passion.

Reading or hearing these lines, one may well wonder just what might have happened to Isabella in the bed of Angelo. How would she have responded? Could he be right in attributing to her a latent sensuality equal to his own? Who wouldn't like to find that out? Does the fact that Angelo, who was once immune to sex and is now obsessed with it, suggest that Isabella might fall too? Claudio has informed us that

> Liberty,
> As surfeit, is the father of much fast;
> So every scope by the immoderate use
> Turns to restraint. (I, ii, 117–20)

So might not the reverse prove true for his sister, as it already has for Angelo? Could her restraint turn to immoderate use? Does her initial desire for more severe restraints within the convent suggest that there is something to restrain? Why does Isabella embrace martyrdom in such passionately sexual terms? Why her special emphasis on woman's frailty? Everyone I've pestered for opinions on her lines says that they seem perfect, exactly in character. I agree, but why so unless the line between saint and sinner, martyr and masochist, righteous severity and sadism – in short, the borderline between angelic and demonic extremes of virtue and of vice – is indeed a very narrow one, and all too easy to cross. At this moment in the play, the psychology, the characterization, and the poetry alike raise all sorts of impious and lurid questions. Who, in an audience listening to inflammatory speeches about stripping and whips, about beds that longing had been sick for, about sharp appetites, sensual races, fit consent, and so on, has a mind so pure but some 'uncleanly apprehensions' 'might 'in sessions sit' with meditations lawful?

Far from finding in it affirmations of orthodox pieties, moralists, from Plato to Gosson and Collier, have condemned the drama for inflaming passions and raising impious speculations that they thought ought to be suppressed. Twentieth-century commentators like Kirsch, who tend to presuppose an inveterate piety on the part of Elizabethan audiences, would seem to ignore the obvious fact that there are certain moments in the drama when most members of any audience – Christian or pagan, Elizabethan, modern, or, for that matter, Greek – are virtually forced to join the devil's party, perhaps without knowing it. Given the choice, 'you can watch Marlowe's Faustus go forward, or you can watch him repent', how many people would choose the latter? Do we not join forces with Lucifer and Mephistopheles in urging Faustus on towards the midnight hour, to the very heart of darkness? Sometimes, at crucial moments in many works wherein the protagonist has decided to pursue a course of action known by his audience to be dangerous, evil, or inevitably tragic in its consequences, he may be offered an opportunity to desist or turn back. He can then decide (in the words of Macbeth) to 'proceed no further in this business'. 'Ask me no more', pleads Teiresias to Oedipus: 'I mean to spare you, and myself', and later on Jocasta implores Oedipus to abandon his tragic quest. Yet who, in the *audience*, wants Oedipus to leave the terrible truth unknown? Shortly before their final encounter with the White Whale, the virtuous Starbuck begs, and momentarily almost persuades, Captain Ahab to return to Nantucket. But does any reader really want Ahab to reverse course? Having come this far, would we not feel, to say the least, let-down, if, at this point, Ahab decided to abandon all thoughts of revenge, forget Moby-Dick, and return to his dear wife and children? Similarly, had Faustus heeded the

Old Man and managed an eleventh-hour repentance, many members of the audience might well storm out of the theatre demanding refunds from the box-office, and complaining, with good cause, about 'cop-outs' on the part of Faustus and Marlowe alike.

In certain works, the author arouses a desire, on the part of his audience, for climax, not anticlimax. Thus – sometimes – for the audience, as well as for certain dramatic heroes and heroines, there can be no contentment but in going all the way. Indeed, fictional characters of various kinds may serve as surrogates for our own desires to 'try the utmost', to experience whatever it is we most desire, or fear. It is, therefore, satisfying to watch such characters proceed to the outer limits of human experience, and, finally, to watch them face the truths and consequences inherent in our own dreams and nightmares, desires and fears. These facts of dramatic experience seem true regardless of the theological assumptions of the poet's age. So far as *Measure for Measure* is concerned, one may either relish or deplore the psychological and sexual reverberations of Shakespeare's confrontation between a fiery saint and a fallen angel, yet who would not be fascinated by them? Who would not wonder what might have happened, had Isabella yielded herself to Angelo? Where's that palace whereinto 'foul things' sometimes intrude not? In the audience? On the stage? Why, incidentally, are Isabella's last lines in the play about Angelo's desire for her?

Given the subsequent course of action, there's no knowing. Shakespeare himself apparently decided, at mid-point in *Measure for Measure*, to proceed no further in this business – or, as Dryden would put it, having first prescribed a purge, he immediately orders us to take restringents. There is, clearly, a deliberate and virtually complete withdrawal from this (his and our) fascination with the sexual and psychological proclivities of his

villain and his heroine. Perhaps significantly, he never again permits them a moment alone together on the stage. He abruptly and conspicuously parts company with his sources, wherein the counterpart to Isabella *always* yields up her body, for one night, to Angelo's counterpart. But, then, in none of his sources is the sexual and emotional situation anything like so highly charged. Perhaps partly to avert a conflagration, Shakespeare resorts to a series of elaborate intrigues. He drags in the tepid Mariana to play the bed-trick, thus assuring that Angelo is securely fettered to another woman by the bonds of holy wedlock, and then – ever widening the safety-zone between his incendiary pair – he has the Duke claim Isabella for his own. Thus, officially at least, Shakespeare precludes further speculation about a sexual moment-of-truth between Isabella and Angelo. In short, the subsequent action of the play, like many scholarly discussions of it, would seem designed to encourage us to efface from the memory the extraordinary psychological and sexual reverberations of the earlier scenes. Assuming (only assuming) that Shakespeare himself wants us to disregard that dramatic evidence which he himself introduced previously, is it, in the last analysis, possible to do so?

Obviously, a master-poet like Shakespeare may consciously, or unconsciously, incite powerful emotional responses from us in any number of different ways. But it is sometimes impossible for even the greatest writer to suppress strong emotional responses which he has already, either in intent or in effect, aroused in his audience. Shakespeare's leading expert on the permanent effect of provocative sexual imagery is, of course, his very own devil-in-the-flesh, Iago. Precisely like an unethical counsel-for-the-prosecution of Desdemona, Iago intrudes all sorts of inflammatory images into Othello's mind, and then tells Othello to take no further notice of them:

> I do beseech you –
> . . . that your wisdom yet,
> From one that so imperfectly conceits,
> Would take no notice, nor build yourself a trouble
> Out of his scattering and unsure observance.
>
> (III, iii, 148–55)

> My lord, I would I might entreat your honour
> To scan this thing no further; . . .
> Let me be thought too busy in my fears –
> As worthy cause I have to fear I am –
> And hold her free, I do beseech your honour.
>
> (III, iii, 244–8)

Thus, in legal terms, Iago 'objects' to his own testimony, and instructs Othello to 'disregard the evidence'. Or, in common parlance, he advises Othello to lock the barn doors of his imagination after having already loosed the wild horses. As his own rhetoric implies (he deliberately protests too much), Iago knows the answer to that age-old court-room question: 'How can a jury disregard evidence already presented to it?' The answer is, 'It can't'. Potent evidence may finally be out-weighed by equally potent evidence, emotions can be countered by equally powerful emotions, but no one can, by taking thought, obliterate from the imagination associations implanted in it by the very command to do so: 'Try to count to ten without thinking of a rabbit.' Thus, even as he urges him to put them out of mind, Iago effectively sears his 'dangerous conceits' into Othello's imagination and memory:

> Dangerous conceits are in their natures poisons,
> Which at the first are scarce found to distaste,
> But with a little act upon the blood,
> Burn like the mines of sulphur. I did say so.
>
> (III, iii, 325–8)

Iago spoke these lines before a court audience on 1 November 1604. It goes without saying that the creator of Iago knew – none so well as he – all about the survival power of sexually and emotionally charged 'conceits'. And he certainly knew it when Isabella first spoke her inflammatory lines to Angelo at the court of King James on 26 December 1604. Had he

wished to, surely he could have – and would have – toned down those confrontation scenes.

Yet he didn't. Why not? He certainly had reason to, if he wished to provide us with easy solutions to the problems posed. For that matter, why doesn't Angelo say that his lust for Isabella represented a perverted appetite, and that he has finally realized his true love for Mariana? Why doesn't Isabella say that she has learned what it means to be a woman from Mariana and therefore accepts the Duke's proposal of marriage? Why did Shakespeare leave it to scholars, centuries later, to provide these solutions for him? Surely an obvious problem with the text as it stands is that the subsequent intrigues do not serve to set what has gone before in a new light, nor to over-whelm us (as Emilia overwhelmed Othello) with a new blaze of truth, but perfunctorily and ineffectually to contradict the earlier characterization and action and so, perhaps, confuse and frustrate us. Coleridge, for one, found the ending too good to be true. Seeing in this play something 'horrible', seeing sadism and criminal sexuality in him, it was impossible for Coleridge to accept 'the pardon and marriage of Angelo': 'For cruelty, with lust and damnable baseness, cannot be forgiven, because we cannot conceive of them as being morally repented of.'[1] Whatever Shakespeare might wish him to do at the end of a play

---

[1] See *Coleridge's Shakespearean Criticism*, ed. T. M. Raysor, 1 (1930), 131. Kirsch castigates Dr Johnson for his 'specifically un-Christian' lack of charity towards Angelo (p. 90). Coleridge, by Kirsch's standards, is equally 'un-Christian'. But, then, so would be Dryden, who, in *An Essay of Dramatic Poesy*, refused to accept the conversion of the Usurer in *The Scornful Lady*: that he should 'so repent, we may expect to hear in a sermon, but I should never endure it in a play'. Ben Jonson, in *Volpone* and in *The Discoveries*, also deemed certain vices incorrigible: 'They would love nothing but the vices . . . It was impossible to reforme these natures . . . They may say, they desir'd to leave it; but doe not trust them. . . they are a little angry with their follies, now and then; marry they come into grace with them againe quickly.'

ostensibly concerned with forgiveness, Coleridge (who, like Dr Johnson, was a devout Christian as well as a great critic) cannot do this: cannot forgive, cannot conceive, cannot imagine. Neither could most commentators until the twentieth century.

In recent years, Shakespeare's scholarly jury has been hopelessly split between those who can, and those who cannot, those who will, and those who will not, accept the ending of *Measure for Measure*. Those who cannot (like Coleridge) tend to be concerned with the major characters, with the consistency (or inconsistency) of their psychology, their motives, and their behaviour, and with the powerful emotional responses which they elicit. Critics who approve of the ending (like Kirsch) tend to be primarily concerned with the play's tragicomic form, its themes, and its religious overtones.

This critical deadlock surely results from problems inherent in the text itself. For though he clearly sets out to explore them, here, as elsewhere, Shakespeare was not about to subordinate his apprehension of a most protean reality to any single doctrine, dogma, or dramatic form. Throughout *Measure for Measure* there is a kind of firelight flamenco dance between comedy and tragedy, piety and impiety, virtue and vice, wherein one may threaten, arouse, change places with, embrace, or repulse, the other. So far as sexual vices and virtues are concerned, Shakespeare would seem to have here developed the photo-negative reversals, the strange changes and interchanges between benefactors and malefactors that he describes in *Romeo and Juliet*:

> For nought so vile that on the earth doth live
> But to the earth some special good doth give,
> Nor ought so good, but strain'd from that fair use,
> Revolts from true birth, stumbling on abuse.
> Virtue itself turns vice, being misapplied;
> And vice [sometime's] by action dignified.
>
> (II, iii, 17–22)

The sexual act between Claudio and Julietta, the one most severely condemned throughout the play, is, paradoxically, the only one in it that is dignified by mutual love. What is commonly deemed the 'vilest' form of sex, commercial prostitution, with all the diseases it entails, seems comparatively harmless when set beside Angelo's 'sharp appetite' and 'salt imagination', that is, when set beside the diseases of the soul.

Sometimes to avoid 'all profanation in the world' is to invite disaster. As J. C. Maxwell put it, it is certainly possible, 'without manifest distortion', to see the germs of twentieth-century psychological ideas in this play: 'I have even been told of untutored playgoers who thought that it was Jonathan Miller and not Shakespeare who conceived the notion of setting it in Vienna.'[1] For that matter, the fact that sexual repression could result in neurosis, in a diseased imagination, in sexual aberrations, was as obvious to Freud's Elizabethan predecessor, Robert Burton, as it was to Shakespeare.

In *The Anatomy of Melancholy*, Burton (very like Shakespeare in *Measure for Measure*) brings together 'Great precisians' and 'fiery-spirited zealots' as well as certain types that (by the way) surely composed a substantial part of Shakespeare's audience: there are the 'good, bad, indifferent, true, false, zealous, ambidexters, neutralists, lukewarm, libertines, atheists, etc.'.[2] In Burton, as in Shakespeare,

[1] See Maxwell, '*Measure for Measure*: The Play and the Themes', *Proceedings of the British Academy*, 60 (1974), 3.

[2] See *The Anatomy of Melancholy*, ed. Holbrook Jackson (1972) – page references are cited in my text. Surely Shakespeare's audience might have contained *some* neutralists, atheists, and libertines like Lucio, or like the ale-house keeper who, charged with having said that he would rather be in bed with his girlfriend than in heaven with Jesus Christ, compounded his offence when interrogated (in 1650) by saying 'A pox on Jesus Christ' or who, like Thomas Webbe,

Continued on p. 95.

virtue itself may turn to vice: 'Howsoever they may seem to be discreet', the 'preposterous zeal' of great precisians (like Angelo) can result in forms of madness that may break out 'beyond all measure' (III, 372). In sexual matters, by seeking to avoid Scylla, one may fall into Charybdis, and 'Venus omitted' may do as much damage to the body and mind as 'Intemperate Venus': it may cause 'priapismus, satyriasis, etc.' and 'send up poisonous vapours to the brain and heart'. If the 'natural seed be over-long kept (in some parties) it turns to poison' (I, 234). For that matter, the tyranny of religious 'superstition' seemed as terrible as the tyranny of princes: 'What power of prince or penal law, be it never so strict', asks Burton, could enforce men, and women like Isabella, to do that which they will voluntarily undergo, 'As to fast from all flesh, abstain from marriage, whip themselves . . . abandon the world?' (III, 332). Zealots of this kind will endure any misery, 'suffer and do that which the sunbeams will not endure to see, *religionis acti furiis*', endure 'all extremeties', 'vow chastity', 'take any pains', 'die a thousand deaths' (III, 350).

Might not organized religion itself, rather like the Duke – or like oversimplified, 'Christian' interpretations of *Measure for Measure* – provide solutions that are false, ways out that are too easy? Discussing, and deploring, the 'general pardons' issued by Catholics (their 'easy rates and dispensations for all offences') Burton observes how 'their ghostly fathers' so 'easily apply remedies . . . cunningly string and unstring, wind and unwind their devotions, play upon their consciences with plausible speeches and terrible threats, . . . settle and remove, erect with such facility and deject, let in and out' (III, 403–4). I have never seen, anywhere, a better gloss on the dubious contrivances of Shakespeare's Duke-disguised-as-a-friar than this. Even in the end, when the organization of the play seems to encourage it,

the characterization seems to subvert an acceptance of the Duke's far too facile settlements and solutions: Angelo asks only for death, never for marriage to Mariana; Isabella's response to the Duke's proposal is silence. In the end, as in the beginning, they seem, oddly, two of a kind.

Moreover, by way of their counterparts on the stage (Claudio, Lucio, Barnardine) this play might seem quite sympathetic to the ordinary sinners in Shakespeare's audience. Markedly unlike the Duke, Shakespeare's play does not 'repel a fornicator, reject a drunkard, resist a proud fellow, turn away an idolator, but entertains all, communicates itself to all' (Burton, III, 413). It is in this spacious humanity, and, perhaps, only in this, that Shakespeare might be said to reflect the ultimate grace of God. Yet he also gives the Devil his due. In the confrontation scenes, as Coleridge observed, he confronts us with things that are 'horrible'. He crosses the boundary between the angelic and the demonic to remind us that God's temple itself may contain the Devil's chapel. Through his recalcitrant characters, he challenges the assumption that human nature can be made to perform according to a scenario of the Duke's contriving. Critical efforts to exorcize the play's demons, to disregard Shakespeare's illumination of the darker regions of the soul, in effect deny the play one of its boldest claims to truth. And to impose any external – thematic, formalist, or theological – solutions on the manifold and enduring problems posed within it is, in fact, to deny this play its rightful claim to greatness. Finally, it seems impertinent to consider it the duty of criticism to solve problems that Shakespeare himself refused to solve. What remain pertinent are the problems posed.

Continued from p. 94
might have concluded that 'There's no heaven but women, nor no hell save marriage' (see Hill, *Irreligion in the 'Puritan' Revolution*, above, p. 106, note 1).

TROILUS AND CRESSIDA[1]

KENNETH MUIR

Troilus and Cressida has always been something of a puzzle. The title-page of the Quarto described it as a History, the Epistle to the Reader spoke of it as a Comedy, and the Folio as an afterthought put it between the Histories and the Tragedies. Oscar J. Campbell calls it a comical satire. John Palmer spoke of it as a tragedy in 1912, and as a comedy in 1914. To Hazlitt it was loose and desultory; Coleridge found it hard to characterize; Swinburne said it was a hybrid which "at once defies and derides all definitive comment". Heine said much the same thing more decoratively:

It is as though we should see Melpomene dancing the Cancan at a ball of grisettes, with shameless laughter on her pallid lips, and with death in her heart.[2]

The stage-history has been equally baffling. We do not know whether it was ever performed in Shakespeare's lifetime and the first recorded performance—apart from those of Dryden's adaptation—was at Munich in 1898. We do not know whether the play was Shakespeare's contribution to the War of the Theatres; we do not know whether Achilles was intended as a portrait of Essex; we do not even know when the play was written. After the first modern performance in England, *The Times* said that the play was better left unacted; and after the first performance in New York, as recently as 1932, most of the critics said the same thing. If the play has now become relatively popular on the stage, and if modern critics have come to appreciate it more in the study, we may suspect that audiences and critics have been taught by two world wars and by changes in society to see what Shakespeare was trying to do.

Mutability is a common subject in Elizabethan poetry, and the power of Time is one of the main themes in Shakespeare's *Sonnets*, besides being the subject of a not wholly relevant digression in *The Rape of Lucrece*. Whatever the literary genetics of the theme, Shakespeare seems to have been poignantly conscious of the irreparable outrages of Time. Time is mentioned in about a third of the *Sonnets*, and in many of them it is the implacable enemy of youth and beauty, of fame, and even of love. Shakespeare's beloved "among the wastes of Time must go". In the early sonnets the poet declares that marriage is the one sure way of making war "upon this bloody tyrant, Time" and in the later ones that beauty may live for ever in his "eternal lines":

you shall shine more bright in these contents
Than unswept stone besmear'd with sluttish time.

Time becomes a symbol, almost a synonym, for mortality:

Since brass, nor stone, nor earth, nor boundless sea,
But sad mortality o'er-sways their power,
How with this rage shall beauty hold a plea,
Whose action is no stronger than a flower?

> O, how shall summer's honey breath hold out
> Against the wrackful siege of battering days,
> When rocks impregnable are not so stout,
> Nor gates of steel so strong, but Time decays?

The poet protests that he will remain constant despite Time with his scythe, and proclaims that:

> Love's not Time's fool, though rosy lips and cheeks
> Within his bending sickle's compass come.

But he is agonizingly aware, as Troilus is, that he cannot expect constancy in others. He knows that although his own love would not alter when it alteration found, love is often "converted from the thing it was".[3]

Here in the *Sonnets*, then, whether they are fact or fiction, or a blend of both, we have a fore-runner of the Troilus situation—an obsessive concern with the power of Time and a realization of the vulnerability of constancy. In *Lucrece*, it may be observed, the heroine's tirade against Opportunity and Time (ll. 876–1024) precedes the long and vivid description of the painting of Troy Town (ll. 1366–1568). Time is described as "mis-shapen", "carrier of grisly care", "eater of youth", "virtue's snare", "the ceaseless lackey to Eternity". Some of the imagery used in the poem links up with four famous speeches in *Troilus and Cressida*:

> Thou grant'st no time for charitable deeds...   (l. 908)
>
> Time's glory is to calm contending kings...   (l. 939)
>
> To ruinate proud buildings with thy hours,
> And smear with dust their glitt'ring golden towers...   (ll. 944–5)
>
> To feed oblivion with decay of things...   (l. 947)
>
> Let him have time a beggar's orts to crave,
> And time to see one that by alms doth live
> Disdain to him disdained scraps to give.   (ll. 985–7)

Ulysses's speech on Time[4] is spoken in answer to Achilles's question: "What, are my deeds forgot?" And in the course of his reply Ulysses mentions "good deeds past", the scraps which are "alms for oblivion", the charity which is subject to "envious and calumniating time", and the "gilt o'er-dusted" which is no longer praised. In the next act, when Troilus parts from Cressida, he makes use of Lucrece's epithet:

> Injurious time now with a robber's haste
> Crams his rich thievery up, he knows not how:
> As many farewells as be stars in heaven,
> With distinct breath and consign'd kisses to them,
> He fumbles up into a loose adieu,
> And scants us with a single famish'd kiss,
> Distasted with the salt of broken tears.   (iv, iv, 44–50)

Here we have the same image of Time with a wallet, and also the cooking imagery first pointed out by Walter Whiter,[5] to the significance of which we shall have occasion to return. When Ulysses prophesies the destruction of Troy, Hector replies:[6]

> the end crowns all,
> And that old common arbitrator, Time,
> Will one day end it.

The fourth speech having links with the lines quoted from *Lucrece* is spoken by Troilus after he has witnessed Cressida's unfaithfulness:

> The fractions of her faith, orts of her love,
> The fragments, scraps, the bits and greasy relics
> Of her o'er-eaten faith, are bound to Diomed.   (v, ii, 158–60)

Some of the food images in *Lucrece* and the *Sonnets* are connected with the Ovidian idea of devouring Time; the remainder associate sexual desire with feeding, and its satisfaction with surfeiting. The association is a natural extension of the various meanings of the word *appetite*. Tarquin considers that

> the profit of excess
> Is but to surfeit;

his lust is compared to the "sharp hunger" of a lion; and he is described after his crime as "surfeit-taking":

> His taste delicious, in digestion souring,
> Devours his will, that liv'd by foul devouring.

A few lines later, we have another image of surfeiting:[7]

> Drunken Desire must vomit his receipt,
> Ere he can see his own abomination.

There are some twenty-five food images in *Lucrece* and more than three times that number in *Troilus and Cressida*. In the poem there is a link between the Time imagery and the Food imagery: Time is not merely a devourer, but also a bloody tyrant; and the ravisher is not merely a devourer of innocence, but a tyrant as well.

The painting of Troy enables us to compare Shakespeare's early attitude to the story with that he held at the turn of the century, when he may be supposed to have written *Troilus and Cressida*. In both, of course, he adopted the traditional medieval and Elizabethan view of the matter. He sympathized with the Trojans, and he was critical of the Greek heroes. Achilles is not described in the painting. In Ajax is to be seen "blunt rage and rigour". Ulysses is "sly". Pyrrhus is a brutal killer, as he is in *Hamlet*. Sinon is a hypocrite. On the other side Helen is "the strumpet that began this stir", and the lust of Paris is said to be the firebrand that destroyed Troy. Priam is blamed for not checking his son in time and for being deluded by Sinon:[8]

> Priam, why art thou old and yet not wise?

But the Trojans as a whole ought not to have been punished for the sins of Paris:

> Why should the private pleasure of some one
> Become the public plague of many moe?
> Let sin, alone committed, light alone
> Upon his head that hath transgressed so;
> Let guiltless souls be freed from guilty woe:
>> For one's offence why should so many fall,
>> To plague a private sin in general? (ll. 1478–84)

The main difference in *Troilus and Cressida* is that both sides are presented more critically. The debate in Troy enables the poet to show that the blame must be shared by all the Trojan leaders; and the Greek heroes are all presented in as unflattering light as possible. Even in the *Iliad* Hector is a more attractive figure than his killer; but in the play, even if we discount the railings of Thersites, Achilles is singularly unpleasant, and his murder of Hector is more brutal than the account given in Shakespeare's sources. Caxton's Achilles catches Hector partially unarmed and kills him single-handed. For this incident Shakespeare substituted the murder by Achilles and the Myrmidons, which he took from the Caxton-Lydgate story of Troilus's death.

The difference between Shakespeare's attitude to his lovers and that of Chaucer may largely be explained by the hardening of opinion towards Cressida in the intervening two hundred years. She had become a type of inconstancy, as Pandarus was the archetypal pimp. There is another reason: Chaucer, in writing a narrative poem, was able to slide over uncomfortable facts. We do not see Cressida's actual surrender to Diomed. It takes place after a lapse of time; it is 'distanced' by the poet and given excuses and motives—all except the obvious one. But once the story was dramatized—and it had been put on the stage before Shakespeare tried his hand— the evasions of narrative were no longer possible. The tempo was necessarily quickened, and Cressida's rapid capitulation stamps her as a daughter of the game so clearly that we hardly need the official portrait by Ulysses. To make her fall plausible Shakespeare has to suggest in the early scenes that she is something of a coquette. But she is as genuinely in love with Troilus as her shallow nature will allow, and Dame Edith Evans was wrong to play her as a Restoration heroine.[9] We are told that in the scene in which she parts from Troilus she was shown

pinning on her hat, visibly intent on her looks and on her change of fortune, while Troilus is boring her with his repeated "But yet be true". "Oh, heavens! be true again!" retorts the lady in her impatience to get his entreaties done with.

But Cressida means her protestations of eternal faithfulness, as Troilus means his.

Nor is Troilus the "sexual gourmet" with the "educated sensuality of an Italianate English roué" described for us by Oscar J. Campbell.[10] He fears, it is true, that the joy of intercourse will be too subtle for him to appreciate, "tuned too sharp in sweetness for the capacity" of his "ruder powers", and he is afraid of losing distinction in his joys.[11] But in this speech he is expressing precisely the same feelings as those of the chaste Portia when Bassanio chooses the right casket.[12] Campbell thinks that the bawdy benchers would have laughed at Troilus's later speech in which he answers Cressida's wise saw about the incompatibility of love and wisdom:

> O that I thought it could be in a woman—
> As, if it can, I will presume in you—

To feed for aye her lamp and flames of love;
To keep her constancy in plight and youth,
Outliving beauty's outward, with a mind
That doth renew swifter than blood decays!
Or that persuasion could but thus convince me,
That my integrity and truth to you
Might be affronted with the match and weight
Of such a winnow'd purity in love;
How were I then uplifted! but, alas!
I am as true as truth's simplicity
And simpler than the infancy of truth.   (III, ii, 165–77)

These lines, underlined in Keats's copy of the play and partly quoted by him in a letter to Fanny Brawne,[13] can hardly be taken to mean that Troilus fears that Cressida "will never be able to satisfy the demands of his discriminating, if voracious, sensuality".[14] Nor is Troilus a Mr Pinchwife who married only because he could never keep a mistress to himself. The whole point of the story is that Troilus is a faithful lover and that Cressida proves unworthy of him. He is not exactly a Romeo; Donne, it may be said, had intervened. The audience at one of the Inns of Court—if the play was performed there, as several critics have thought— would recognize Troilus as one of themselves. If he is satirized, it is not as a lecher but as an idealist. Indeed, some of his most characteristic speeches are concerned with the contrast between the idea and the reality, and with the inadequacy of the flesh to express the desires of the heart:

This is the monstruosity in love, lady, that the will is infinite and the execution confined, that the desire is boundless and the act a slave to limit.   (III, ii, 87–90)

Troilus the idealist is displayed in the debate in Troy. He speaks, as Hector points out,

                    not much
Unlike young men, whom Aristotle thought
Unfit to hear moral philosophy: (II, ii, 165–7)

for he brushes on one side all considerations of wisdom and justice, arguing merely from Helen's beauty:

                    a Grecian queen, whose youth and freshness
Wrinkles Apollo's, and makes stale the morning...
Is she worth keeping? why, she is a pearl,
Whose price hath launch'd above a thousand ships,
And turn'd crown'd kings to merchants.   (II, ii, 78–83)

Earlier in the play Troilus had spoken scornfully of Helen as a war-aim; but the full extent of his unwisdom in this scene is revealed later in the play. We may discount Diomed's bitter attack, as that hard-boiled cynic is likely to be prejudiced:

> For every false drop in her bawdy veins
> A Grecian's life hath sunk; for every scruple
> Of her contaminated carrion weight,
> A Trojan hath been slain. (IV, i, 69–72)

But the devastating scene at the beginning of the third act makes it clear that the face that launched a thousand ships[15] belongs to a woman of extreme silliness and affectation. Troilus is as unlucky in his idealizing of Helen as he had been in his idealizing of Cressida—though, to be sure, it might be said that Troilus, like many who fix their affections on an unworthy object, is not quite so blind as he tries to be. He has suspicions that Cressida is not quite as innocent as she pretends, and if he were certain of her constancy he would not exhort her quite so much.

The function of Pandarus throughout the play and of the Helen scene is to show that Troilus's love is thwarted not merely by Cressida's unworthiness but also by his environment. "Sweet love is food for fortune's tooth"[16] partly because of human frailty:

> something may be done that we will not:
> And sometimes we are devils to ourselves,
> When we will tempt the frailty of our powers,
> Presuming on their changeful potency. (IV, iv, 95–8)

but partly because Troy is an amoral world, and because the house of Pandarus is a place where bedding is more important than wedding.

We have seen how Shakespeare would have found the matter of Troy associated with the imagery derived from time and food in his own *Lucrece*. Ulysses's great speech on Time does not merely serve as part of his device to arouse the sulky Achilles: it also illuminates the coming together and the parting of the lovers, the scenes which precede and follow it. Love, we are warned, is subject to envious and calumniating Time. But we have just heard the lovers swear they will be true for ever; and we are about to hear Troilus's description of injurious Time. Cressida's frailty and the accident of war speeds up what Ulysses regards as an inevitable process. This Time-theme has, of course, been analysed by G. Wilson Knight, D. A. Traversi, Theodore Spencer and L. C. Knights;[17] but it should, perhaps, be said, that there are more references to Time in twenty-eight of the plays than in *Troilus and Cressida*, and only seven with fewer references. *Macbeth* has twice as many, though it is a much shorter play. The critics are nevertheless right to stress the Time-theme in *Troilus and Cressida* since Time makes a memorable and significant appearance at the key-points of the play in the passages to which I have referred.

As we have seen, the food imagery is linked with the Time-theme. It is because sexual desire is an appetite that it is bound to fade with its satisfaction, and because love is linked with desire that it is likely to be involved in its decay. The "fragments, scraps, the bits and greasy relics" of Cressida's faith are given to Diomed; and Menelaus, in seeking to recover Helen, "would drink up The lees and dregs of a flat tamed piece".[18] Troilus is right to claim that his fancy is

> More bright in zeal than the devotion which
> Cold lips blow to their deities, (IV, iv, 28–9)

but therein lies his tragic error. His mad idolatry is criticized by Hector in his speech on Value:

> value dwells not in particular will;
> It holds his estimate and dignity
> As well wherein 'tis precious of itself
> As in the prizer: 'tis mad idolatry
> To make the service greater than the god;
> And the will dotes that is attributive
> To what infectiously itself affects,
> Without some image of th'affected merit.   (II, ii, 53–60)

The food imagery is not confined to the love-scenes; there are about twice as many food images in the other scenes, those relating to the war; and it is reasonable to assume from this, either that Shakespeare was showing that the appetite for glory was as liable as the sexual appetite to lead to revulsion, or else that the atmosphere of the love scenes is carried over, whether deliberately or accidentally, into the remainder of the play. There is, for example, a sexual undertone in the dialogue between Ulysses and Nestor in I, iii: "conception", "shape", "seeded", "blown up", "rank", "nursery", "grossness", "barren", "palate", "pricks", "baby figure", "mutual act", "a man distill'd Out of our virtues", "miscarrying". The appetite for power is a wolf that at last eats up itself, as lechery eats itself. It is still common to apply the sexual term of rape to wars of conquest; and Sartre in *Le Sursis* juxtaposes in the same sentence the rape of his heroine and the signing of the Munich agreement which led to the rape of Czechoslovakia.

Certainly the play is meant to expose the false glamour of sex and war.[19] Both Helen and Cressida are worthless. The war is fought about "a cuckold and a whore; a good quarrel to draw emulous factions and bleed to death upon".[20] The Homeric heroes are vain, self-seeking, beef-witted, brutal individualists; and the great deed at the climax of the *Iliad* is converted into a cowardly murder. On the Trojan side, Priam is an ineffective chairman of committee; and Hector, who is wise enough to make an eloquent plea for the restoration of Helen, suddenly decides against his own arguments:

> For 'tis a cause that hath no mean dependance
> Upon our joint and several dignities.   (II, ii, 192–3)

He deliberately jettisons justice in favour of prestige. His sudden *volte-face* provides a theatrical surprise more effective than A. P. Rossiter's ingenious rearrangment of the speeches.[21] In the last act, Troilus chides Hector for the "vice of mercy" he displays in battle.[22] The "fair play" proper to a medieval tournament is unsuitable in war. Hector, for all his charm and heroism, is doomed: he does not realize that the age of chivalry is dead. Indeed, as the Elizabethans would be acutely aware, all the Trojans are doomed; and it is partly because of the doom which hangs over them that we are willing to judge them leniently.

Wilson Knight, Theodore Spencer and S. L. Bethell[23] are right in suggesting that the debates in Troy and in the Greek camp are designed to present the values which are violated in the action. Just as Hector is the spokesman for sanity in Troy, so Ulysses speaks for sanity in the camp. But in both cases what they say has little effect. Ulysses makes a superb diagnosis of the chaos caused by the lack of order, but his Machiavellian stratagem to put an end to Achilles's sulking has no effect on the action, since the latter is roused only by the death of Patroclus. Shakespeare characteristically suppresses all mention of the genuine grievance that Homer gives Achilles; instead, there is a belated and casual revelation that he is in love with Polyxena.[24]

That the play is concerned with the nature of Value is borne out by the imagery relating to distribution and exchange—there is similar imagery in *Cymbeline*[25]—though in fact the presentation of values is done directly as well as by means of imagery, and there are three other groups of images of greater importance. The numerous images related to sickness are concerned partly with sex, and partly with the sickness of anarchy in the Greek camp, so that these images serve to link the two plots together. The group of images connected with movement suggests the continual revolutions of Time and the agitated striving of Emulation's thousand sons. Even larger is the group of animal images, the great majority of which are confined to the Greek scenes. As Audrey Yoder has pointed out in *Animal Analogy in Shakespeare's Character Portrayal*,[26] the satiric portraiture is mostly put into the mouth of Thersites, and

there is little doubt that satire implemented by animal characterization does play a great part in the depreciation of such characters as Achilles, Ajax, Patroclus, Menelaus, and Thersites, who receive the greatest amount of such characterization.

However much we discount Thersites's railings, some of the mud he throws is bound to stick; and after we have heard Ajax compared to a bear, an elephant, a mongrel, an ass, a horse, and a peacock; after we have heard Achilles compared frequently to a cur; after Menelaus has been described as worse than a herring without a roe or than the louse of a lazar—they cannot climb again on to their Homeric pedestals. The greater sympathy we feel for the Trojans is partly due to the fact that they are largely spared Thersites's satire. Yet Wilson Knight exaggerates when he suggests that[27]

The Trojan party stands for human beauty and worth, the Greek party for the bestial and stupid elements of man, the barren stagnancy of intellect divorced from action, and the criticism which exposes these things with jeers.

For the only real intellectual in the Greek camp is Ulysses, and even *his* speeches are no more intellectual than those of Hector. Hector's actions, moreover, have little relation to his considered opinions, while Ulysses does carry out the one plan he proposes, futile as it is. Nor can it be said that the Greeks stand for intellect and the Trojans for emotion; for pride and the pursuit of self-interest are no less emotional than sexual desire and the pursuit of honour. The motives of Achilles are love, both of Polyxena and Patroclus, and excessive pride. Ajax is moved merely by brutish vanity. Diomed is moved by a sexual desire that is uncontaminated by respect or affection for the object of the desire. Wilson Knight in the course of his essay makes or implies some of these qualifications. But his assumption that Shakespeare's two primary values were Love and War, and that in *Troilus and Cressida* they "exist in a world which questions their ultimate purpose and beauty"[28] seems to make the mistake of replacing the idols Shakespeare was anxious to overturn. Whatever views one may deduce from a study of the whole canon, Hector and Priam, as well as Diomed and Thersites, agree that Helen is an unsatisfactory war-aim; and the one glimpse we have of her only confirms their opinion. Whatever else Shakespeare was doing he was not setting her up as an absolute value.

T. W. Baldwin, for reasons which are both learned and unconvincing, believes that Ulysses's speech on Order is unShakespearian.[29] At least it has a very Shakespearian purpose. It is dramatically necessary to build up a conception of Order, so that its destruction by Cressida's unfaithfulness may be the more devastating. In several of the books suggested as possible sources of the speech, it is Love, rather than Order or Law, which preserves the universe from chaos. It is so in Chaucer's *Troilus and Criseyde*. Order is more appropriate than Love to the war-plot, but the background of the speech facilitated its application to the love-plot. Ulysses argues that the stars in their courses obey the same ultimate laws as the people and classes in a well-ordered State, and he goes on to state that with the removal of degree civil war and anarchy on earth will be reflected in great natural upheavals. The life of man becomes "nasty, brutish and short". If the order is disturbed at one point, chaos everywhere results. Cornwall blinds Gloucester, and nothing but divine intervention can prevent the return of chaos:

> Humanity must perforce prey on itself,
> Like monsters of the deep.   (IV, ii, 49–50)

"When I love thee not", cries Othello[30] while he still loves Desdemona, "Chaos is come again." So chaos comes again to Troilus:

> If beauty have a soul, this is not she;
> If souls guide vows, if vows be sanctimonies,
> If sanctimony be the gods' delight,
> If there be rule in unity itself,
> This is not she. O madness of discourse,
> That cause sets up with and against itself!
> Bi-fold authority! where reason can revolt
> Without perdition, and loss assume all reason
> Without revolt: (V, ii, 138–46)

Cressida's unfaithfulness upsets order both in the microcosm and in the macrocosm—or so Troilus thinks. But before the end of the play he has apparently forgotten his feud with Diomed; he is concerned only with wreaking vengeance on the great-sized coward, Achilles, for the murder of Hector.

Shakespeare, I believe, was more detached than some critics have allowed, though less detached, I hope, than Oscar J. Campbell believes. Charles Williams seemed to imply that the crisis expressed in Troilus's speech was in some sense Shakespeare's own.[31] Even Una Ellis-Fermor argues[32] that the content of the poet's thought is "an implacable assertion of chaos as the ultimate fact of being", though the "idea of chaos, of disjunction, of ultimate formlessness and negation, has by a supreme act of artistic mastery been given form." We may agree about the artistic mastery, but not that Shakespeare was asserting that life was meaningless. He was asserting something much more limited, and much less pessimistic. He was saying that men are foolish enough to engage in war in support of unworthy causes; that they are deluded by passion to fix their affections on unworthy objects; that they sometimes act in defiance of their consciences; and that in the pursuit of self-interest they jeopardize the welfare of the State. He was not saying, as far as one can judge, that absolute values are illusions. He was certainly not saying that all women are Cressids; for Troilus himself, at the very moment of disillusionment, dissociates himself from any such position:

> Let it not be believed for womanhood!
> Think, we had mothers; do not give advantage
> To stubborn critics, apt, without a theme,
> For depravation, to square the general sex
> By Cressid's rule.
>
> (v, ii, 129–33)

T. S. Eliot's early critics, confronted with the unflattering picture of modern civilization given in *The Waste Land*, generally assumed that the poet was expressing his own disgust and disillusionment, though we can see now that it should not have been difficult to recognize the religious implications of the poem. In a similar way, the violation of order and the betrayal of values in *Troilus and Cressida* do not mean that the Order does not exist, or that all values are illusions. There is clearly a strong element of satire in the play, though it is tragical rather than comical satire. We sympathize with Troilus and Hector: we do not laugh at them. Even Campbell has to admit that the half-grim, half-derisive mood expected in comical satire was not suited to Shakespeare's genius:[33]

His mind was unable to assume the required flippancy in the face of human aberrations capable of producing as serious results as those issuing from the abysmal follies of the Greeks and Trojans. The sustained intensity of his mind...lent to the play a depth of tone which makes his satire ring with universal meanings.

One of the reasons why *Troilus and Cressida* has been interpreted in so many different ways is that we are continually made to change our point of view. In nearly all the other plays we look at the action through the eyes of one or two closely related characters. We see *Hamlet* through Hamlet's eyes, never through those of Claudius; *King Lear* through Lear's eyes—or Cordelia's, or Kent's—but never through the eyes of Goneril; *The Tempest* through Prospero's eyes. It is true that another point of view is often given, and a character such as Horatio or Enobarbus may sometimes act as a chorus. But in *Troilus and Cressida* the point of view is continually changing. At one moment we watch events through the eyes of Troilus, and the war seems futile. In a later scene we see the events through the eyes of Hector, and Troilus in advocating the retention of Helen seems to be a romantic young fool. In the Greek camp we see everything from Ulysses's point of view; and then, a little later, however much we despise and dislike Thersites, we become infected with his views on the situation:

Lechery, lechery; still, wars and lechery; nothing else holds fashion: a burning devil take them!

(v, ii, 196–7)

It is this shifting of emphasis which makes the play so difficult to grasp as a unity; but although Tillyard complains[34] that Shakespeare failed to fuse his heterogeneous materials into a unity, I believe the unity is there. Yet we distort the play if we make any one character to be Shakespeare's mouthpiece. The worldly standards of Ulysses are not Shakespeare's, though Shakespeare apparently shared, until the end of the sixteenth century, some of his views on Order. In general Ulysses appears more of a Baconian than a Shakespearian in his attitude. Others have argued that Shakespeare speaks mainly through the mouth of Thersites, though Thersites was renowned for his knavish railing in all Shakespeare's sources, including the *Iliad*, and also in Heywood's play about the Trojan war, written afterwards. Shakespeare could enjoy writing his curses, as we can enjoy hearing them, without sharing the bitterness of his creature. Others, again, suppose that Hector is Shakespeare's real spokesman, though perhaps his attitude to the character was not unlike his attitude to Hotspur.

Tillyard thinks that Shakespeare was "exploiting a range of feelings more critical and sophisticated than elemental and unfeignedly passionate", that he plays "with the fire of tragedy without getting burnt", and that "he meant to leave us guessing". We may agree with him that the play provides "a powerful if astringent delight", but doubt whether it is necessary to make all these qualifications.[35] It is quite possible to be critical and sophisticated at the same time as one is elemental and unfeignedly passionate. This, surely, is what the metaphysical poets accomplish when they are at their best; and if we are to place *Troilus and Cressida* it is not with the banned satirists, or even with the satirical plays of Marston and Jonson, it is rather as Shakespeare's excursion into the metaphysical mode. The most remarkable thing about the play is perhaps the way in which the poet managed to fuse thought and feeling, to unify an extraordinary mass of materials, and to counter the sense of chaos and disruption, not so much by the sense of order implicit in the artistic form, as by his establishment of the values denied or corrupted in the action. Cressida does not stain our mothers. In reading most of Anouilh's plays we feel that the sordid compromises of adult life make suicide the only proper solution for an idealist. As we quaff our dose of hemlock we murmur: "But for the grace of God (if there were a God) we might have gone on living." But although *Troilus and Cressida* is a kind of *pièce noire*, we should never be in danger, after seeing it performed, of thinking that it gives Shakespeare's verdict on life, at any rate his permanent verdict. Cressida did not cancel out Rosalind and Viola or make it impossible for him to create Desdemona or Cordelia. He did not "square the general sex by Cressid's rule".

The play, from one point of view, in its exposure of 'idealism', might be regarded as the quintessence of Ibsenism as interpreted by Shaw. From another point of view, as we have seen, it is a dramatic statement of the power of Time. From a third point of view it shows how "we are devils to ourselves": the world and the flesh make the best the victims of the worst. We may admit that the fusing of these themes required extraordinary imaginative power—a power which Shakespeare on the threshold of the tragic period amply demonstrated. The real problem about the play is the failure of most critics to appreciate it.

NOTES

1. A lecture delivered to the Shakespeare Conference at Stratford-upon-Avon, 18 August 1953.
2. Cf. the New Variorum *Troilus and Cressida*, edited H. N. Hillebrand and T. W. Baldwin (Philadelphia, 1953), pp. 382, 554, 520, 522, 523.
3. *Sonnets* XII, XVI, XVIII, LV, LXV, CXVI, XLIX.
4. *Troilus and Cressida*, II, ii, 145 ff.
5. *A Specimen of a Commentary* (1794), p. 136.
6. *Troilus and Cressida*, IV, v, 224–6. Lucrece had said that her words in railing on Time were "weak arbitrators".
7. *The Rape of Lucrece*, ll. 138–9, 421–2, 699–700, 703–4.
8. *Lucrece*, ll. 1398–9, 1467, 1471, 1550.

9. Cf. New Variorum, p. 218.

10. *Comicall Satyre* (San Marino, 1938), p. 212.

11. *Troilus and Cressida*, III, ii, 22 ff.

12. *The Merchant of Venice*, III, ii, 111 ff.

13. C. F. E. Spurgeon, *Keats' Shakespeare* (1928), p. 165; Keats, *Letters*, ed. M. B. Forman (1935), p. 501.

14. Campbell, *op. cit.* p. 213.

15. *Troilus and Cressida*, II, ii, 82.

16. *Troilus and Cressida*, IV, v, 293.

17. G. Wilson Knight, *The Wheel of Fire*, ed. 1949, pp. 65 ff.; D. A. Traversi, *Scrutiny*, VIII (1938), 301–19; T. Spencer, *Studies in English Literature*, XVI (Tokyo, January 1936), 1 ff.; L. C. Knights, *Scrutiny*, XVII (1951), 144–57.

18. *Troilus and Cressida*, IV, i, 61–2.

19. Cf. Bonamy Dobrée (ed.), *Troilus and Cressida* (1938), p. xii.

20. *Troilus and Cressida*, II, iii, 78–80.

21. *T.L.S.* 8 May 1948, p. 261.

22. *Troilus and Cressida*, v, iii, 37.

23. S. L. Bethell, *Shakespeare and the Popular Dramatic Tradition* (1944), pp. 98–105.

24. *Troilus and Cressida*, III, iii, 208.

25. Cf. A. A. Stephenson, *Scrutiny* (1942).

26. *Op. cit.* (New York, 1947), pp. 41–3.

27. *Op. cit.* p. 47.

28. *Op. cit.* p. 47.

29. New Variorum, p. 410.

30. *Othello*, III, iii, 92.

31. *The English Poetic Mind* (Oxford, 1932), pp. 60 ff.

32. *The Frontiers of Drama* (1945), pp. 71–3.

33. Campbell, *op. cit.* p. 234.

34. E. M. W. Tillyard, *Shakespeare's Problem Plays* (1950), p. 86.

35. *Op. cit.* p. 86. I have produced the play for an audience which was both unsophisticated and unbewildered.

15. *Troilus and Cressida*, Act III, scene i. Pandarus' song (Max Adrian), with Helen (Elizabeth Sellars), Paris (David Sumner) and Paris' servant (Roy Dotrice). Directed by Peter Hall and John Barton, 1960.

16. *Troilus and Cressida*, Act III, scene ii. Pandarus (David Waller) brings Cressida (Helen Mirren) to Troilus (Michael Williams). Directed by John Barton, 1968.

17. *Troilus and Cressida*, Act III, scene ii. Troilus (Mike Gwilym) and Cressida (Francesca Annis) plight their troth. Directed by John Barton and Barry Kyle, 1976.

18. *Troilus and Cressida*. Thersites (Norman Rodway) and Achilles (Alan Howard). Directed by John Barton, 1968.

19. *Troilus and Cressida*, Act v, scene ii. Cressida (Dorothy Tutin) and Diomedes (David Buck) are watched by Troilus (Denholm Elliott) and Ulysses (Eric Porter). Directed by Peter Hall and John Barton, 1960.

20. *Troilus and Cressida*, Act v, scene viii. 'Look, Hector, how the sun begins to set'; Hector (Derek Godfrey) surrounded by Achilles (Patrick Allen) and the Myrmidons. Directed by Peter Hall and John Barton, 1960.

'SONS AND DAUGHTERS OF THE GAME': AN ESSAY ON SHAKESPEARE'S 'TROILUS AND CRESSIDA'

R. A. YODER

Of all Shakespeare, *Troilus and Cressida* is our play. It could be rediscovered only by a sensibility tuned to artistic discontinuity and preoccupied with the realities of love and war; and so it had to wait for cubism and atonality, for fascism and Freud. So given over to 'philosophy' and debate, it had to wait for Shaw to rescue this dramatic mode, and probably for the kind of painstaking analysis of texts apart from performance that modern criticism has indulged. In a narrower sense, it is our play because it makes sense to Americans in the 1970s. We know, albeit still in a remote and mostly vicarious way, the meaning of a protracted seven years' war. We know how the designs of war fail in their promised largeness and how the Greeks must have felt tented in a foreign land, so many hollow factions, with their great engine Achilles useless in seeming mockery of their very designs. Like the Trojans, too, we have heard endlessly the arguments for carrying on a war of doubtful justification, and we know what it really means to settle only for an 'honorable peace'. We have seen good men who spoke truth in council, even in public, suddenly capitulate to save the corporate image. Within the walls of our capital cities – or more accurately, in their gilded suburbs – we may observe an elegant and seething triviality to match the palace society of Troy. Last and worst, we know what this society and its war has done to our best youth – those not literally destroyed have suffered a degradation of spirit, and of those whose ideals

are not fully corrupted, many have chosen a life of irreconcilable alienation. There is no doubt, *Troilus and Cressida* gives back our own world.

Not surprisingly, then, some of the most acute Shakespearian criticism of the past decade concerns this play, and these interpretations have been generally pessimistic: the play in some way ridicules or diminishes every character, and ultimately the human character, man himself; no one any longer seems to accept Ulysses's 'degree' speech as the established value of the play, yet for all the times I have read that Thersites is right about this or that incident, no one comfortably or categorically asserts that he speaks for Shakespeare. Instead, there is a tendency to philosophize about this philosophical drama, to gather it all up into one large design and stress the symmetry of parallels and contrasts between settings, persons, and arguments. Then 'multiplicity' rather than any one character's ideas governs the viewpoint of the play. And most of the traditional dichotomies – like Trojan/Greek, love/war, passion/reason, extrinsic/intrinsic theories of value, tragic/comic – are seen as 'complementary' and resolved in more encompassing generalizations.[1] Thus for Norman

[1] Contemporary notions about *Troilus and Cressida* go back certainly to Theodore Spencer, *Shakespeare and the Nature of Man*, first published in 1942, and to Una Ellis-Fermor's essay in *The Frontiers of Drama* (London, 1946). The trend toward 'complementarity' may have begun as a reaction against G. Wilson Knight's positive preference for Trojan intuition over

Rabkin the great issues of the play all point toward the realization that 'value is a function of time', and time a process growing of its own accord without regard to the desires of any man.[1] Or in Terence Eagleton's account *Troilus and Cressida* is epitomized in the inference Ulysses draws from his reading:

> ... No man is the lord of anything,
> Though in and of him there be much consisting,
> Till he communicate his parts to others
> (III, iii, 115–17)

The characteristic action of the play, describing or evaluating someone to someone else, and the imagery of merchants, mediators, and go-betweens show us that 'individual identity is a public creation', that we have no intrinsic identities apart from our relationships; thus Troilus who never objectifies himself in a public role or identity inevitably fails.[2] Particular man appears to dissolve in a discourse on the fallacy of simple location. For all the confusion on stage, the characters transcend the ordinary limitations of life – Troilus, Cressida, Pandarus would define themselves as mythical beings 'in the world to come' (III, ii, 171–203).[3]

This larger, philosophical view of *Troilus and Cressida* provides some relief from taxing ideological quarrels and from any lingering sense of aesthetic chaos. Yet its great virtue, I think, is to startle us with still another profound question, as all good philosophy does: Why in a play that so richly evokes an atmosphere, a sense of the here and now, are we asked to look so far beyond it, into the dim abstract, for answers? Why, in short, should we desert the world that is for 'the world to come'? A look at the actual world of Troy, and we may learn why its inhabitants – and following them, the audience – might find refuge in a time outside of time and in a space that relieves them of an identity apart from public role.

I

What is going on at Troy is no secret. Some time ago the 'princes orgulous' came from Greece to meet the courteous Trojans in honorable battle, all over a point of honor in love. Now, 'after seven years' siege' (I, iii, 11) – 'after so many hours, lives, speeches spent', and 'honour, loss of time, travail, expense,/ Wounds, friends, and what else is dear that is consumed/ In hot digestion of this cormorant war' (II, ii, 1, 4–6) – they are still at it. Trojans

Greek cunning (*The Wheel of Fire*, 1st ed., London, 1930). Derek Traversi's treatment in *An Approach to Shakespeare* (1st ed., London 1938), Kenneth Muir's '*Troilus and Cressida*', *Shakespeare Survey 8* (Cambridge, 1955), pp. 28–39, and L. C. Knights's essay in *Some Shakespearean Themes* (London, 1959) are all in this vein. More recently, R. A. Foakes, '*Troilus and Cressida* Reconsidered', *University of Toronto Quarterly*, XXXII (1963), 142–54, Mary Ellen Rickey, '"'Twixt the Dangerous Shores": *Troilus and Cressida* Again', *Shakespeare Quarterly*, XV (1964), 3–13, make similar assumptions. The most philosophical exposition of complementarity is Norman Rabkin, *Shakespeare and the Common Understanding* (New York, 1967), pp. 31–57. Apart from this rather general point, these essays are not always similar. It should be clear that I have no quarrel with what I have called 'philosophical' criticism as a method; the only question is which philosophy to apply.

[1] Rabkin, *Shakespeare and the Common Understanding*, p. 53. His view does not take account of differences, particularly between the lovers' sense of time in III, ii, and Ulysses's in III, iii. Inevitably, Rabkin's stress on a philosophical theme resolved underplays the pessimistic tone of the whole play.

[2] *Shakespeare and Society* (New York, 1967), pp. 14–22, 34–7. My view of Troilus is almost the reverse of Eagleton's. Eagleton, in effect, shows how the dramatic techniques explored by Rudolf Stamm, 'The Glass of Pandar's Praise: The Word-Scenery, Mirror Passages, and Reported Scenes in Shakespeare's *Troilus and Cressida*', *Essays and Studies*, XVII (1964), pp. 55–77, can be interpreted as controlling the theme.

[3] Foakes, '*Troilus and Cressida* Reconsidered', pp. 149–54, argues that this passage shows the play is not de-bunking myth, but myth is modifying the play, directing us to the noble values that time has preserved from the somewhat ignoble action and diminished personages the play presents.

and Greeks are still playing the game according to the rules of knightly combat and the courtly lover's code. Yet nowhere in Shakespeare is the official standard of conduct more at odds with the action and language of the play.[1] Even Troilus, at the beginning, dissociates himself as a lover from this absurd war:

> Fools on both sides! Helen must needs be fair,
> When with your blood you daily paint her thus.
> I cannot fight upon this argument   (I, i, 92–4)

But he finds it easier to brush off this truth than to escape the war. Troilus, youngest son of Priam, a prince raised in the Trojan court, has inherited its code, though, to be sure, his courtly stance is still a bit awkward: he wallows – to use his own egregious verb – in a morass of conceits that invariably betray a less idealistic basis for love than Troilus realizes.[2] Not only do sensuous and financial images undercut his romantic protestations, but the strained pitch of his language leads him to absurd exaggerations – in the parting speeches, for example:

> Nay, we must use expostulation kindly,
> For it is parting from us.
> I speak not 'be thou true', as fearing thee,
> For I will throw my glove to Death himself
> That there's no maculation in thy heart;
> But 'be thou true' say I, to fashion in
> My sequent protestation: be thou true,
> And I will see thee.   (IV, iv, 60–7)

The challenge to death fits a code that joins love with honor in the field – that is why Troilus cannot escape the war. This extreme personification and the Latinized diction, which is a repeated device in the play,[3] suggest that Troilus has over-reacted to Cressida's twitting response. Were he able to know Cressida, Troilus would not need the merchant bark, 'this sailing Pandar' (I, i, 105) – and later in a grimly ironic figure 'my Charon' (III, ii, 10) – as a go-between. For the lovers the courtly role is inappropriate; somehow they have been miscast, or misplaced. In the climax of the play, when he is faced with Cressida's infidelity, Troilus himself razes the structure of their love:

> The bonds of heaven are slipped, dissolved and
>   loosed,
> And with another knot, five-finger-tied,
> The fractions of her faith, orts of her love,
> The fragments, scraps, the bits and greasy relics
> Of her o'ereaten faith are given to Diomed.
>   (V, ii, 156–60)

Here the subdued coarseness of Troilus's love poetry surfaces: the 'thing inseparable' is blasted to pieces, and her divine drapery shredded to scraps of fat for a Greek appetite.

In public the Greek and Trojan generals loyally act out their roles. Hector's challenge delivered by Aeneas exactly suits the conventions of the tiltyard, wholly ignoring the causes of strife while twining the themes of love and war in their formal courtly relation:

> If there be one among the fair'st of Greece,
> That holds his honour higher than his ease,
> That seeks his praise more than he fears his peril,
> That knows his valour and knows not his fear,
> That loves his mistress more than in confession
> With truant vows to her own lips he loves,
> And dare avow her beauty and her worth
> In other arms than hers – to him this challenge!
>   (I, iii, 265–72)[4]

[1] A paraphrase of Spencer, *Shakespeare and the Nature of Man* (New York, 1949), p. 111.

[2] Spencer, *ibid.*, pp. 115–17, rightly contrasts the imagery of Troilus and Romeo; but consciously Troilus is trying to imitate the high-flown courtly style. See also Traversi, *An Approach to Shakespeare* (New York, 1956), pp. 63–71, and more recently Raymond Southall, '*Troilus and Cressida* and the Spirit of Capitalism', in Arnold Kettle (ed.), *Shakespeare in a Changing World* (New York, 1964), pp. 222–31.

[3] See T. McAlindon, 'Language, Style, and Meaning in *Troilus and Cressida*', *PMLA*, LXXXIV (1969), 29–43.

[4] See the note on this passage in Alice Walker (ed.), *Troilus and Cressida* (Cambridge, 1963), p. 159. My references are to this edition.

After this prolixity and more posturing, when the duel finally comes off and Ajax, according to Ulysses's scheme, is representing the Greeks, Hector declines to continue the fight on the ground that he and Ajax are kin. With flourishing oratory (IV, v, 119–39)[1] he puts up his sword, the two contestants embrace, and the Trojan lords are invited to the Greek tents where Agamemnon's welcome aspires to Hector's own courtesy:

> Worthy of arms! as welcome as to one
> That would be rid of such an enemy –
> But that's no welcome; understand more clear,
> What's past and what's to come is strewed with husks
> And formless ruin of oblivion;
> But in this extant moment, faith and troth,
> Strained purely from all hollow bias-drawing,
> Bids thee, with most divine integrity,
> From heart of very heart, great Hector, welcome.
>
> (IV, v, 163–71)

This strained purity, akin to the lover's (cf. Troilus, IV, iv, 24), lifts the present moment out of time; it is the ceremony that holds off chaos. The public world of *Troilus and Cressida* teems with these ceremonial gestures of respect, friendship, and affection: Ulysses's deference to Agamemnon and Nestor in the Grecian camp (I, iii, 54–69); Agamemnon's greeting to Aeneas in the same scene (I, iii, 304–9), much like the later welcome to Hector; Hector's surprising reversal in deference to Troilus in the Trojan council (II, ii, 189–93, 205–13); the diplomacy surrounding the exchange of prisoners (IV, iv, 109–39), and the ceremonial salute, the kissing game, that welcomes Cressida to the Greek camp (IV, v, 16–53); and the profusion of oaths and prophecies, the insistent promises that mark almost every stage of the play (II, ii, 101–12, implicit in II, ii, 139–41, III, ii, *passim*, III, iii, 15, V, iii, 6–25).[2] All these gestures culminate in Hector's gallant refusal to take Achilles's life (V, vi, 13–21) – here, indeed, is the embodiment of the code, and Hector a

paragon of 'fair worth and single chivalry'. But the culmination is in fact merely a foil to the scenes that follow, where in shocking contrast the code is betrayed. Hector, suddenly stirred by an acquisitive and bloodthirsty lust, tracks down a Greek 'beast' and kills him for his 'sumptuous' armor (V, vi, 27–31; V, viii, 1–4).[3] Then, having disarmed, he is set upon by Achilles and the Myrmidons. A parallel is explicitly drawn when Hector cries, 'I am unarmed; forego this vantage, Greek' (V, viii, 9); but he is viciously cut down, and in Achilles's closure to the scene the omnipresent jaws of appetite return: 'My half-supped sword that frankly would have fed,/ Pleased with this dainty bait, thus goes to bed' (V, viii, 19–20).

The plots of love and war are obviously parallel: Hector's death carries us to the same conclusion as the disillusionment of Troilus, namely, that the ugly realities of this world are at cross-purposes with the codes of courtly love and honor that seem to govern it. Shakespeare's panorama of the Trojan war is an ela-

[1] McAlindon, 'Language, Style, and Meaning', p. 29, finds the diction incongruous and the speech mere bombast.

[2] Most of these are in Stamm's discussion of mirror passages ('The Glass of Pandar's Praise', pp. 62–8); see also McAlindon, 'Language, Style and Meaning', pp. 30–1, on gestures and vows.

[3] Cf. J. Oates Smith, 'Essence and Existence in Shakespeare's *Troilus and Cressida*', PQ, XLVI (1967), 172–3, and for a contrasting view on this point, R. J. Kaufmann, 'Ceremonies for Chaos: The Status of *Troilus and Cressida*', ELH, XXXII (1965), 151. I think that the two can be reconciled if we consider that an aristocratic code always distinguishes between the treatment of generals or heroes and of common soldiers like the nameless Greek. Thus Hector is playing the ceremonial game of war, as Kaufmann argues, but the incident shows up the intrinsic worth of the code. The next scene is a comment on its extrinsic value, its relevance to the way men actually behave. The essays by Smith and Kaufmann add a nihilistic and existential dimension to philosophical interpretations of the play. Smith's stress on infidelity and Kaufmann's view of ceremonies accord with my notion of evasion.

boration of his own famous epigram, 'Something is rotten in the state of Denmark' – or of the germ in a contemporary analyst's report of the Elizabethan scene: 'I do here grossly fashion our commonweal, sick or diseased.'[1] What is worse, as the disease progresses, cross-purposes do become complementary purposes. The sick world Shakespeare fashions is like the world of *Julius Caesar* or of *Hamlet*: its ceremonies and formal rhetoric disguise the actual condition of life; the truth, told in images of disease and devouring appetite and by the successive, unveiling actions of the play, is an unpleasant truth, and so to avoid seeing their world for what it is, Trojans and Greeks cling desperately to the superstructures they have erected to deny it.

Time itself serves this mechanism of evasion. Time is a complex notion, regarded with both fear and reverence. Everyone in the play holds a proper Elizabethan distrust for time conceived as mere process or in process; the process is too clearly one of decay. What they reverence is time considered teleologically – the process completed, somehow ended so that durable judgments can be made. Such a completed Time is allegorized in Hector's remark to Ulysses:

Hector.   The end crowns all;
  And that old common arbitrator, Time,
  Will one day end it.
Ulysses.   So to him we leave it.   (IV, v, 224–6)

There is an odor of empty circularity or tautology in the exchange, because time in this sense confers value upon objects and renders them meaningless – the end is all, but the end is also empty, nothing. It is like the 'formless oblivion' that comprises past and future for Agamemnon (IV, v, 167), whose prescription is to lift the 'extant moment' out of the process, elevating it with chivalry. Thus the code is called into service to combat decay. As in *Julius Caesar* the great defense is Roman constancy and

honor, illuminated by images of a soldier's polished metal. So Agamemnon harangued his council,

    Why then, you princes,
  Do you with cheeks abashed behold our works,
  And call them shames, which are indeed nought
                            else
  But the protractive trials of great Jove
  To find persistive constancy in men?
  The fineness of which metal is not found
  In fortune's love: for then the bold and coward,
  The wise and fool, the artist and unread,
  The hard and soft, seem all affined and kin;
  But, in the wind and tempest of her frown,
  Distinction with a broad and powerful fan,
  Puffing at all, winnows the light away,
  And what hath mass or matter, by itself
  Lies rich in virtue and unmingled.   (I, iii, 17–30)

Here is the official, religiously orthodox view of temporal process – tending toward decay, but only as a means for God to weigh the fortitude of men. The hard, undiluted mass will stand the test. And so, in figures of hardened, shiny surfaces, does Ulysses explain to Achilles the nature of lasting virtue:

  Nor doth he of himself know them [his virtues]
                           for aught
  Till he behold them forméd in th'applause
  Where they're extended; who, like an arch,
                      reverberate
  The voice again; or, like a gate of steel
  Fronting the sun, receives and renders back
  His figure and his heat.   (III, iii, 118–23)

Continuous deeds of heroism may outrun 'emulation' – 'Perseverance, dear my lord,/ Keeps honour bright' (III, iii, 150–1) – and similarly, in Ulysses's degree speech, only an order and authority constantly maintained can hope to withstand the downward spiral of time.

Time and timelessness are equally the concern of lovers. Both Troilus and Cressida

[1] From a report by Armigail Waad, 'The Distresses of the Commonwealth, With the Means to Remedy Them', quoted by Southall, '*Troilus and Cressida* and the Spirit of Capitalism', p. 229.

observe, in the early scenes, that love is a process working gradually toward its goal (Pandarus to Troilus, I, i, 15–30, Cressida in I, ii, 287–94), and in the maxim tossed off by Pandarus – 'Well, the gods are above; time must friend or end' (I, ii, 77–8) – lies the same sense of tautology and impotence in the face of time that is found later in the play. Impotence of this sort runs through the love plot: when Cressida says, 'Things won are done – joy's soul lies in the doing', she means that from a woman's viewpoint the stage of courtly wooing is more satisfactory than the consummation; and at the very point of union Troilus seems obsessed with the failure of achieved love to live up to its promise (III, ii, 18–29, 76–82). Like the generals they fear the ruinous process of decay, and so they too would look beyond to the end, or very nearly the end of time, when with assurance in their judgment 'True swains in love shall in the world to come/ Approve their truths by Troilus' (III, ii, 172–3). Then as myths and metaphors they will have no need to fear, and they will outrival all the hardened similes – steel, iron, the stones of Troy, the sun, and the very earth itself (III, ii, 176–8, 184–8) – as figures of constancy.

Time, then, is not a philosophical theme above the play, containing and unifying the dramatic action; nor are the speeches about time analytical rather than dramatic.[1] The characters of *Troilus and Cressida* share a special and heightened awareness of time, which is appropriate to the world they live in: who would not, after seven years of destruction, fear the procession of time passing before them? Their appeal to ultimate Time, the process ended, is a means of escape from the present.

II

If Time as the arbitrator of all value is tautological, at once all and nothing, and if the dramatic function of time is to serve as a means of evading the present, then what becomes of the debate over values in the play? The most common exposition of this problem has been to contrast the extrinsic theory proposed by Troilus, in which value is conferred by the evaluator, by the price he offers, with the intrinsic theory set out by Hector, which assigns value according to the inherent worth of the object. The first might also be called subjective, in that it requires no public reasons, and the second objective, since it is assumed to depend upon an impartial, reasoned judgment; hence the first is linked with will, the second with reason, reinforcing this larger dichotomy in the play. Moreover, the problem of value described in this way draws a parallel between the two camps: as Hector and Troilus represent opposite ways of evaluating Helen, so Ulysses and Achilles stand as extremes in judging the hero (the hero being Achilles himself, whom Achilles over-rates much as Troilus does Helen).[2] Valuable as this analysis is, it does disguise something of what happens. In the first place, this contrast has only limited importance in the debate over values because both parties in the Trojan camp shift their grounds, Hector most obviously and Troilus more subtly. Thus, although a rhetorical question like 'What's aught, but as 'tis valued?' (II, ii, 52) suggests that value is determined by 'particular will' (and Hector would gladly fix on Troilus this appearance of serving appetite), Troilus's argument is actually quite different. It does not really concern Helen at all, for Troilus

[1] Knight, *Wheel of Fire* (London, 1965), p. 51. While he points out the dramatic appropriateness of various speeches, Knight values the metaphysical inquiry for its own sake. Rabkin also tends to elevate the speculation about time above the drama, though his notion of time is diametrically opposed to Knight's: for Rabkin (*Shakespeare and the Common Understanding*, p. 53) time determines value, while for Knight (p. 65) time destroys values.

[2] Fully described by Rabkin, *Shakespeare and the Common Understanding*, p. 43.

is quite willing to accept Hector's theory and defend Helen's intrinsic merit: '– why, she is a pearl/ Whose price hath launched above a thousand ships/ And turned crowned kings to merchants' (II, ii, 81–3). Cressida, too, was a pearl (I, i, 102–6) and a desirable commodity. What really matters for Troilus, in questions of love and war, is not the woman involved but the 'manhood and honour' (II, ii, 47) at stake. Will may or may not fix value in Helen, that is irrelevant:

> – how may I avoid,
> Although my will distaste what it elected,
> The wife I chose? There can be no evasion
> To blench from this and to stand firm by honour.
> (II, ii, 65–8)

What is relevant is one's word, one's honor, and more, the fact that 'our several honours' are all engaged (II, ii, 124) in this enterprise. Hector, it seems to me, misrepresents Troilus and Paris when he contrasts their 'raging appetites' with the 'moral laws/ Of nature and of nations' (II, ii, 181–6), and perhaps because they are not so merely willful as he makes out, Hector finds it easier to go over to their side in the end.

> Yet, ne'ertheless,
> My sprightly brethren, I propend to you
> In resolution to keep Helen still;
> For 'tis a cause that hath no mean dependence
> Upon our joint and several dignities.
> (II, ii, 189–93)

Those are precisely Troilus's terms – 'our several honours' – and behind Hector's reversal may be a feeling he shares with his opponents: what they really want to keep is the 'well-ordered nation' Hector admires, and this state, they know, depends more on the consistency with which its honor is defended than on moral laws or abstract questions of value. Consistency, after all, is what Troilus and Paris have insisted upon; their argument is perhaps the Trojan counterpart to the Greek constancy

expressed in images of hardness and metals. After Hector has capitulated, Troilus shifts his focus from past to future; no longer needing the pearl as a standard of value, he paints Helen as a means to great possibilities:

> But, worthy Hector,
> She is a theme of honour and renown,
> A spur to valiant and magnanimous deeds,
> Whose present courage may beat down our foes,
> And fame in time to come canonize us;
> For I presume brave Hector would not lose
> So rich advantage of a promised glory
> As smiles upon the forehead of this action
> For the wide world's revenue. (II, ii, 198–206)

We have already seen in other circumstances how Troilus's religiosity, this desire to be canonized, culminates in an appeal to the 'time to come' (cf. III, ii, 172–3), and how this appeal lures men away from things as they are.

Consistency, unity – in a word, 'order' in the nation is the underlying desideratum in the Trojan council, and the code of honor, as the concluding agreement indicates, is the means to that end. These assumptions about honor, shared implicitly by Troilus and Hector, are explicitly set forth by Ulysses among the Greeks. When his extraordinary portrait of cosmic order, the famous degree speech, finally boils down to the specific complaint, Ulysses attributes the failure of the campaign to social impropriety – the Greek soldiers haven't proper respect for their superiors:

> The general's disdained
> By him one step below, he by the next,
> That next by him beneath; so every step,
> Exampled by the first pace that is sick
> Of his superior, grows to an envious fever
> Of pale and bloodless emulation –
> And 'tis this fever that keeps Troy on foot ...
> (I, iii, 129–35)

And like Hector, Ulysses tries to identify this situation in which 'degree is shaked' with 'appetite' (I, iii, 119–24), while his own concept of hierarchic order takes on the name of reason (I, iii, 210). But it is not reason, no more than Troilus's argument was purely appetite; rather it is a kind of reasoning that promotes order and unity, just as the code of honor, imposing deference upon inferiors and consistency upon superiors, cements the *status quo*. These appeals to 'reason' and to 'honor' are essentially nominal or arbitrary standards: Ulysses's social order originates in 'The primogeniture and due of birth,/ Prerogative of age, crowns, sceptres, laurels' (I, iii, 106–7) without reference to merit, and for Troilus honor demands constancy (II, ii, 84–92), as if to say that holding the course chosen is the best proof of a wise choice. Thus both depend upon the assumption of an infallible or omniscient authority, and that authority is stressed in the third important discussion of value, between Achilles and Ulysses. Achilles, bolstering his now unattended pride, would exempt himself from the run of men who are governed by a merely nominal concept of honor:

> And not a man, for being simply man,
> Hath any honour but honour for those honours
> That are without him – as place, riches, and
>   favour,
> Prizes of accident as oft as merit;
> ... But 'tis not so with me.   (III, iii, 80–3, 87)

But Ulysses cautions him that virtue, so far as men are concerned, lies in actual deeds, not in sheltered qualities; that laud goes to 'dust that is a little gilt' rather than to 'gilt o'er-dusted' (III, iii, 178–9) reminds us that 'Degree being vizarded,/ Th'unworthiest shows as fairly in the mask' (I, iii, 83–4). So Achilles puts aside this public world that seems to belong entirely to 'envious and calumniating Time', and pleads private reasons for his retirement. To this Ulysses answers, in effect, there is no private world:

> The providence that's in a watchful state
> Knows almost every grain of Pluto's gold,
> Finds bottom in th'uncomprehensive deeps,
> Keeps place with thought and almost like the gods

> Does thoughts unveil in their dumb cradles.
> There is a mystery, with whom relation
> Durst never meddle, in the soul of state,
> Which hath an operation more divine
> Than breath or pen can give expressure to.
>   (III, iii, 196–204)[1]

Nothing is unknown to the state, which is 'almost like the gods', and all authority, all honor and reputation, derive from it. What budding love there may have been in Achilles for Priam's daughter gives way to his pride which can be fed only by the official histories of Greece. In time to come – always this concern for an indefinable, 'eternal' future – 'When fame shall in our islands sound her trump' (III, iii, 210), Achilles's name must be inscribed as 'potent and heroical'. Patroclus, too, though he has 'little stomach to the war' (III, iii, 220), urges his lover Achilles to yield their privacy to the call of honor.

Ulysses's speech on the providence of the state, more sharply than any other, discovers the centripetal pull of all the philosophy and rhetoric in *Troilus and Cressida*. Beneath an apparent disparity, all the theories converge in a way that is more obvious if we consider the total action of the play: they all support, at the expense of privacy, a collective, public order which is absolute in its authority and which is geared to continuing the long, absurd war that stretches across the stage, infecting if not devouring the entire cast. Call it the state, or

[1] See W. R. Elton, 'Shakespeare's Ulysses and the Problem of Value', *Shakespeare Studies*, II (1966), 107, who explains with citations the medieval concept of monarchical sacred omniscience on which this speech is based. Elton argues that Ulysses's views are nominalistic and relativistic, significantly like the philosophy of Hobbes. Thus for Ulysses value is relative to human desires, a marketable quantity, and this is exactly the kind of relative or subjective evaluation Troilus makes in the debate over Helen. What Elton doesn't stress is implied in his discussion of the 'mystery of the state', namely, that the relativism of Ulysses, and of Troilus for that matter, is, like that of Hobbes, used as a defense of political absolutism.

call it the system, it is a subtle network that both 'reason' and 'honor' serve: it is what supposedly justifies the parleys and games between opposing generals in the midst of slaughter; it is the apology for awful sacrifices on the part of men forever hoping that Time will somehow redeem them; it is a part of the 'necessary form' of history, a Grand Mechanism rising above men, directing them to roles they are hardly conscious of – and not just the mechanism of political struggle, but the superior machinery of war that unifies society while squeezing out its very life. In *Julius Caesar*, and to an extent in the earlier history plays, the acts of successive political figures in their struggles for power begin to mirror each other as the mechanism gathers momentum.[1] In *Troilus and Cressida* the mechanism is superbly efficient: not only acts, but thoughts converge – as the action is all part of the game of war, so the arguments are all ceremonies of rededication to the code that maintains the war and dissolves all forms of personal expression.[2] What needs to be contrasted is not subtle variations among Greek and Trojan leaders, but rather the single dimension in all their reasoning set over against the prophetic cries of Cassandra and Thersites.

> Cry, Trojans, cry! lend me ten thousand eyes,
> And I will fill them with prophetic tears . . .
>
> (II, ii, 101–2)

> Farewell – yet soft! Hector, I take my leave;
> Thou dost thyself and all our Troy deceive.
>
> (V, iii, 89–90)

Weigh reason against prophecy in this play, and to borrow Thersites's incisive complaint, 'all the argument is a whore and a cuckold' – to the appetite of war.

III

The debate over value, like the descant on time, sustains the illusion fabricated by reason and honor. Bound by their heroic code, Greeks and Trojans march into oblivion; they are caught up in the machinery of a state at war; the only hope they know is that of a timeless, collective memory where reputation – what Cassio, another purveyor of the code, calls the 'immortal part' of man – will be sealed up long after their bodies have turned to dust. In such a world it is natural for Eros to be postponed or channelled to serve the state. And the story of the young lovers, the central characters from whom the play takes its name, reveals the full effect of the grand mechanism at work.

Love and war are traditionally parallel or complementary themes, and in the play the codes of the warrior and the lover are clearly made out to be symbiotic. The motifs are pervasively entwined: for example, when Aeneas delivers Hector's challenge, the beauty and worth of Greek opposed to Trojan women are at stake (I, iii, 268–76); in the witty exchanges between Pandarus and Cressida, love is treated as martial combat (I, ii, 260 ff.); Troilus also thinks of war in anticipating the taste of love – 'I shall lose distinction in my joys,/ As doth a battle, when they charge on heaps/ The enemy flying' (III, ii, 27–9); and in the duet that ends the scene the lovers battle to prove their constancy –

Troilus.
I am as true as truth's simplicity,
And simpler than the infancy of truth!

[1] The 'Grand Mechanism' is introduced by Jan Kott, *Shakespeare Our Contemporary*, trans. Boleslaw Taborski (Garden City, 1966), especially pp. 6–11, 14. He does not mention it in connection with *Troilus and Cressida* though he does make the point that both feudal mystics and rationalists in the play attempt to justify the war (p. 79). I have used Kott's idea to interpret the other plays in 'History and the Histories in *Julius Caesar*', *Shakespeare Quarterly*, XXIV (1973), 309–27.
[2] Kaufmann, 'Ceremonies for Chaos: the Status of *Troilus and Cressida*', pp. 139–59, stresses the inability of all characters to stand free of codes or concepts; by giving themselves to ceremonies that distort reality, they lose the integrity or selfhood that heroism requires.

Cressida.
In that I'll war with you.
Troilus.   O virtuous fight,
When right with right wars who shall be most
right!
(III, ii, 168–71)

War thrives on a kind of love – when knights defend their mistresses whose tokens they bear, and mistresses arm and disarm their knights. But privacy in love, as we have seen with Achilles, is dangerous to the field; it must be rooted out. So, in the moment of love's consummation, Shakespeare contrives that 'the time' should undermine the lovers. And this is not personified Time, but the actual moment, war-time, the here and now: Calchas is prompted by 'Th'advantage of the time' (III, iii, 2) to demand an exchange of Antenor for his daughter, and Paris sums up the plight of the lovers – 'There is no help;/ The bitter disposition of the time/ Will have it so' (IV, i, 49–51). In one of Shakespeare's characteristic dramatic actions, the public world comes knocking early at the private chamber. Troilus and Cressida have awakened, and in lines that recall a similar scene from *Romeo and Juliet* (III, v, 1–42) they lament night's brevity:

Troilus.
O Cressida! but that the busy day,
Waked by the lark, hath roused the ribald crows,
And dreaming night will hide our joys no longer,
I would not from thee.
Cressida.   Night hath been too brief.
Troilus.
Beshrew the witch! with venomous wights she
stays
As tediously as hell, but flies the grasps of love
With wings more momentary-swift than thought.
You will catch cold, and curse me.
Cressida.   Prithee, tarry.
You men will never tarry.
O foolish Cressid! I might have still held off,
And then you would have tarried.   (IV, ii, 8–18)

The young nobleman, who naively accepts the courtly code he has inherited, is frightened that the demands of sexual love will conflict with honor; he is afraid of being discovered and would flee with the night. Cressida pleads with him to 'tarry' – the essential of Pandar's recipe for love (I, i, 15) – for she realizes now in a fuller sense that love grows slowly, that it must struggle against the demands of the world, that men fear when it 'swells past hiding' in a sense more profound than her earlier witticism (I, ii, 270) entailed. This kind of love challenges the order, the mechanism.

But here love loses. Consider the response of Troilus, who was 'mad in Cressid's love' (I, i, 53), to the encroachment of the official world:

Aeneas.
My lord, I scarce have leisure to salute you,
My matter is so rash . . .
. . . within this hour,
We must give up to Diomedes' hand
The Lady Cressida.
Troilus.   Is it so concluded?
Aeneas.
By Priam and the general state of Troy.
They are at hand and ready to effect it.
Troilus.
How my achievements mock me!
I will go meet them; and, my Lord Aeneas,
We met by chance: you did not find me here.
(IV, ii, 59–60, 64–71)

This is far from madness – an off-hand question, a wistful comment, and Troilus departs with Aeneas to join the very council that has dealt the blow. 'The young prince will go mad', cries Pandarus (IV, ii, 75), but he reacts more passionately than Troilus. He is left to console Cressida whose grief, so unlike Troilus's, points toward tragic intensity:

Tear my bright hair and scratch my praiséd cheeks,
Crack my clear voice with sobs and break my heart
With sounding Troilus. I will not go from Troy.
(IV, ii, 106–8)

Thus there is, in this central incident of the play and moment of high passion, an obvious flattening in the character supposedly most susceptible to feeling. It is not an undramatic slip; surprisingly, perhaps, but with psychological precision, Shakespeare shows that Troilus is calmed, even relieved in returning to his public role – he belongs to 'the general state of Troy'.

The bargain that sends Cressida to the Greek camp is just another of the acts of shame war brings. It must therefore be disguised and treated as an elaborate public ceremony, like the ritualized assassination of Caesar or the murder of Desdemona. Like Othello, Troilus borrows imaginary priestly robes for his task:

> I'll bring her to the Grecian presently;
> And to his hand when I deliver her,
> Think it an altar, and thy brother Troilus
> A priest, there offering to it his own heart.
>
> (IV, iii, 6–9)

Cressida will be a sacrifice to the gods. Troilus invites religious sanction, and like Agamemnon who saw adversity as the trials of Jove, he explains this calamity as decreed by the gods:

> Cressid, I love thee in so strained a purity,
> That the blest gods, as angry with my fancy,
> More bright in zeal than the devotion which
> Cold lips blow to their deities, take thee from me.
>
> (IV, iv, 24–7)

Strained indeed, this purity and zeal that sloughs off responsibility on the authority of a world beyond: for we have seen such divine operations before, when the watchful state unveiled, 'almost like the gods', the privacy of lovers. Strained, too, are the phrases of his 'loose adieu', betrayed by the ubiquitous imagery of the market-place (IV, iv, 40) and by that other metaphysical scapegoat, 'injurious Time' (IV, iv, 42), whom Troilus blames for what clearly *the* time and *this* world have done ... and for what *he* is doing, almost in numbed default. Imagine Romeo or Hamlet in his place – would they be tamed to this hollow, passionless performance? But Troilus never sees beyond his part in the ceremony. It is a game he plays at quite seriously – she'll wear his

sleeve, and with the special rights of the rich and noble, he'll go between the warring camps, bribing the Greek sentinels (IV, iv, 70–3). For the exchange proper Troilus flourishes with courtly demeanor:

> Welcome, Sir Diomed! Here is the lady
> Which for Antenor we deliver you.
> At the port, lord, I'll give her to thy hand,
> And by the way possess thee what she is.
> Entreat her fair; and, by my soul, fair Greek,
> If e'er thou stand at mercy of my sword,
> Name Cressid, and thy life shall be as safe
> As Priam is in Ilion.   (IV, iv, 109–16)

Diomedes's refusal to join in the chivalrous pledges and his obvious attentions to Cressida puncture this gesture, leaving Troilus to complain about his lack of courtesy (IV, iv, 121). This rebuke foreshadows Hector's treatment at the hands of Achilles, which is also something less than courteous. It infuriates Troilus, stirring the obsessive fears he broached so insistently to Cressida. He does not realize yet how love has lost, but the extent to which eros has been subordinated to the state by his chivalrous, pseudo-religious act is conveyed in the final dialogue between Aeneas and Paris:

> *Aeneas.*   How we have spent this morning!
> The prince [Hector] must think me tardy and
>   remiss,
> That swore to ride before him to the field.
> *Paris.*
> 'Tis Troilus' fault; come, come, to field with him.
>   · · · ·
> *Aeneas.*
> Yea, with a bridegroom's fresh alacrity,
> Let us address to tend on Hector's heels ...
>   (IV, iv, 140–3, 145–6)

Troilus lingers only momentarily; in the end he is true to the world of his fellow courtiers – the bridegroom casts off his fleshly bride and renews his troth to the spectre of war.

And so Cressida, as perhaps all the words of love have foretold, is finally marketed and sold.

To see her as merely a shallow and experienced 'Trojan drab', as most critics now do, is to miss the significance of this act. Jan Kott's brief but vivid sketch is an appropriate antidote to Cressid's detractors:

This girl could have been eight, ten, or twelve years old when the war started. Maybe that is why war seems so normal and ordinary to her that she almost does not notice it and never talks about it . . . There is no place for love in this world. Love is poisoned from the outset. These wartime lovers have been given just one night . . . Pandarus has procured Cressida like some goods. Now, like goods, she will be exchanged with the Greeks for a captured Trojan general. She has to leave at once, the very morning after her first night. Cressida is seventeen. An experience like this is enough. Cressida will go to the Greeks. But it will be a different Cressida. Until now she has known love only in imagination. Now she has come to know it in reality. During one night. She is violently awakened. She realizes the world is too vile and cruel for anything to be worth defending. Even on her way to the Greek camp Diomedes makes brutal advances to her. Then she is kissed in turn by the generals and princes, old, great, and famous men: Nestor, Agamemnon, Ulysses. She has realized that beauty arouses desire. She can still mock. But she already knows she will become a tart. Only before that happens, she has to destroy everything, so that not even memory remains. She is consistent.[1]

Certainly there is no need to assume Cressida is sexually experienced because of her talk. Playful bawdry and sharp passion are commonly found in the speeches of Shakespeare's virginal heroines, Rosalind or Juliet, for example. Whatever she has done before, for Cressida this morning in Troy is unquestionably a rude awakening. Among the Greeks she is bound to be exposed and degraded; it is, in the cliché of courtly honor, a fate worse than death, and quite expectedly that is what we hear from Troilus: 'Hark! you are called. Some say the Genius so/ Cries "Come!" to him that instantly must die' (IV, iv, 50–1). The ceremony that welcomes her to the Greek camp is a brilliant contrivance – it is drapery that actually reveals her nakedness, and it should bring home the full meaning of her being turned over to the enemy. Despite the elaborate courtesy of begging kisses, the Greek generals are taking what Cressida, essentially a captive, has no real power to refuse. She plays their game with wit and spirit, for that is her best defense.

Rude as it is, Cressida is not shocked or distraught; there is in her less illusion than in Troilus and an adaptive, reserve strength. She is indeed a daughter of the game, but we must be sure what game is being played. Whether or not Cressida knows about sex, she knows about war; she has grown up with it, not as one who seeks its glory, for she disdains the heroic proportions of warriors –

> *Alexander.*
> They say he [Ajax] is a very man per se,
> And stands alone.
> *Cressida.* So do all men, unless they are drunk, sick, or have no legs. (I, ii, 15–18)

– but as an onlooker and victim who must learn to survive with it. That is why Cressida seems so worldly and why she plays so knowingly the courtly game of sweet withholding. Hers is the good training courtly standards provide, good for a war-torn world in which something must always be withheld or restrained. Love is degraded in this world, for the wisdom of survival reduces it to a series of one-night stands: tomorrow the lover is gone to battle, or the beloved is traded off to the other side. Thus what Cressida discovers on rudely awakening is what she has instinctively prepared for. If Troilus submerged his erotic self in honor, Cressida has consistently struggled to keep part of *her* self unengaged:

[1] Kott, *Shakespeare Our Contemporary*, pp. 80–1. The Cressida of the Loeb Theater production at Harvard in the summer of 1968 seemed to me very much like Kott's – young, fresh, attractive, alive to the pleasures of love and knowledgeable in a way that makes the question of her previous sexual experience really irrelevant.

I have a kind of self resides with you,
But an unkind self that itself will leave
To be another's fool. I would be gone.

(III, ii, 147–9)

She knows that secrecy and silence are 'cunning in dumbness' (III, ii, 131), estrangement is a means of self-preservation. She knows that wisdom, in her world, is incompatible with love: 'for to be wise and love/ Exceeds man's might; that dwells with gods above' (III, ii, 155–6).

Cressida surrenders to Diomedes a few hours after leaving Troy. The complex demands of her situation shroud her motives; she is shrewd and practices the wisdom of concealment. What we do know is that Cressida is still very much the divided self that she pictured earlier: dialogue and gestures – giving, taking back, and giving again the sleeve – mark her importunate uncertainty. When Diomedes has left, Cressida examines what she has done, speaking for the last time in the play.

> Troilus, farewell! One eye yet looks on thee,
> But with my heart the other eye doth see.
> Ah, poor our sex! this fault in us I find,
> The error of our eye directs our mind;
> What error leads must err – O, then conclude
> Minds swayed by eyes are full of turpitude.
>
> (v, ii, 107–12)

If passing from one man to another is her role in the ceremony of war, she plays it; but unlike Troilus she holds something back, and in this withholding, this wandering or double vision, her critical faculty is sustained. By her own standards, and surely by the official standards of her world, she is condemned. Yet where minds are so readily corrupted and eyes so irresponsibly blind, it is self-righteous for her world to judge Cressida. After all, she is simply practicing the way of that world as envisioned by Troilus – 'My will enkindled by mine eyes and ears –/ Two traded pilots 'twixt the dangerous shores/ Of will and judgement' (II, ii, 63–4) – and by Ulysses – 'The present eye praises the present object' (III, iii, 180). Perhaps in the sensual pleasure of the here and now, however bittersweet it proves, Cressida has got hold of the only value her world affords. All that is left to her is a little touch of Troilus in the night – or of Diomedes, what does it matter? One or the other will be dead next evening.

IV

The betrayal of Troilus is an extraordinary scene which, together with the closing action of the play, points toward a number of motifs in *Othello*.[1] At the center is ocular proof of Cressid's infidelity. Troilus, whom Ulysses observes to be, like the noble Moor, 'both open and both free' (IV, v, 100), is shocked almost to silence. At first, he tries to stifle any response, his speech reduced to brief utterances –

> by Jove, I will not speak a word.
> . . . I will not be myself, nor have cognition
> Of what I feel. I am all patience. (v, ii, 54, 65–6)

Then, so far from Cressida's reliance on her senses (v, ii, 107–12), he would simply deny what he sees:

> But if I tell how these two did co-act,
> Shall I not lie in publishing a truth?
> Sith yet there is a credence in my heart,
> An esperance so obstinately strong,
> That doth invert th'attest of eyes and ears;
> As if those organs had deceptious functions,
> Created only to calumniate. (v, ii, 118–24)

[1] Stamm, 'The Glass of Pandar's Praise', p. 71, discusses technical aspects of this scene. Brian Morris, 'The Tragic Structure of *Troilus and Cressida*', *Shakespeare Quarterly*, X (1959), 488–9, calls the contrivance of the setting comic, but the development of the scene tragic. Both Morris (pp. 488, 491) and Kott (p. 82) suggest parallels with Othello. Othello naturally denies the 'evidence' of Desdemona's infidelity, but when he begins to believe it his speeches are shortened to perfunctory responses and his whole sense of order collapses. He, too, suffers the divided awareness that afflicts Troilus, and bolsters himself with rhetorical flourishes and the ceremonial sanctions of judge and priest.

For Troilus the 'esperance', a Latinate vision of what might be, has always been more comfortable than reality. Finally his whole world is split open and stood on end. Beginning his own degree speech, Troilus spells out the kind of spiritual hierarchy that reason imagines:

> If beauty have a soul, this is not she;
> If souls guide vows, if vows be sanctimonies,
> If sanctimony be the gods' delight,
> If there be rule in unity itself,
> This is not she.   (v, ii, 138–42)

And yet it is – so reason turns to madness and paradox makes sense. In the tradition of Shakespearian protagonists, not just Othello but Brutus and Macbeth and even Cressida herself, Troilus is a divided soul – the state of man, like a kingdom or a whole world, suffers an insurrection and chaos is come: 'a thing inseparate/ Divides more wider than the sky and earth'; 'The bonds of heaven are slipped, dissolved, and loosed' (v, ii, 148–9, 156). And the speech begun in celestial and Platonic order ends with the 'greasy relics' of appetite. Troilus cannot endure it; he cannot withhold or be 'but half attached' to his passion, as Ulysses counsels (v, ii, 161–2), so that the divisive loss of faith does not become for him, as it did for Cressida, a crippled wisdom accommodated to a corrupt world. Disillusionment paralyzes Troilus only for a moment, and then he begins to swell with hate; he steadies himself with what is most natural and accessible to him, the role of a faithful knight whose 'so eternal and so fixed a soul' swears to avenge its honor. Along with this role comes the rhetoric of *miles gloriosus*, dreadful bombast that should not be mistaken for Troilus coming to his senses:

> Not the dreadful spout
> Which shipmen do the hurricano call,
> Constringed in mass by the almighty sun,
> Shall dizzy with more clamour Neptune's ear
> In his descent, than shall my prompted sword
> Falling on Diomed.
> *Thersites.*   He'll tickle it for his concupy.
>   (v, ii, 171–7)

Troilus is posturing again, and his exercises carry over to the field where he redeems himself with 'Mad and fantastic execution', so careless of his own safety that his luck is to Ulysses the 'very spite of cunning' (v, v, 38, 41). The old 'dog-fox' Ulysses did his best, but in the distracted slaughter of this final movement there is no order, no 'degree', not even of cunning; policy 'is proved not worth a blackberry', and 'the Grecians begin to proclaim barbarism' (v, iv, 11, 15), evidently loosing the kind of savagery that lets Achilles murder Hector. Rising from this dust, Troilus speaks in concluding, funereal tones of Hector's death and the imminent destruction of Troy. 'Hector is dead; there is no more to say' – but Troilus is never at a loss for words –

> Stay yet. You vile abominable tents,
> Thus proudly pight upon our Phrygian plains,
> Let Titan rise as early as he dare,
> I'll through and through you! And thou
>   great-sized coward,
> No space of earth shall sunder our two hates;
> I'll haunt thee like a wicked conscience still,
> That mouldeth goblins swift as frenzy's thoughts.
> Strike a free march to Troy! with comfort go:
> Hope of revenge shall hide our inward woe.
>   (v, x, 23–31)

'Words, words, mere words', Troilus said of Cressida (v, iii, 108), but he cannot say it of himself. This speech is little more than a continuation of his spiteful threats in the betrayal scene and can hardly be construed as tragic recognition. Always what matters is what Troilus does not recognize: that 'after so many hours, lives, speeches spent', another oath of revenge is a terrible folly; that his late heroism and frenzied hatred for the enemy is one more instance of Eros harnessed to the purposes of the state, sublimated into the honorable outlet of duty – and Troilus is, in his own image, 'Mars his heart/ Inflamed with Venus' (v, ii, 164–5); that his world is not governed by the splendid systems and codes rehearsed throughout the play but is pretty much what Ulysses feared it might become:

> Then everything includes itself in power,
> Power into will, will into appetite;
> And appetite, an universal wolf,
> So doubly seconded with will and power,
> Must make perforce an universal prey,
> And last eat up himself. (I, iii, 119–24)

For the state at war 'everything includes itself in power' – all ceremonies, all speeches and all love, all secrets and all hope are drawn into the mechanism that must finally devour itself. The Troiluses, the Hectors, the Achilles and Ulysses of this world and ours, more or less unwittingly, are sons of the game. Thersites has told them the way things are: but will they ever learn?[1]

[1] For Morris ('Tragic Structure of *Troilus and Cressida*', p. 489) Troilus 'begins to find his true self' after his disillusionment at Calchas's tent and returns to the role of heroic warrior. McAlindon ('Language, Style, and Meaning', pp. 33–4) also sees Troilus recovering verbal and behavioral decorum. Stamm, on the other hand ('The Glass of Pandar's Praise', pp. 75–6), discredits such a recovery by calling Troilus's final speech a 'series of hyberbolic images'. Moreover, both rants by Troilus are undercut, first by Thersites's mockery (v, ii, 177) and then by the ending Pandarus gives to the play, especially the song that has much to do with the source of Troilus's wrath:

> Full merrily the humble-bee doth sing
> Till he hath lost his honey and his sting;
> And being once subdued in armed tail,
> Sweet honey and sweet notes together fail.
> (v, x, 41–4)

THE PROBLEM PLAYS, 1920-1970:
A RETROSPECT

MICHAEL JAMIESON

A survey of attitudes since 1920 towards Shakespeare's Problem Plays or Dark Comedies, *Troilus and Cressida*, *All's Well That Ends Well* and *Measure for Measure*, invites two observations neither of which would be true of any other Shakespearian group. First, the plays – particularly *Measure for Measure* and *Troilus* – have undergone a revaluation so radical as to amount to a rediscovery, and this re-assessment itself reflects changes in literary and theatrical taste. Second, the aesthetic validity and critical usefulness of regarding these plays as a group has been increasingly questioned. A third point is that, while the study of texts and sources has advanced, research has unearthed no new fact about the original date of writing or the circumstances of first performance of any of the plays.

Today, when *Measure for Measure* and *Troilus and Cressida* are set books at 'A'-level, and when all three plays come up regularly, not just for a token staging, but for their full quota of performances in repertory at Stratford and elsewhere, it seems incredible that around 1870 William Poel (the first modern director ever to stage all three plays) was recommended by his tutor never to read *Measure for Measure* and *Troilus and Cressida*, as being improper; or that in 1906 townspeople in Oxford opposed an undergraduate performance of *Measure for Measure*; or that in 1913 F. R. Benson had such qualms about himself staging *Troilus* at Stratford that he preferred to invite Poel to revive his production for two performances

on a single day. *Measure for Measure* did, however, inspire Walter Pater's fine essay (1874) and Walter Raleigh's perceptive few pages in *Shakespeare*;[1] and in 1884 Bernard Shaw maintained before Furnivall's New Shakspere Society that in *Troilus and Cressida* Shakespeare 'treated the story as an iconoclast treats an idol'. Shaw later liked to suggest connections between his *Plays Unpleasant* and Shakespeare's: 'in such unpopular plays as All's Well, Measure for Measure, and Troilus and Cressida we find [Shakespeare] ready and willing to start at the twentieth century if the seventeenth would only let him'.[2]

The three plays were first grouped together by Edward Dowden in *Shakespere: his Mind and Art* and subsequent text-books as belonging to Shakespeare's 'third period: *In The Depths*'.[3]

[1] London, 1907.
[2] See Robert Speaight, *William Poel and the Elizabethan Revival* (London, 1954), p. 192; Harold Child, 'The Stage History', New Cambridge *Measure for Measure* (Cambridge, 1922), p. 165; J. C. Trewin, *Benson and the Bensonians* (London, 1960), pp. 197–8; R. F. Rattray, *Bernard Shaw* (Luton, 1951), p. 147; G. Bernard Shaw, Preface to *Plays Pleasant and Unpleasant*, 1 (London, 1898), xxi.
[3] In the first edition (London, 1875), Dowden found *All's Well* 'serious', *Measure for Measure* 'dark', and *Troilus* 'bitter' – and so puzzling that he deferred discussing it till later editions. The phrase 'In the Depths' does not occur in the 1875 text, and the embryonic theory of four periods was later expanded. S. Schoenbaum has stated: 'No biographical pattern imposed on Shakespeare ... has made so profound an impact as Dowden's', *Shakespeare's Lives* (Oxford, 1970), p. 496.

F. S. Boas in *Shakspere and his Predecessors*[1] found links, some of them tenuous, between the three plays and *Hamlet* – 'we are left to interpret their enigmas as best we may' – and borrowed for them from the Ibsenist theatre the term 'problem play'. It did not win currency until recirculated by W. W. Lawrence in *Shakespeare's Problem Comedies*, a sane, slightly old-fashioned book,[2] dedicated to the octogenarian A. C. Bradley. Lawrence's was the first study of *All's Well*, *Measure for Measure* and *Troilus and Cressida* as a group. In each he perceived 'a perplexing and distressing complication in human life ... presented in a spirit of high seriousness' and the problem he defined as ethical in that 'complicated interrelations of character and action' are probed 'in a situation admitting of different ethical interpretations'. Lawrence argued that what is puzzling for modern readers would not have been so for the Elizabethan audience. E. M. W. Tillyard in *Shakespeare's Problem Plays*,[3] though not wedded to 'a highly unsatisfactory term', exploited its analogy with 'problem child' to discuss *All's Well* and *Measure for Measure* as 'radically schizophrenic' and *Hamlet* and *Troilus and Cressida* as dealing 'with interesting problems'. A. P. Rossiter in lectures given in the early fifties (posthumously published as *Angel with Horns*[4]) put forward a rationale for treating the three comedies as problem plays. Ernest Schanzer argued cogently against current uses of the term, himself giving a rigorous definition of 'problem play' which fitted only three of Shakespeare's plays, *Julius Caesar*, *Measure for Measure* and *Antony and Cleopatra*, which are the subject of his *The Problem Plays of Shakespeare*.[5] The term lingers on. Peter Ure, in his pamphlet *Shakespeare: the Problem Plays*,[6] continued to regard it as an accepted label for a group of plays, including *Timon of Athens*, which 'have some features in common'. In *Shakespeare's Problem Plays*[7] William B. Toole used the term only as 'a convenient tag for four plays', including *Hamlet*, in which he traced, with little profit to his readers, the same theological pattern that governs the structure and meaning of the *Divina commedia*.

Biographical assumptions that Shakespeare underwent a psychological crisis in 'the third period' for long coloured some critics' reading of the three plays. E. K. Chambers in three introductions to the Red Letter Shakespeare, 1906–8 (re-issued in *Shakespeare: a Survey*[8]) and in his much-read Shakespeare entry for the *Britannica*,[9] described them as 'unpleasant' and 'embittered' – 'the three bitter and cynical pseudo-comedies'. C. J. Sisson in his British Academy lecture 'The Mythical Sorrows of Shakespeare' (1934) demolished all such biographical fallacies, and his defence of *Measure for Measure*, 'one of Shakespeare's finest acting plays', contributed to that re-instatement of the problem plays which G. Wilson Knight had championed since 1929 in a changing climate of opinion. Bonamy Dobrée, reviewing *The Wheel of Fire* in *The Criterion*,[10] said that to his generation these plays and *Timon* did not seem 'incomprehensibly gritty; most of us prefer them to the romantic comedies'.

'All's Well That Ends Well'

G. K. Hunter lamented in 1959 that 'criticism of *All's Well* ... has failed to provide a context within which the genuine virtues of the play can be appreciated'. Certainly the New Cambridge edition[11] found *All's Well* the most neglected play in the canon by editors ('There

[1] London, 1896.
[2] London, 1931. [3] London, 1950.
[4] London, 1961. [5] London, 1963.
[6] London, 1961; revised 1964.
[7] The Hague, 1966.
[8] London, 1925.
[9] 11th edition (Cambridge, 1911).
[10] January 1931.
[11] Cambridge, 1929.

is no money in it, since it is never read in schools and very rarely in universities') and possibly in the theatre. Dover Wilson looked on the Folio text as a Jacobean revision 'by Shakespeare and a collaborator' of 'an Elizabethan play perhaps by Shakespeare but . . . probably containing pre-Shakespearean elements', a view which induced neither editorial caution nor critical respect. Quiller-Couch dismissed the play as 'one of Shakespeare's worst', preferring Boccaccio's story as straighter and more dignified. He disliked 'the inept business with Parolles', thought Lafeu had 'no business in the play', that Lavache was 'nothing to any purpose' and Bertram ultimately 'a stage puppet'.

When 'Q' wrote his patronising introduction, G. P. Krapp's interesting article 'Parolles' had been published[1] and W. W. Lawrence's first thoughts on *All's Well* had appeared.[2] Lawrence traced two movements, centred on Helena and based on folk-themes: the Healing of the King and the Fulfilment of the Tasks. He showed that all the sources and analogues exalt the resourcefulness and devotion of the Clever Wench, and thus maintained that for the Elizabethans there was no impropriety in the bed-trick and Helena was wholly admirable. For Dr Tillyard *All's Well* was 'in some sort, a failure' – though probably not on the stage. He praised its construction, but followed Lawrence in stressing the rift between realistic characterisation and fairy-tale plot.

Three essays of the early fifties advanced the critical study of *All's Well*. M. C. Bradbrook in 'Virtue is the True Nobility'[3] surmised that 'the dramatist and the poet . . . were pulling different ways': for her, the structure revealed a serious moral debate on 'the question of blood and descent versus native worth'. Clifford Leech, writing on 'The Themes of Ambition',[4] found 'the folk-tale stories and the Christian colouring . . . strongly companioned

by other elements' – including satire. His reaction to the ambitious Helena was critical. Harold S. Wilson in 'Dramatic Emphasis in *All's Well That Ends Well*'[5] defended its deliberate artifice as a play on the wronged wife, and as stage entertainment rather than something that stands up to reflection.

In the spate of articles from the later fifties and the sixties there are three currents.[6] Many writers seek to establish the unity of the play by exploring the Age/Youth/Regeneration complex, or by teasing out the imagery (including the erotic), or by developing the view that our response to characters is more ambiguous than Lawrence imagined. The defence of Bertram has been accompanied by a blackening of Helena, shown up as having comic faults to match his, as aggressive where he is snobbish, or as sensual and predatory like the Venus of *Venus and Adonis*. Critics tend to quote in title or epigraph: 'The web of our life is of a mingled yarn, good and ill together . . .' (IV, iii, 68–9). The vitality of Parolles, and his acceptance of life on any terms has also been related to the play's themes.

Dramaturgical analyses include discussion of *All's Well* as a 'prodigal son' piece, and Bertrand Evans's discussion in *Shakespeare's Comedies*[7] of Helena's manipulative control

[1] In *Shakespearian Studies*, ed. Brander Matthews (New York, 1916).

[2] *Publications of the Modern Language Association of America*, XXXVII (1922).

[3] *Review of English Studies*, XXVI (1950).

[4] *Journal of English Literary History*, XXI (1954).

[5] *Huntington Library Quarterly*, XIII (1949–50).

[6] See John Arthos, 'The Comedy of Generation', *Essays in Criticism*, V (1955); J. L. Calderwood, 'The Mingled Yarn of *All's Well*', *Journal of English and Germanic Philology*, LXII (1963) and 'Styles of Knowing in *All's Well*', *Modern Language Quarterly*, XXV (1964); Robert Hapgood, 'The Life of Shame', *Essays in Criticism*, XV (1965); and R. Y. Turner, 'Dramatic Conventions in *All's Well*', *PMLA*, LXXV (1960).

[7] Oxford, 1960.

over the action which finally 'borders on witchery'. By contrast a third approach has stressed religious, even mystical reverberations. 'The Third Eye', Wilson Knight's long suggestive essay in *The Sovereign Flower*[1] is in his own late manner. He discerned two antithetical concepts of honour, one masculine and military (Bertram), the other feminine (chaste love). The active Helena unites or transcends both; Shakespeare, with the creative bisexuality of genius, presented her as his supreme expression of feminine love, as 'miracle worker' and 'medium'. Robert Grams Hunter has written rewardingly and more soberly of the play as 'a secular comedy ... for a Christian audience' with Bertram as *humanum genus* in *Shakespeare and the Comedy of Forgiveness*.[2]

Different approaches sometimes yield contradictory conclusions. Richard David, reviewing in *Shakespeare Survey 8* (1955), a stage production which guyed the older generation, welcomed 'the lightening and depersonalizing of the story' which revealed the play's kinship with the last romances. C. J. Sisson in 'Shakespeare's Helena and Dr William Harvey'[3] presented material to prove that Helena's medical conduct and her status as a female practitioner would have struck the Elizabethans 'as consonant with the realities of contemporary life and not an element of fairy tale invention'.

The most accessible account of the play's source, text etc., is G. K. Hunter's excellent new Arden edition[4] which defines the play's 'strongly individual quality' as 'a quality of *strain*'. His tentative dating of the play is 1603–4, just before *Measure for Measure*, but Josephine Waters Bennett in 'New Techniques of Comedy in *All's Well That Ends Well*'[5] thinks that this 'wise, tolerant, and beautiful play' is both later and technically superior.

Joseph G. Price has dealt comprehensively with the theatrical and critical fortunes in *The Unfortunate Comedy*[6] and has shown that *All's Well* was adapted first as a farce about Parolles and then as a sentimental play about Helena. His own scene-by-scene defence of the play always keeps theatrical presentation in mind.

Barbara Everett in her edition[7] has defined the tone as 'mature, subtle, haunting', and 'sober' and 'elegiac rather than saturnalian'. A different view occurs in R. A. Foakes's recent *Shakespeare: from satire to celebration*:[8] 'What a stage performance reveals is the degree to which the tonality ... is governed by ... figures like Parolles and Lavache, who persuade us ... we are in a comic world.' Criticism has often taken *All's Well* too seriously and exaggerated its problems. After all, as Kenneth Muir has maintained, 'if the Clown were given better jokes and Bertram a better speech at the end, the play would leave us with feelings of greater satisfaction'.[9]

'Measure for Measure'

The bulk of criticism on *Measure for Measure* since 1930 almost rivals that on *Hamlet*. Much of it makes great claims for Shakespeare's achievement and some of it raises theoretical questions about the interpretation and evaluation of Renaissance plays. Writers fall into two categories: 'new critics' of different persuasions – there never was a 'School of Knight' – who regard the text as self-sufficient; and various 'historical critics' who assume that the meaning of the play, or important parts of it, can be elucidated only by recourse to prior knowledge about genres, Renaissance ethics,

[1] London, 1958.
[2] New York, 1956.
[3] *Essays and Studies*, n.s. XIII (1960).
[4] London, 1959.
[5] *Shakespeare Quarterly*, XVIII (1967).
[6] Liverpool, 1968.
[7] New Penguin Shakespeare (Harmondsworth, 1970).
[8] London, 1971.
[9] *Shakespeare's Sources*, I (London, 1957), p. 101.

medieval or Renaissance theology, or Elizabethan law.[1]

The New Cambridge edition no longer serves the general reader. Dover Wilson held that the Folio text incorporated theatrical revisions and was corrupt. 'Q' in his critique ('What is wrong with this play?') judged the characters by the criterion of psychological consistency. Some of his points were restated with greater ebullience and critical sophistication by William Empson in 1938 as a reaction against the idealisation or deification of the Duke, whom Empson saw as 'playing God'.[2]

Wilson Knight's by now classic essay, '*Measure for Measure* and the Gospels',[3] approached the play as 'a parable' and 'a studied explication' of the theme 'Judge not, that ye be not judged'. Knight found that it *tended* 'towards allegory or symbolism', saw the Duke as 'the prophet of an enlightened ethic', and Isabella as a self-centred saint. W. W. Lawrence, however, postulated a *stage* Duke and a blameless Isabel. R. W. Chambers's forensic British Academy lecture, 'The Jacobean Shakespeare and *Measure for Measure*' (1937), represents, with C. J. Sisson's earlier one, the Establishment's rehabilitation of the play as a doctrinally Christian work of art. It defended Isabella.

Three separate studies appeared in *Scrutiny* during 1942. L. C. Knights, analysing words like 'scope', 'liberty', and 'restraint',[4] sensed in the play 'not paradox but genuine ambiguity', and was puzzled by both Claudio and Isabella, finding Angelo 'the admitted success of the play'. His qualified evaluation provoked from his co-editor, F. R. Leavis, an assertion of the play's value, 'The Greatness of *Measure for Measure*'.[5] Leavis maintained that there ought to be 'an element of the critical' in the way we regard Isabella, endorsed Wilson Knight's high view of the Duke 'the more-than-Prospero', and viewed Angelo sympathetically. In the third *Scrutiny* essay D. A. Traversi located a poetic tension between Claudio's consciousness of the 'ravening' process of self-destruction and Lucio's 'great speech on Claudio's love'. In '*Measure for Measure*: A Footnote to Recent Criticism',[6] J. C. Maxwell found no imperfection in Isabel 'beyond that involved in creaturely limitation'; the play seemed 'one of Shakespeare's most perfect works of art'.

Their views on Isabella split critics into camps. By Warren D. Smith's count in 1962 'fourteen critics praise her nobility in the prison scene and thirteen ... charge her with inhumanity towards her brother'.[7] Some have developed the parallel between her and Angelo with differing emphases. While to one critic they were 'those senators of virtue', Philip Edwards has seen them as 'trapped by their own kind of ethical idealism'.[8] Angelo has been sensitively presented as a tragic protagonist by W. M. T. Dodds, now Mrs Nowottny,[9] and exposed as a Puritan by D. J. McGinn.[10] Ernest Schanzer discussed the five main

[1] See O. J. Campbell, 'Shakespeare and the "New" Critics', *J. Q. Adams Memorial Studies* (Washington, 1948); L. C. Knights, 'Historical Scholarship and the Criticism of Shakespeare', *Further Explorations* (London, 1965); Robert Ornstein, 'Historical Criticism and the Interpretation of Shakespeare', *Shakespeare Quarterly*, X (1959); J. M. Newton,' *Scrutiny*'s Failure with Shakespeare', *Cambridge Quarterly*, I (1966).

[2] *The Structure of Complex Words* (London, 1951).

[3] *The Wheel of Fire* (London, 1930).

[4] Ernest Leisi in his semanticist's 'old spelling and old meaning edition' (1964), lists as key-words: *authority, scope, liberty, restraint, mercy, grace, weigh* and *seem*.

[5] *The Common Pursuit* (London, 1952).

[6] *Downside Review*, LXV (1947).

[7] 'More Light on *Measure for Measure*', *Modern Language Quarterly*, XXIII (1962). Smith also claimed that Isabella's 'More than our brother is our chastity' is the only non-royal use of *our* save for Julius Caesar's. J. C. Maxwell noted earlier that the Folio printed it as a *sententia*.

[8] *Shakespeare and the Confines of Art* (London, 1968).

[9] *Modern Language Review*, XLI (1946).

[10] In *J. Q. Adams Memorial Studies* (Washington, 1948).

characters and their interplay, and revealed that German scholarship anticipated some American and British interpretations.

Miss Bradbrook in 'Authority, Truth, and Justice in *Measure for Measure*'[1] detected a medieval Morality structure: 'The Contention between Justice and Mercy, or False Authority unmasked by Truth and Humility.' A learned and extreme allegorical interpretation, with the Duke as the Incarnate Lord, by Roy W. Battenhouse in '*Measure for Measure* and Christian Doctrine of the Atonement'[2] has lately been faulted by the combative Roland Mushat Frye[3] on the grounds that Battenhouse drew on patristic and scholastic rather than Renaissance authorities. Elizabeth Marie Pope's paper, 'The Renaissance Background of *Measure for Measure*',[4] presented material from text-books and sermons of Shakespeare's day to suggest that the play is concerned with the duties of the Prince or Ruler and his privilege to use extraordinary means in tempering justice with mercy. This kind of approach produced a rejoinder from Clifford Leech 'The "Meaning" of *Measure for Measure*'[5] in which he argued against the narrow interpretation of plays as 'embodying theses' and demonstrated how complex this play is. More recently Marco Mincoff has denounced critical orthodoxies by declaring that as Providence the Duke 'is even less satisfactory than as ideal ruler'. In the closely argued '*Measure for Measure*: Quid pro Quo?' A. D. Nuttall showed that the Duke is a White Machiavel and that Angelo is morally 'worth four Dukes'. He also distinguished a different atonement pattern.[6]

Lawrence found law in Shakespeare 'a queer business'. Scholars have explained Claudio's 'offence' with Juliet and Angelo's betrothal to Mariana in the light of Elizabethan law, ecclesiastical and secular. Others have clarified Escalus's mid-way stance between Angelo (Justice) and the Duke (Mercy) by reference to Renaissance concepts of Equity.[7]

O. J. Campbell extended his theory about *Troilus and Cressida* to include *Measure for Measure* as a 'comicall satyre'.[8] R. G. Hunter discerned a pattern by which the main characters judge one another and are judged in 'a comedy of forgiveness'. Two dramaturgical analyses confirm Tillyard's view that the play 'changes its nature half way through'. Herbert Weil, Jr claims that Shakespeare deliberately terminated 'the dramatic intensity of his early acts' and that the play's 'descending action' ought to be played 'in a light comic, even farcical vein.'[9] Bernard Beckerman also sees the dramatic shift as deliberate but the play as a not entirely successful experiment in tragicomedy.[10]

Some critics have felt that Shakespeare never reconciled his vivid characterisation or his new learning with the pre-existing plot. The rela-

[1] *RES*, XVII (1941).
[2] *PMLA*, LXI (1946).
[3] *Shakespeare and Christian Doctrine* (Oxford, 1963), pp. 35–6. Frye attacked less scholarly men than Battenhouse for their union of subjective criticism with a naive understanding of theology. He also showed that Father William Sankey, the English Jesuit, excised the whole of *Measure for Measure* from the Folio, *c.* 1641–51, at the English College at Valladolid, Spain.
[4] *Shakespeare Survey 2* (Cambridge, 1949).
[5] *Shakespeare Survey 3* (Cambridge, 1950).
[6] *Shakespeare Studies*, II (1966) and IV (1968) respectively.
[7] See Davis P. Harding, 'Elizabethan Betrothals and *Measure for Measure*', *Journal of English and Germanic Philology*, XLIX (1950); Ernest Schanzer, 'The Marriage Contracts in *Measure for Measure*', *Shakespeare Survey 13* (Cambridge, 1960); S. Nazarjan, '*Measure for Measure* and Elizabethan Betrothals', *Shakespeare Quarterly*, XIV (1963); John Wasson, 'A Play of Incontinence', *ELH*, XXVII (1960); and J. W. Dickinson, 'Renaissance Equity and *Measure for Measure*' and Wilbur Dunkel, 'Law and Equity in *Measure for Measure*' – both in *Shakespeare Quarterly*, XIII (1962).
[8] *Shakespeare's Satire* (New York, 1943).
[9] 'Form and Contexts in *Measure for Measure*', *Critical Quarterly*, XII (1970).
[10] 'The Dramaturgy of *Measure for Measure*', *The Elizabethan Theatre*, II, ed. David Galloway (Toronto, 1970).

tion between *Measure for Measure* and various possible sources, discussed by L. Albrecht (1914) and W. W. Lawrence, has been further explored by Mary Lascelles, Madeleine Doran, Kenneth Muir, J. W. Lever, and Geoffrey Bullough, whose *Narrative and Dramatic Sources*,[1] includes the relevant materials. Mary Lascelles's humane and penetrating *Shakespeare's 'Measure for Measure'*[2] is responsive to the departures Shakespeare made, and to the distinctive role of the heroine, denied the self-revelation of soliloquy. J. W. Lever's compressed, informative introduction to the new Arden edition[3] copes with such folk-themes as 'the Disguised Duke', and with the play's ideas. He finds much less textual corruption than his predecessors and dates the play between May and August 1604, before its performance at Court on 26 December.

David Lloyd Stevenson in *The Achievement of 'Measure for Measure'*[4] gives an undoctrinaire, open, ahistorical account of a 'schematic' and 'disturbing' play about living people. Historically informed, he is ironic about 'neotheologians' and 'historical reconstructionists'. He relegates to an appendix, as irrelevant to our understanding the play, his revival of the theory that the Duke reflects King James.[5] Josephine Waters Bennett in *'Measure for Measure' as Royal Entertainment*[6] builds the many-tiered hypothesis that Shakespeare as author–actor–director complimented King James, who is shadowed in the Duke, whom Shakespeare played. Some of her insights were anticipated by Miss Lascelles and chime with suggestions by Anne Righter.[7] Acceptance of the theories would give us a light-toned, topical, witty comedy, centred on absurd situations 'like *The Mikado*'.

Writers have not agreed about the tone, meaning, or value of *Measure for Measure*. To Miss Lascelles it is 'this great, uneven play', to Dr Lever 'a flawed masterpiece', to Dr Leavis 'one of the very greatest of the plays'.

Its shrewdest critics believe that it possesses that *complexity* in which Miss Lascelles found 'the very proof of its integrity'.

'Troilus and Cressida'

Both *All's Well* and *Measure for Measure* have a two-part structure, source-materials in folklore and Italian literature, and comedic resolutions which involve the bed-trick. Virgil K. Whitaker has linked *Troilus and Cressida* with *Measure for Measure* ('radically faulty as drama, but ... the most explicitly learned plays that Shakespeare ever wrote'[8]), but J. C. Maxwell's view that *Troilus* is 'the most isolated of the Middle Plays' has won assent. To Sir Walter Greg it was 'a play of puzzles, in respect of its textual history, no less than its interpretation'.[9]

Bibliographical and theatrical speculations about Bonian's and Walley's Quarto and the play's ultimate position in the Folio have led to disagreement over the play's genre. Scholarship has now established that the first title-page of the Quarto was cancelled *before* publication and that the Folio printers originally intended *Troilus* to follow *Romeo and Juliet*. Thus two factions can each claim some Jacobean authority for regarding *Troilus* as comedy or as tragedy. Nevill Coghill's questioning of the credibility of the Bonian and Walley preface led to correspondence in *The Times Literary Supplement* in

[1] Vol. II (London, 1958).
[2] London, 1953.
[3] London, 1965.
[4] Ithaca, 1966.
[5] That the *Basilicon Doron* was a source had been suggested by George Chalmers (1779) and by L. Albrecht (1914) who did not convince W. W. Lawrence. Peter Alexander, who believed that 'Shakespeare did not neglect ... to show his knowledge of his sovereign's philosophy', found James often 'muddle-headed and inconsistent', *Shakespeare* (London, 1964), p. 152.
[6] New York, 1966.
[7] *Shakespeare and the Idea of the Play* (London, 1962).
[8] *Shakespeare's Use of Learning* (San Marino, 1953) p. 194.
[9] *The Shakespeare First Folio* (Oxford, 1955).

1967. E. K. Chambers in 1906 had speculated that *Troilus* might have been produced for an academic audience at Cambridge, and Peter Alexander, to explain the nature of the copy for the Quarto, conjectured that the play was commissioned for some Inns of Court festivity.[1] Alfred Harbage is adamant that there is 'no recorded instance . . . when a regular play was bought, rehearsed and acted by a professional company exclusively for a special audience'.[2] That the first audience could tell a true argument from a false remains an attractive hypothesis; that they could also distinguish between histrionics and sincerity is suggested by Patricia Thomson's essay 'Rant and Cant in *Troilus and Cressida*'.[3] A remarkable feature in the rediscovery of the play since 1920 has been its undergraduate appeal.

Unlike *Measure for Measure* this play seems to have had no early enthusiasts. Wilson Knight implicitly suggested its new importance in 'The Philosophy of *Troilus and Cressida*' in *The Wheel of Fire* where he elucidated its central idea – 'almost a "thesis"' – as the opposition between 'intuition' and 'emotion' (the Trojans) and 'intellect' and 'reason' (the Greeks). His coherent if over-simplified reading is imaginative and exciting alongside W. W. Lawrence's more cautious source-study of The Love-Story and The Quarrels of the Chieftains. William Empson's deeper perceptions about the operation of double plots[4] and Caroline F. E. Spurgeon's detailed charting of the iterative imagery of food and disease[5] also gave methodological leads. Theodore Spencer mentioned aspects of the play that were 'sympathetic to a generation that found expression in *Ulysses* and *The Waste Land*' in a long 'Commentary'[6] which he regarded as superseded by *Shakespeare and the Nature of Man*.[7] There he found in the case of Troilus 'a worse kind of tragedy than death . . . continued existence after everything that matters has been destroyed'. At the end of the war Una Ellis-

Fermor wrote of her own revised view of *Troilus and Cressida* as a unity, and was reprimanded by Harley Granville-Barker for ceasing 'to distinguish between Shakespeare's better plays and his worse'.[8] Her essay, 'The Discord of the Spheres', suggested the paradox that, though the play's thought 'is an implacable assertion of chaos as the ultimate fact of being', its form testifies to order.[9]

The antithesis in content and in structure, and the play's preoccupation with Time, have led to other schematic and thematic readings along lines adumbrated by Wilson Knight. D. A. Traversi's analysis, written for *Scrutiny* in 1938, re-appeared without the limiting evaluation 'not, on any view, a successful play' in the enlarged editions of *An Approach to Shakespeare*.[10] He regarded the play as 'a dramatic statement of the emotional ambiguity whose resolution was to be the motive of the great tragedies'. L. C. Knights in 1951, taking Appearance and Reality as the theme, viewed the play as vital in the development of Shakespeare's thought.[11] In a subtle reading, '"Opinion" and "Value" in *Troilus and Cressida*', W. M. T. Nowottny saw between Ulysses and Troilus the 'great antithesis between two approaches to life, that of the statesman and that of the individual creative imagination'.[12] Frank Kermode replied in 1955 by suggesting a different antithesis, itself 'a simplification of something appallingly diffi-

---

[1] *The Library*, 4th series, IX (1929).
[2] *Shakespeare and the Rival Traditions* (New York, 1952), p. 116
[3] *Essays and Studies*, n.s. XXII (1969).
[4] *Some Versions of Pastoral* (London, 1935).
[5] *Shakespeare's Imagery and What it Tells us* (Cambridge, 1936).
[6] *Studies in English Literature* (Tokyo, 1936).
[7] New York, 1942.
[8] *RES*, XXII (1946).
[9] *The Frontiers of Drama* (London, 1945).
[10] New York, 1956; 2 volumes (London, 1969).
[11] *Some Shakespearean Themes* (London, 1959).
[12] *Essays in Criticism*, IV (1954).

cult'. A. S. Knowland[1] accused critics of over-simplifying and over-conceptualising the play and of over-stressing the Time theme, in his own effort to establish 'our total dramatic experience of the play'. R. J. Kaufmann's 'Ceremonies of Chaos: the Status of *Troilus and Cressida*'[2] shows that a thematic approach can still yield insight.

In *Comicall Satyre and Shakespeare's 'Troilus and Cressida'*[3] O. J. Campbell connected the play with the satirical plays of Jonson and Marston which flourished from 1599, but his response to the text, especially in *Shakespeare's Satire*,[4] was insensitively moralistic: the lovers' 'adventures ... exemplify lust' leading to 'deserved disaster'. That the play is a tragedy was argued by Brian Morris in 'The Tragic Structure of *Troilus and Cressida*'; he complained that the problem plays 'have been forcibly and unequally yoked together' and he regarded the 'monolithic design' of the generals' plot as the 'backcloth against which the lovers' tragedy is played out'.[5] Alice Walker in 1957 endorsed Campbell's view. R. A. Foakes, reconsidering the play, first in *The University of Toronto Quarterly*[6] and later in *Shakespeare: from satire to celebration*,[7] put the emphasis on the comical-satirical tone, on the play's 'three endings', and on the part played by the audience's prior knowledge of a familiar story. Bertrand Evans from a technical standpoint reported that 'our advantage over Troilus, Cressida, and Pandarus ... depends upon our extra-dramatic knowledge of outcomes', thus establishing a distinctive technique. Earlier G. F. Reynolds had proved that the play makes no elaborate stage-demands.[8]

The massive Variorum edition by H. N. Hillebrand and T. W. Baldwin[9] is replete with secondary materials. The New Cambridge editor, Alice Walker, admits a bias towards the Folio text; hers is the main critical edition.[10] Robert Kimbrough's *Shakespeare's 'Troilus and Cressida' and its Setting*[11] is a comprehensive

study and it relates *Troilus* to works in the repertory of public and coterie theatres. A wide range of sources, studied before 1920 by J. S. P. Tatlock and Hyder E. Rollins, has been reconsidered by, amongst others, R. K. Presson in *Shakespeare's 'Troilus and Cressida' and the Legends of Troy*[12] which stressed the Homeric influence through Chapman. Geoffrey Bullough, for reasons of space rather than genre, dealt with the sources in his volume on *Other 'Classical' Plays*.[13] Miss Bradbrook has suggested that 'What Shakespeare did to Chaucer's *Troilus and Criseyde*' included the 'lacerative destruction of Chaucer's whole vision'.[14] The 'play of puzzles' continues to be seen as comedy, 'comicall satyre', tragedy, and tragic satire.

Any outline of the critical fortunes of the three plays has to be selective, and much comment in books on the comedies and in wider studies has here been ignored. Writers on the separate plays or on three works 'which ingenious absurdity has thrown together' have no monopoly on critical insight; indeed anyone taking as his subject Shakespeare's word-play or his bawdy, his use of learning or of stage-convention, or his treatment of the Renaissance concept of honour, is bound, from that perspective, to see something distinctive in each of the three. Do we persist in seeing differences between these and other plays of Shakespeare's where his contemporaries saw none? Have critics in the Age

[1] *Shakespeare Quarterly*, X (1959).
[2] *ELH*, XXXII (1965).
[3] San Marino, 1938.   [4] New York, 1943.
[5] *Shakespeare Quarterly*, X (1959).
[6] XXXII (1963).
[7] London, 1971.
[8] '*Troilus and Cressida* on the Elizabethan Stage', *J. Q. Adams Memorial Studies* (Washington, 1948).
[9] Philadelphia, 1953.
[10] Cambridge, 1957.
[11] Cambridge, Mass., 1964.
[12] Madison, 1953.
[13] London, 1966.
[14] *Shakespeare Quarterly*, IX (1958).

of Anxiety over-valued these three plays?[1] In 1944 T. S. Eliot remarked 'At a particular moment ... certain of the less popular plays may have a particular appeal'; and he went on to recall 'the limited but significant interest in *Troilus and Cressida* a few years ago'.[2] Interest in all three plays has not abated amongst critics and men of the theatre. It has increased. They are no longer Problem Plays, and no longer unpopular.

[1] See John Russell Brown, *Shakespeare Survey 8* (Cambridge, 1955), p. 13.
[2] Introduction to S. L. Bethell's *Shakespeare and the Popular Dramatic Tradition* (London, 1944).

© MICHAEL JAMIESON 1972

A SELECTION FROM
REVIEWS OF THE THREE PLAYS

RICHARD DAVID
ON
ALL'S WELL THAT ENDS WELL,
OLD VIC, 1953

To the Old Vic goes the credit for the one production of the season that was full of interest and excitement throughout–*All's Well That Ends Well*. By every test it should have been a thoroughly bad one, and I have heard that a young actor–producer of talent walked out half-way through the performance declaring that he had never seen a worse. Faced with a difficult play to put over, Michael Benthall resorted to all the most disreputable tricks of the trade – drastic cutting, transposing, the masking of awkward speeches with music or outrageous buffoonery. Yet it was not only in spite of these tricks but partly because of them that the producer was able to offer a coherent, convincing, and, as far as I know, a new view of Shakespeare's play, at least to those who are prepared to allow that in theatrical affairs the end may justify the means.

The difficulties of the play are rather conceptual than verbal. We have had it drummed into us by every commentator that this is a problem play, and that its subject is 'unpleasant'–in Shaw's sense or worse. No modern audience, we are told, can stomach a hero as priggish and as caddish as Bertram, or sympathize with a heroine who like Helena is determined that a man who does not love her shall accept her as his wife, and who resorts to the most ignoble tricks to cheat him into

doing so. The comic subplot of the Braggart Parolles is despicable in its barrenness, and the only characters in the play that deserve attention and respect are the King of France and the Countess Rousillon, who both possess a wise nobility worthy of a better play.

Benthall's first step was to take the King and the Countess down a peg. The King became a figure of fun and the affairs of his court pure farce. He was attended by a couple of comic doctors, one fat, one thin, and by a friar who kept up a running Paternoster in a high monotone. His speeches were punctuated by sudden grimaces and yowling cries as his ailment griped him. Even his lucid intervals were diversified by similar 'business'. During the long speech to Bertram in which the King recalls his youth, the courtiers began to chatter among themselves, growing louder and louder until he was driven to shout them down. When he made a joke he would pause until the court had duly acknowledged it with forced laughter. After his cure at Helena's hands he still remained something of a caricature, with the tetchiness of Old Capulet and the blether of Polonius. The Countess was not ragged to this degree, but Fay Compton played the part not as the aristocratic paragon of tradition but as a very human old woman whose nobility appeared rather in what she did than in the doing of it. She was bent and crabbed, her gestures had an arthritic awkwardness, her utterance was creaky, abrupt, arbitrary. By such treatment both King and Countess became more homely, nearer to earth, and their judgements on the action more humanly convincing from their being more than a little touched with human frailty.

To this roughly individual and 'de-idealized' Chorus was added a powerful reinforcement in the shape of Michael Hordern's Parolles, which should have utterly shattered the theory that Shakespeare's Braggart is a more than usually inept version of the dullest of all stock figures. This Parolles was brimful of vitality, and a masterpiece of comic invention. As befits one who is to be found a sheep in wolf's clothing, he began by looking the opposite, his long hungry face in itself a comic contrast to the gay Florentine doublet with its huge hanging sleeves. The wolf soon begins to look a good deal sillier, and Hordern was brilliant in inventing a series of mimes to express Parolles's attempts to maintain his dignity in face of Lord Lafeu's quizzing – hurt, and chilling at the first suspicion, a scraggy cockerel when trying to outface his tormentor, at last swallowing with anguish the sour plum of his inability to answer back without calling down retribution. His gait was as expressive as his face. His entry in procession with the victorious Florentine army, himself in dudgeon over the disgrace of the lost drum, brought down the house– a jobbling, uncoordinated motion, head bobbing forward between limp shoulders from which the arms dangled, feet flapping carelessly down in the abandonment of utter disgust. Equally satisfying was his return, in apparent eagerness to recapture the drum singlehanded, the beaky nose uplifted and seeming to draw the rigid, gawky body after it in over-acted determination. And in the climax to this subplot, the interrogation of Parolles by the practical jokers who have ambushed and blindfolded him, every move and every tone was deft and delightful: the anxious gabbling of the numbers as he

tumbles over himself to betray the military strength of his own side, the confidential becking of his interrogator in order to impart one extra titbit of lying scandal about his superior officers, the self-hugging satisfaction at getting through the interview, he thinks, so adroitly. When Parolles is finally unblindfolded, and discovers his captors to be his own comrades, Hordern managed an immediate and breathtaking transition from farce to deadly earnest. At the discovery he closed his eyes and fell straight backward into the arms of his attendants; then, as with taunts they prepare to leave him, he slithered to the ground, becoming wizened and sly on the instant, and with 'simply the thing I am shall make me live' revealed an essential meanness not only in Parolles but in human nature as a whole. For effect the moment is akin to Lear's 'unaccommodated man is no more but such a poor, bare, forked animal as thou art'; but whereas it is the physical insignificance of man that Poor Tom shows us in a flash, Parolles gives us his spiritual degradation.

Having provided a rough and realistic framework to the drama, the producer could afford to play down the awkward facts of life in its main argument. Accordingly the story of Helena and Bertram was given the remoteness of a fairy-tale, or at least of the medieval fabliau from which Shakespeare took it. The sets immediately suggested the sense in which the story was to be read. Behind the three arches of the permanent façade a backcloth with a country scene that might have come from an illuminated manuscript created Rousillon; an equally stylized view of Florence transported us to Italy. When the action shifted to Paris, sliding panels of Notre Dame quickly blotted out the country, while in Florence the undisguised manipulation of hinged screens composed the Capilet interior. Against such ingenious and delicate stage-contraptions it was appropriate that Claire Bloom should play Helena as Cinderella. Opinions about this actress differ, and I was prepared to find no more than a beginner of talent whom youth, beauty, and an appearance in a notable film had magnified into a star. I am still in two minds about her. She moved with admirable grace, she had an appealing and ingenuous charm, and–except for a few tiresome mannerisms–she spoke musically and with authority, even managing the awkward couplet soliloquy in her first scene with a skill that made an insult of the instrumental accompaniment officiously provided by the producer. And yet her performance made no coherent impression, and the spectator was left in irritated puzzlement as to what exactly the actress had been driving at. Her vehemence in the early soliloquies–was it impulsiveness and the sudden abandon of passion long pent up? Her almost hysterical reaction when trapped by the Countess into revealing her secret love for Bertram (a scene to which Fay Compton's motherly shrewdness gave a rare tenderness) – was this violence the index of a gentle nature torn between love and loyalty, or of a wayward obstinacy? Did the aggressiveness of her rejoinders to Parolles's innuendoes come from the self-confidence of innocence or the hardness of a worldly-wise little bourgeoise? No doubt some of these conundrums are implicit in Shakespeare's lines, but it is the business of the actress to resolve them; and slowly the conviction dawned that Claire Bloom was not even attempting the task, that her emphasis came of nothing more than an eagerness to inject the maximum of feeling into every phrase and word. To be blunt, I think she was ranting–and yet she ranted distinctly, there was music if not meaning in her rant; and again what should have been a blemish turned out to be a positive contribution to the total effect of the play.

A fairy-tale princess should not be too closely accountable for her actions, and the wildness of this Helena's regrets, even that trick of making her exit lines trail off on a rising intonation, like a great bird taking wing, gave an other-worldly quality to her story.

Bertram's task was easier. He had only to look like Prince Charming (which John Neville did) and to speak handsomely (which he did also). Such distinction, even unaided, might have overborne all our scruples as to the decency of Bertram's conduct, even to the shameless shifts of excuse to which he betakes himself in the last scene. This Bertram, however, was given every assistance by the producer who, taking a hint from Lafeu's 'No, no, no, your son was misled with a snipt-taffeta fellow there', made Parolles responsible for all Rousillon's misbehaviour. Bertram, too much a schoolboy still to be allowed by the French King to go to the wars, was shown taking his cue at every step from his unsavoury pedagogue. It was Parolles whose nods and becks strengthened Bertram in his first resistance to the King's command that he should marry a commoner. Having married her, he appeared to soften towards her, and would have given her the kiss she so pathetically begs at parting had not a 'Psst!' from Parolles recalled him to his previous resolution. Shakespeare makes Parolles the factotum in Bertram's arrangements for the disposal of his wife; Benthall made him the prime mover as well.

King and Countess as Disney dwarfs, the hero and heroine reduced to decorative pasteboard, Parolles taking over the play as a sort of amateurish Mephistopheles–no wonder the orthodox were disapproving. Yet to me at least this lightening and de-personalizing of the story, this removal of the play into the half-world of pantomime and Grimms' Fairy Tales, suddenly revealed its kinship not, as is usually supposed, with *Measure for Measure* and *Troilus*, but with the last romances. With these it shares the theme of paradise lost and paradise regained: the penitent Bertram recovers the wife he has cast off as surely as do Leontes and Posthumus, and his restoration to Helena makes her as much amends as the meeting of Ferdinand and Miranda does to Prospero. Here, however, it is themselves that the losers lose and find, and their redemption is their own and not the work of another more innocent generation. The pattern in this condensed form does not perhaps make so good a play as in its extended shape, where the processes are more clear-cut; but it does make a play, a much better play when seen as a first sketch for *Winter's Tale* than as a botched *Measure*.

JOHN RUSSELL BROWN
ON
ALL'S WELL THAT ENDS WELL,
STRATFORD, 1959

Tyrone Guthrie, directing *All's Well That Ends Well* at Stratford in 1959, made some additions to the dialogue to fill out those scenes which had particularly attracted him: so a major-domo instructs lesser servants about 'hastening the musicians' and moving a platform 'more to the left', a courtier inquires about the 'good old king' and there are many 'Quite so's', 'Hear, hear's', petty oaths, orders and exclamations; more ambitiously, the Duke of Florence enquires 'Is this the machine?' But Guthrie's invention—in keeping with the present reluctance to accept rewriting—was more plainly shown in numerous dumb-shows, excisions, actions in contradiction to what is said, and deliberate and effective mis-speaking of Shakespeare's lines.

Yet after he had taken all this trouble, it was hard to see his leading purpose in adapting the play. During the first half, the scenes in which the Countess appears were set in and around an elegant Chekhovian mansion: in a tender, brownish light, a grove of bare and slender trees bend gracefully, from both sides of the stage, towards a summer-house, and, while its inhabitants are voguish and precise in dress, from classical urns dead leaves and tendrils hang untended. At the end of the play the same house becomes, surprisingly, a vast hall, sketchily furnished in trivial blue, white and gilt. The King's Court at Paris is a dark ballroom, glittering occasionally with lights and dancing figures but, more often, empty and comfortless, so that its inhabitants protect themselves with tall leather screens. All these scenes were presented as if the action took place just before the First World War, but in later scenes among the soldiers in Florence the stage was set as for the Second World War: there is a microphone and a megaphone of the latest design, and the men are dressed in khaki shorts, the officers in tunics, black ties and berets. The widow's household was presented in a mixture of the two periods: for, gaping and giggling at the soldiers, the girls are dressed in housecoats and headscarves, and one sucks a fruit lolly; but for travelling, Diana appears in an Edwardian coat and hat, to match Helena's, who has come, unchanged in her style of dress, from the other part of the play.

The treatment of the text was as various as that of the setting. At one extreme, Lavache, the old clown, is cut completely, and at the other, the Countess is played by Edith Evans with assured dignity, feeling and intelligence, in keeping with the sense and music of Shakespeare's lines. The King, both when dying and when restored to health, is a tetchy princeling: in Robert Hardy's performance, he has nothing of the Countess' assurance, but strives continually to exert himself; he toys with

Helena and pats his courtiers; his lines are ingeniously spoken so that 'I fill a place, I know't' is a petulant rebuke, 'My son's no dearer' an affected self-advertisement, and 'the inaudible and noiseless foot of Time' a jest that amuses its speaker. Diana, who is called a 'young gentlewoman ... of most chaste renown' and claims to be descended from 'the ancient Capilet', is played by Priscilla Morgan for restless comedy: on her first entrance she looks as if she passed her days reading cheap magazines and staring at men, and this appearance is half-reconciled with her lines about virginity, virtue and pity in that she speaks them with a pert and knowing avidity. Angela Baddeley, as her widowed mother, keeps the audience laughing by little tricks which emphasize her decrepit old-age and prudence to the exclusion of everything else. The bizarre effect of mingling these interpretations may be exemplified from the final scenes: here Parolles takes his proper place as Lafeu's fool without the encounter with Lavache to establish his new status; the King does not sit in judgement, but moves continually among his courtiers, so that he often steps up to a character before addressing him; only the Countess is unmoving and dignified and so, in the continual bustle, draws all eyes to herself – but there seems to be little purpose in this, for Shakespeare has written few words for her in this scene. In this disorder, some expectancy is awakened for Helena's final entry by sweet and soothing music played off-stage.

Guthrie's liveliest invention was reserved for an interpolated dumb-show in Act III, sc. iii. In Shakespeare's play this is a brief moment when the audience is shown the Duke of Florence welcoming the boy Bertram as a man and soldier of worth, and without any of the references to his father's virtues which he has always heard before. As such it is a step forward in the presentation of Bertram, but Guthrie has used it for introducing an entertaining episode in which a comic duke (a grotesque caricature of General Smuts, short-sighted and falsetto) inspects a comic army (a pair of trousers threaten to fall down, someone catches a sword between his legs, a flag slips from its staff as the general salutes, and most of the words are inaudible); this farce lasts six or seven minutes, in which time less than a dozen of Shakespeare's lines are heard, or partly heard. Similar comic invention was utilized every time the soldiers appeared after this, so that the braggart Parolles is shown up as a coward and liar among soldiers that could never fight a battle, and the audience has to suppose that Bertram achieves 'the good livery of honour' in a crazy-gang army. Of course the whole economy of Shakespeare's play has been altered, its proportions, tempo, tensions, emphases, and its comic spirit.

Shakespeare's progressive presentation of the relationship between Helena and Bertram is particularly subtle, yet Guthrie has freely changed this in accordance with his own conception. In the original, Helena hesitantly approaches each of the King's other wards before she confronts Bertram, and then, realizing the presumption of demanding him as husband, she only gives herself to him:

I dare not say I take you; but I give
Me and my service, ever whilst I live,
Into your guiding power.

In Guthrie's version, Helena's choice is made while she engages in a series of lively and sentimental dances: Bertram offers himself, unprompted, as her partner for the last dance and Helena of course is delighted, and, when the dance concludes, addresses him in modest joy, not in fearful resolution; Bertram relinquishes her hand later, only when the King insists that he must call her wife. Here Guthrie has lessened the nervous embarrassment of Helena, and directed the audience's attention away from her and her feelings; he has also introduced some entertaining *divertissements* and heightened the sense of surprise. When the King demands their marriage, overriding everyone's wishes, Guthrie has directed Bertram to walk right across the stage in a general silence and, after a pause, to say the line Shakespeare has given him, very deliberately: 'I cannot love her, nor will strive to do't.' Again this heightens the dramatic excitement through suspense, but it alters Shakespeare's portrayal of Bertram, making him appear so deliberate that it is no longer credible that, in his inexperience, his action is 'but the boldness of his hand . . . which his heart was not consenting to'. Next, Guthrie played confidently for pathos: numerous courtiers take silent leave of Bertram, as if sympathizing with him, and then Bertram and Helena walk together across the empty hall towards the marriage ceremony, and are followed by the far brisker steps of Longaville who has been ordered to conduct them. Shortly afterwards an entirely new scene has been added, the re-entry of Helena and Bertram as from their marriage, holding ceremonial candles and attended by a priest. In all these mute actions, Bertram treats Helena with a quiet, dazed tenderness which is in direct contrast with the brusque, reiterative words Shakespeare has given to him: 'I take her hand. . . . Although before the solemn priest I have sworn, I will not bed her. . . . O my Parolles, they have married me! I'll to the Tuscan wars, and never bed her.' For immediate dramatic gains of suspense or pathos, or in order to introduce dance and movement, the director has altered the presentation of Helena and Bertram.

Whether he was following Shakespeare's text, or deliberately misconstruing it, or intro-ducing some new incident, Guthrie was continually in command of the whole stage; and if his adaptation fails (like Davenant and Dryden's *Enchanted Island*) to sustain any comprehensive dramatic interest, it is always (again like the earlier adaptation) diverting, varied and spirited. If this was the full scope of Guthrie's intentions, he has been brilliantly successful – with the proviso that his version is seen once only. The third or fourth time it is seen, the additions and alterations cease to hold the playgoer's attention, and those parts where he has followed Shakespeare most closely tend to dominate everything else: Zoe Caldwell's tense and emotional Helena in the earliest scenes and Anthony Nicholls's unvariedly elegant Lafeu both gain in stature and interest when they are seen without the new distractions, and Edith Evans's Countess still more realizes the human understanding and poetic utterance which have always been the hall-marks of Shakespeare's original plays.

RICHARD DAVID
ON
MEASURE FOR MEASURE
STRATFORD, 1950

[The production of *Measure for Measure* was reviewed following a consideration of a production of *Love's Labour's Lost*.] The niceties (if they may be so called) of a few passages of bawdry are unintelligible without notes, but their general drift is plain and in any case does not affect the action. There are some startling leaps of imagery and syntax, but nothing to nonplus an audience acquainted with *Hamlet* and *Lear*. A dozen textual confusions require straightening out. Peter Brook did not scruple to make cuts in all these, and emendations in the last, but he made them fairly and firmly. The worst sufferers were deservedly the banter of Lucio and his two gentlemen, and the long-winded prose in which the Duke expounds his plot to Isabella – at worst reviser's stuff, at best an experiment, superseded by Shakespeare's later work, in contriving a measured prose to link scenes of highly-wrought verse. There was less excuse for the drastic compression of the last scene (no apology by the Duke for the circuitousness of his proceedings, no Barnardine); the aim here was clearly to remove anything that might dull either the climax and point of the play, or the Duke's nobility. In this it was no longer the minor difficulties of his text that the producer was tackling but, with equal hardihood, his main problem – what *is* to be the total effect of the play?

The simplicity of the text of *Measure for Measure*, as compared with that of *Love's Labour's Lost*, is a function of its more serious mood. It is a play of ideas rather than of impressions and is concerned more with lines of conduct followed out to their logical conclusions than with the confusions and compromises of real life. There is still controversy as to how far these ideas form a coherent argument, and *Shakespeare Survey* has already given space to notable pleadings on either side. The one maintains that *Measure for Measure* is Shakespeare's considered opinion on the apparent conflict in Renaissance theory between the Christian duty of the Ruler to secure Justice, and that of the individual to be merciful. The other finds in the purpose and character of Isabella and the Duke as many dislocations as in the time-scheme, and holds that Shakespeare, here more even than usual, was concerned only to contrive a series of fine dramatic moments, heightening the effect of each as best might be, without regard to the philosophic or psychological coherence of the whole. A modern producer is apparently faced with the alternative of abandoning any totality of effect for the sake of the incidental

beauties, or of clouding these by the imposition of a 'programme' that will be bewildering to his audience.

Peter Brook's solution of the conundrum was symbolized in the setting that he himself devised for the play. This was a double range of lofty arches, receding from the centre of the stage on either side to the wings upstage. These arches might remain open to the sky in those scenes where some air and freshness is required – the convent at night where Isabella hears from Lucio of her brother's plight, Mariana's moated grange, and the street scene in which all odds are finally made even; or, in a moment, their spaces could be blanked out, with grey flats for the shabby decorum of the courtroom, with grilles for the prison cells. Downstage, at either side, stood a heavy postern gate, also permanently set, serving as focus for the subsidiary scenes to which the full stage would have given undue emphasis, or those, such as the visiting of the imprisoned Claudio, which gain by a cramped setting. The single permanent set gave coherence to the whole; its continuous shadowy presence held together the brilliant series of closet-scenes played on a smaller section of the stage, that glorious succession of duets, Lucio–Isabella, Isabella–Angelo, Claudio–Duke, Isabella–Claudio, in which Shakespeare conceived the action. These were given all the more definition, and urgency, by the apparently confined space in which they were played, although their scope was restricted more by lighting than by any material barrier, and at any moment the whole span of the stage might spring to life and remind us of our bearings in the play. The occasions for such a broadening of effect are not many, but the producer made the most of them. To the progress of Claudio and Juliet to prison, with all corrupt Vienna surging and clamouring about them, and to the final marshalling of all the characters for judgement, he added a third full-stage scene, in which the prisoners, processing through the central hall of the prison, brought its holes and corners for a moment into relation with each other. Shakespeare's text gives only the slimmest pretext for this, in Pompey's enumeration of the old customers whom he has met again in his new employment; but the expansion–in both senses–came happily as a central point of relief in a chain of scenes each requiring a confined attention.

The great duets largely play themselves. It is they that make the play memorable, and such tense and moving writing is found elsewhere in Shakespeare only in the great tragedies. There is of course the notorious danger that to a modern audience Isabella may appear unbearably self-centred and priggish. Isabella knows, and a Jacobean audience took for granted, that there can be no compromise with evil, that, though the only road to right may appear to lie through wrong, the taking of it can do no one any good. Claudio acknowledges it, when not blinded by his panic, for he finally begs his sister's pardon for suggesting otherwise; and we know it, too. But we are shy of being dogmatic about it in the manner of the Jacobeans; though we may admit Isabella's reasons we find it hard to swallow her matter-of-fact schematization of them–'More than our brother is our chastity.'

The producer and Barbara Jefford together saved our faces. Miss Jefford's was a young Isabella, a novice indeed, with no mature *savoir-faire* with which to meet her predicament, but only the burning conviction that two blacks cannot make a white. When she came to the perilous words she turned, from speaking full to the audience, to hide her face passionately against the wall behind her, as if herself ashamed that her intellect could find

no more adequate expression of her heart's certainty. In the same way her tirade against her brother, when he begs her to save his life at any cost, was made to appear as much anger with her own failure as a witness to truth, her own inability to communicate it to others. It was indeed skilful, and a good illustration of one kind of 'translation', to substitute the pathos of the inarticulate for an affronting insensitivity, and convert what is often an offence to modern playgoers into the very engine to enforce their sympathy. Altogether it was a moving performance, that found its perfect foil in the suppressed and twisted nobility of John Gielgud's Angelo. With such interpreters the producer could risk the boldest effects. The climax of the play was breathtaking. Mariana has passionately implored Isabella to kneel to the Duke for Angelo's pardon; the Duke has warned her that to do so would be 'against all sense'–'He dies for Claudio.' The pause that followed must have been among the longest in theatre history. Then hesitantly, still silent, Isabella moved across the stage and knelt before the Duke. Her words came quiet and level, and as their full import of mercy reached Angelo, a sob broke from him. It was perfectly calculated and perfectly timed; and the whole perilous manoeuvre had been triumphantly brought off.

Yet it is not Isabella, still less Angelo, that is the crux of the producer's problem, but the Duke. If the play is to mean anything, if it is to be more than a series of disjointed magnificences, we must accept the Duke's machinations as all to good purpose, and himself as entirely wise and just. Peter Brook presented Vincentio rather as Friar turned Duke than as Duke turned Friar, and maintained throughout the impressiveness of his appearance at the cost of rendering his disguise completely unconvincing. He had found in Harry Andrews a Duke whose commanding presence could dominate the play, as the half-seen arches the stage, and whose charm of manner could convince us of his integrity and wisdom. If his speaking could have been more measured, more confident, more natural ease and less careful manipulation, we might have had the Vincentio of a generation.

It remains (since *Measure for Measure* is still a comedy) to say something about the comics. In refreshing defiance of tradition, Pompey, Elbow, and Abhorson were left to make their proper effect as natural English 'characters', instead of being reduced, as in most productions of the play, to circus clowns and fantastics. Peter Brook has not always escaped censure for that over-emphasis on 'business' which I have already denounced as the fatal Siren of modern producers. Here, where so much depended on control, the supporting elements in the play were not allowed to get much out of hand. The Viennese mob was extremely loud and energetic, but then the outrageousness of its manners (a motif echoed in the Brueghelesque grotesquery of Brook's costumes) is an essential contrast to the nobility of the play's main themes. Pompey was assiduous in distributing advertisements of Mistress Overdone's establishment to all with whom he came in contact, a 'turn' for which the cue can only be wrung from the text with difficulty; but it is in character, and was carefully confined to those moments when no 'necessary question of the play was then to be considered'. It was permissible, too, having provided a pit from which an admirable Barnardine emerged with his true effect, to use it for a tumultuous 'exeunt omnes' at the end of the scene. The only real excrescence was some buffoonery with Pompey's fetters that for a moment put the Duke's dignity in jeopardy. This must be forgiven a producer of such restraint elsewhere that he could keep the crowd in the background of his prison scenes silent and motionless through almost an entire act; could dispense with music, save a tolling bell and the herald's trumpet; and at the close could allow his couples merely to walk, 'hand in hand, with wandering steps and slow', in silence from the stage–and to what great effects!

PETER THOMSON
ON
MEASURE FOR MEASURE,
STRATFORD, 1970

Nothing unthought happens in a play directed by John Barton. The Duke's desk, in the opening scene of *Measure for Measure*, is piled high with dusty books, probably the overspill of this endearing eccentric's untidy library. Angelo uses the same desk in II, ii, but there are no books on it. He loves neither dust nor scholarship. The desk has become a judgement table. Angelo is busy at it when Isabella is first admitted. 'You're welcome' he announces tonelessly, then looks up, *sees* her, and continues, 'what's your will?' The pause is not a long one, but a lot of work is done in it. The process begun there is confirmed in II, iv, when Angelo, admitting his lust, moves from behind the judgement table impulsively towards Isabella, and she, in escaping, replaces him. Isabella, at that moment, judges Angelo. (It was, I think, at II, iv, 125.) There is some danger that, in the pursuit of significant detail, Barton will shy away from Shakespeare's larger gestures. There is nothing certainly wrong in having Claudio (in a blonde wig suggestively similar to Angelo's) eat a prison meal whilst the Duke exhorts him to 'Be absolute for death', but, in offering an alternative object of attention, such an action is, I think, false to the text. Such falseness is less obvious where the pursuit of truth is less meticulous; and it should be stressed that this *Measure for Measure* is serious, intelligent, and sometimes dull. The dullness gathers around Sebastian Shaw's Duke. To the Shakespeare Conference, John Barton described the Duke as a 'complex, inconsistent man', adding that 'the *point* of the part is its inconsistencies'. Shaw spoke it like a man conscious of his own complexity and willing to keep slow pace with it. He found prose rhythms even in the octosyllabics of III, ii, but only by blurring stress and unstress and placing the words round pauses. If the pipe-smoking eccentric of I, i, seemed wise, it was partly because his sniggering councillors behaved foolishly; and if the good humour remained with him, even embracing a quizzical fondness for Lucio, it wasn't always distinguishable from simple-mindedness. Certainly the gravity with which this Duke followed his own thought processes exposed more triteness than sagacity in his pronouncements. At the end of the play Isabella was left alone on stage, puzzled still for an answer to the Duke's proposal. Such an ending, is, of course, a rejection of comedy convention in the pursuit of psychological consistency – unnecessary but not uninteresting. Estelle Kohler's Isabella was always imperfectly aware of her real feelings. I am uncertain whether Miss Kohler was acting the character's uncertainty or making drama out of her own uncertainty about the character. Something was missing, although a lot was there. Neither the Duke nor Isabella held me as Mariana and Angelo did. Watching Sara Kestelman this season, as Jane Shore, Mariana and Hippolita/Titania, I have felt in touch with future greatness. Mariana is given unusual prominence in this production. She is, writes Anne Barton in a programme note, the one character who 'exists as an uncriticized absolute', and, by placing the interval immediately before the play's move to the

moated grange, John Barton has reinforced his view that *Measure for Measure* undergoes a radical shift of emphasis with the introduction of Mariana. Hers is the dominant presence in act v (should it be?), a pale, auburn-haired, pre-Raphaelite beauty whose dejection has produced in her no hesitancy. Angelo was given a less helpful introduction. The Duke's announcement of his deputy was met with concerted chuckles by the assembled officers. (Even stranger was the giggle with which Friar Thomas greeted the Duke's,

> hence shall we see,
> If power change purpose, what our
> seemers be.)

I was disturbed by this. Right government was *not* a serious issue in I, i, so that Claudio's subsequent condemnation lacked political definition. It seemed as peripheral as the trial of Froth and Pompey, a scene that was neither funny nor controlled in this production. It was left to Ian Richardson to establish his own authority as Angelo. Richardson's individuality is strongly marked in this company. Dangerously so, perhaps. Buckingham, Proteus and now Angelo stood out as cold-blooded, precise figures whose disdain for baser men was signalled in the carriage of the head, the subtle modulation of the voice, and the sparse, carefully expressive gestures. All accurately acted, they were all improbably similar. But the theatrical delight of such accomplished playing is irresistible – the greeting of Isabella in II, iv, when, seated on his desk, he pulls a chair towards him with his foot and indicates with a flick of the right hand that she should sit; the distaste with which he handles the Duke's dusty books in I, i; the fastidious wiping of his fingers, which becomes an image of his misanthropy, later to be parodied in the Abhorson/Pompey scene; the desperate phrasing of,

145

Would yet he had liv'd!
Alack! when once our grace we have
  forgot,
Nothing goes right: we would, and we
  would not.

(IV, iv, 35–7)

There must be some questioning of so physically 'beautiful' an Angelo, and of Barton's
decision to have him seize Isabella's hair in
II, iv, to pull her down on to the judgement
table and stroke her body from breast to groin,
but there is no doubt of the continuing
control of Richardson's performances. John
Barton suggested to the Shakespeare Conference that *Measure for Measure* is 'Isabella's
play'. Timothy O'Brien's set pushed it further
towards Angelo. The wall-blocks of panelled
wood indicated, but did not complete, a box-
set. Continued into semi-parquet flooring and
slung, wooden ceiling, they had a clinical
(puritanical?) cleanliness and a forbidding
solidity. But the perspective was sharply
exaggerated, a distortion of the geometrical
form it adumbrated, and a realization almost
of Angelo's mentality. It must have been a
beautiful model. Full-size, it tended to crush
the play.

ROGER WARREN
ON
MEASURE FOR MEASURE,
STRATFORD, 1978

Without concealing the unevenness of the play,
Barry Kyle achieved the astonishing feat of
unifying the uneven *Measure for Measure*,
something I have never seen happen before
nor thought was possible. Mr Kyle did not
achieve this by sensational means, nor by
following the drastic expedients of others
(huge cuts, changes like Isabella refusing to
marry the Duke, or sheer extraneous fantasies
like playing the Duke as a pantomime demon

king), but by a very wary, careful, sensitive
exploration of what the text actually says,
combined with bold, imaginative interpretation.

The design scheme set out the play's concerns clearly but without forcing: the 'precise'
Angelo was properly dressed in Puritan
homespun grey, and once in power he re-
placed the red robes of the Duke's counsellors
with black ones; the Provost and his officers
wore tall black Puritan hats; Lucio by contrast
was a laughing cavalier in red leather; between
the two extremes, the Duke was a sober
Jacobean gentleman. At the start, he gave
Angelo a white robe of office edged with red
flames, a symbol of his prerogative of 'mortality and mercy'. Angelo promptly made all
his victims wear this device, Claudio on his
Inquisition-style pointed cap as he was paraded
through the streets, the bawds on the smocks
which they were compelled to wear after being
dragged into prison and their clothes (even
wigs) torn off and piled in a huge heap centre-
stage. For the trial of Pompey, Angelo sat on a
specially elevated black seat high above the
others, the symbolic 'deputed sword' of
justice across his knees, absolute image of
'proud man,/Dress'd in a little brief authority'.

Christopher Morley's distinguished set ingeniously provided both palace and prison.
A three-sided black box contained a series of
doors for the palace which became stable-like
cells for the prisoners, from the upper half of
which they could watch the action. This
sharply defined, without restricting, the acting
area, and, like the costumes, emphasised the
issues: the box's moveable walls swung in to
enclose Angelo at his black-draped table for
the first scene with Isabella, and an overhead
spotlight picked out his first sign of weakening: 'She speaks, and 'tis/Such sense that my
sense breeds with it.' After she had gone, he
tried to work at his papers to keep his mind

off her, and tried again after the soliloquy. He seemed trapped, cornered, by his physical situation which reflected his internal tension, caught between the demands of his office and those of his desires; a nervous glance towards those walls at 'O cunning enemy' suggested that he imagined the enemy all around him. Thus set up, Jonathan Pryce took command of the stage, powerfully expressing the turmoil and confusion of Angelo, especially his self-loathing even while giving his 'sensual race the rein', spitting the lines against the enclosing walls, not towards Isabella, and even showing a kind of concern for her: 'I talk not of your soul' was not a gibe, but a genuine wish not to endanger it. It was quite consistent for this Angelo to play the final scene in a daze, overcome by what he had done.

Elsewhere, too, the director sought consistency of character where others have failed to find it: John Nettles's excellent Lucio delivered his apparently out-of-character speech about 'full tilth and husbandry' as if he thought this was language which a novice might understand better. But the real achievement in this respect was to make coherent sense of the Duke. In Michael Pennington's gentle, thoughtful performance, the Duke seemed genuinely to be seeking practical solutions to the problems of his office, not playing God. He obviously cared for his subjects, and his urgent attempts to reconcile Claudio with death gave the impression that the Duke felt that people had to be made to *experience* the gravity of breaking the law (whose 'bits and curbs' are, after all, '*needful*') so that his ultimate mercy might be appreciated at its true worth, and this obviously prepared us to accept his apparently gratuitously cruel treatment of Isabella later.

A similar sense of the need for practical solutions emerged in the excellent treatment of

Escalus's examination of Pompey, where Raymond Westwell's Escalus showed beautiful comic timing and also a ripe humanity as he gently sought to replace Elbow with a more competent constable without offending him: 'to your worship's *house*?' replied Elbow, overwhelmed at the honour. There was a very strong sense that, as Anne Barton put it in the programme, 'justice is best served by the unassuming, empirical evaluations of old Escalus', who significantly leant Angelo's symbolic sword of justice casually against the table, and who, while 'it grieves me for the death of Claudio', had to admit that there was yet 'no remedy', banging the table in frustration as, like the Duke, he stressed that the severity of the law is 'needful'.

From the point of his intervention ('a remedy presents itself' was enthusiastic), this Duke vigorously applied himself to working out the kind of pragmatic course needed: Michael Pennington's ability to deliver formal couplets formally and yet make them seem like developing thought-processes ('*Craft* against vice I must apply') meant that he involved us in his plans. His vigour re-appeared at the moated grange: amongst a pile of straw, under a large straw sun, Mariana lay drinking her sorrows away, listening to half-naked rural urchins singing 'Take O take those lips away'. She indicated the half-consumed bottle at 'I have sat here all day', and the Duke later poured himself a drink. This general lightening of the tone got the maximum humanity, and a hint of a warmly relaxing countryside outside the harsh city, from what can seem a perfunctory scene, as well as underlining the play's shift from intensity to intrigue.

There were important results: the Duke's humanity was established; Isabella, mapping out Angelo's garden and vineyard cheerfully and practically with pieces of straw, seemed willing to enter the intrigue as a secular operator, a noticeable development from her reverent, dedicated kissing of the nun's robes presented to her at her first arrival at the convent, and developed further when she tore off the veil in despair at Claudio's supposed death; most important for the general progress of the play, she and the Duke seemed to be drawn into a natural relationship through their shared activity.

The play's development was further assisted by making Angelo's distracted soliloquy in IV, IV, a kind of fevered climax to the prison sequences, watched over as if in a nightmare by the prisoners who were his victims. Then this entire world was disposed of as the front section of the floor rose up to become a fourth wall to block it from sight; and, on a pure white carpet at the very front of the stage, the resolution seemed able to merge the symbolic and realistic aspects into single, highly-charged moments. Claudio, his face bandaged and in a shroud-like prison smock, returned pale and shaken from his ordeal, naturally, but with the additional suggestion that he had come from the grave: Isabella even touched him to make sure he wasn't an apparition. The tension was enormous, the sequence intensely moving, with magical echoes and yet the work of man. It was natural that Isabella should respond to her friar/Duke/preserver and that he should propose to her. After his unmasking, the Duke wore his friar's robe half-on, half-revealing his secular clothes, to sustain his ambiguous role; yet nothing seemed forced, largely because, although pushed to desperate (and sometimes harsh) measures in achieving a pragmatic solution, the Duke seemed an essentially *kind* man, tenderly uniting Juliet and Claudio, and gently urging the others to faith and happiness. In its sense of hard-won harmony, and its secure combining of realism and symbol, the play strongly resembled the 'lawful magic' of the late romances rather

than, as it often seems, merely aspiring towards them: an exceptional achievement.

RICHARD DAVID
ON
TROILUS AND CRESSIDA,
OLD VIC, 1956

Tyrone Guthrie's *Troilus and Cressida* was, as expected, lively, gay and shrewd. Frederick Crooke's Edwardian *décor* certainly pointed up some characteristics of the play. Morning-coat and top-hat of Ascot grey were fair enough for the smart worldliness of a Pandarus who was, nevertheless, more Chaucerian than Shakespearian, and his dialogue with the riding-habited Cressida, as they took turns with his field-glasses to view the returning army, appeared in its proper perspective as small-talk in the paddock. The Prussian severity of the Greeks contrasted aptly with the Ruritanian Trojans, and the solemn absurdity of the council of war came nearer home with Ulysses in admiral's frock-coat and Menelaus as a be-monocled Staff Officer Operations. And I have never seen a happier Nestor (Dudley Jones again) than this fiery little old man, whom even the vast military great-coat, the profusion of whisker, and the peaked cap many sizes too big, could not extinguish. Helen's conservatory was a model of decadent silliness. Cassandra, as a half-crazy devotee of séances, in sack tunic, much embroidered, and waist-long strings of beads, was essentially right, though not royal; and Thersites as war-correspondent, in cloth cap, knickerbockers, and brown boots, if not right was at least more definite than the nothing of most productions. Yet there were disadvantages. It was a pity to place this play, of which a main subject is war, in a period that emphasized only war's glamour and never its reality. Ceremonial uniforms filled the scene, and the battles, including the killing of Hector, were perfunctory. The producer, indeed, had not really come to grips with the play. A programme-note read: 'Shakespeare, we believe, was concerned to shew that the causes of the war, so far as causes of any event can ever be determined, were utterly confused and unreasonable. . . . The Trojans are shewn to be undermined by frivolity; the Greeks by faction.' Even if we accept this as far as it goes (and 'frivolity' is not the right word for the Trojans' fault) it leaves out too much—notably the hero and heroine. They were indeed shabbily treated, reduced to a mere subplot of thoughtless undergraduate seduced by bitch. Their first meeting was trifled away, for as Pandarus Paul Rogers was unforgiveably allowed to distract the audience with foolery and a shawl. Their parting was a little better, though the violence of Cressida's sobs and Troilus' hasty pinning of her into her dress added a stronger dash of the comic than the moment can rightly stand. Even then the lovers were not allowed to claim undivided attention, for the scene was played on a double set, bedroom above, hall below, with the impatient escort quite as prominent as the protagonists. Another expressionist trick destroyed the end of the affair. The audience, tittering at the elegant game of blind man's buff played, in full light, by Cressida, her wooer, and the two parties of eavesdroppers, could hardly spare a serious thought for Troilus' passion. In place of the play's advertised subject we were offered some curious decorations by the producer: a flirtation between Cressida and her groom, and a psychopathic enlargement of Patroclus. Though it was an amusing evening, it was also an infuriating one.

JOHN RUSSELL BROWN
ON
TROILUS AND CRESSIDA,
STRATFORD, 1960

Peter Hall had the fullest showing at the Memorial Theatre, Stratford-upon-Avon, with a *Two Gentlemen of Verona*, a *Troilus and Cressida* (in which he had the assistance of John Barton) and a revival of a *Twelfth Night* from two years earlier. This director came to Shakespeare after staging twentieth-century plays, and the experience is mirrored in his work. It is most obvious in his attitude to speaking Shakespeare's verse and prose: he is determined to avoid stuffiness, or solemn staginess, and seeks instead liveliness, humour and point—in a word, vitality. He has had an apron built over the orchestra pit and uses it for direct and forceful contact with the audience. The clear gains of this policy are in certain comic passages where the actors have sufficient skill to sustain the size of their delivery without crudeness. . . . Such acting is well served by Peter Hall's quest for vitality. And so is the quick, restless art of Max Adrian. As Pandarus he sometimes spoke with a running laugh or simper, or invented excited gestures to indicate the prurience and childishness of an impotent *voyeur*; short phrasing, over-emphasis, repetitions, proverbs, images— 'she fetches her breath as short as a new-ta'en sparrow'—were explained, illustrated, heightened, made to seem inevitable by the actor's invention and performance; he could point his lines, standing right down stage, and bear any scrutiny. Although Pandarus has direct address to the audience, he did not involve them in his thoughts; rather they watched him among others, and at the end were given a spectacle of self-pity and purposeless anger, not a demand for sympathy. . . .

Among the rest of the Stratford Company,

Dorothy Tutin gained most by Peter Hall's treatment of the dialogue. Visually her Cressida may have been too obviously or too early a seductress from an exotic film – would it not explain Troilus' talk of 'purity' if for a time she were successful in keeping her vow, 'nothing of that shall from my eyes appear'? – but the liveliness and humour she found in the part – the vitality her director seeks – was finely judged and enacted with control and intensity: 'he will weep you, an't were a man born in April', promises Pandarus, and Cressida momentarily stills the mockery with, 'And I'll spring up in his tears', and then releases it with, 'an't were a nettle against May'. A Shakespearian heroine thus becomes a creature of impulse and quick intelligence.

Equally clear is Peter Hall's pursuit of visual elaboration. . . . *Troilus* was set on an irregular, raised and raked octagon, covered with pale sand. By itself this would have suggested a play-pit or a tray from a bird-cage. But behind it stretched a vast abstract backcloth designed by Leslie Hurry in copper-reds with black hieroglyphic markings; it suggested a furnace, a volcanic cliff, an ancient palace hung with undecipherable trophies, a storm, a dragon's wing. In front of this the sanded platform seemed a torrid desert or an arena for gladiatorial combat. Peter Hall had modified, not changed his policy: so far as the structure of Stratford's theatre would permit he had provided a simple platform stage, but placed it within a wide, emotive setting. He even repeated his interest in small visual details by the eye-catching novelty of the sand: Cressida languorously made it flow through her fingers and the action traced changing patterns across it as in a bull-ring. Moreover banners, stools, a high throne, carpets and one of the director's favourite potted trees were used to 'dress' the arena, controlled by a hand practised in more obviously elaborate settings. So the stage was capable of varied emphases: after Æneas had gone off with Troilus to meet Diomede for the first time, Pandarus was suddenly alone on a stage of desert-like emptiness; when Achilles at last spoke to Hector after the duel with Ajax, he did so from beside a tall, black standard to the back and right of the stage, a position of ominous emphasis created for this moment. The most spectacular effects were in the last battle-scenes where smoke hung low around a darkened stage, illuminated with sulphurous and glaring lights; the simplest mechanisms had been used for the detailed pictorial quality which is one of this director's most evident marks.

A further one is a constant pursuit of business. . . . [For example] Achilles and Thersites share a chicken leg. . . . These inventions are often in character, as when Agamemnon, who is said to speak 'like a chime a'mending', rises between two discourses from Ulysses as if to speak himself, but instead crosses in front of Ulysses to drink from a goblet, conveniently placed on the floor. But however well this fits the character it is questionable whether it serves the scene as a whole; the primary task at this moment is to interest the audience in what Ulysses is saying. This aspect of Peter Hall's direction can be distracting, especially when business is allowed to obliterate the connexions, contrasts and emphases suggested by the text of a play. . . .

But any director's achievements must be judged by his handling of complete plays. . . .

Troilus and Cressida had the advantage of a far less fussy and more appropriate setting, and the liveliness, humour and point of the speaking served the satirical elements well, and the vaunting encounters of the soldiers. The two difficult council-scenes failed, however, to hold a close attention. The Greek was slow and too uniformly stressed; in particular,

Ulysses spoke too weightily for a man of his acute (or fox-like) intelligence. In Troy the princes seemed to try too hard to sustain the longer speeches and two opportunities for variety were lost by giving Priam to a small actor placed on a rickety throne and by allowing Cassandra to look and sound uncomfortable rather than terrible and commanding; the scene lacked a shape and a centre. Yet generally, the fire and the absurdity of love and warlike preparations were clearly delineated, and this play, unlike the other two, seemed to sweep forward, broadening and defining its scope, finding its energy from within the characters and situations, rather than from the director's hand. Pandarus and Paul Hardwick's Ajax were comic performances, and Derek Godfrey's Hector and Patrick Allen's Achilles heroic, which had vitality appropriate to their language and their characters. And Miss Tutin's Cressida, particularly when she had parted from Troilus, showed her complaisance to be her 'plague', her will and memory unable to change her desires; silence among the Greeks and then the mocking of Menelaus became eloquent of her 'quick sense', and the last scene with Diomede showed her to be both cunning and helpless.

Yet the end of the play was disappointing. First Troilus (Denholm Elliott) did not sustain interest after Cressida's last appearance. Throughout he had been striving for an impression of energy–he even tried to endow 'a strange soul upon the Stygian banks' with a kind of brightness. A more tender Troilus, with a more pitiable Cressida, would have been well within this actor's powers, but in the vital idiom of the production his voice seemed lacking in size and range, his movements consistently nervous. He had no reserve of power to transform himself into a cold, resolved 'savage' for the last scenes; he could only become tense and shout his anger. The

second disappointment was caused by the director giving way to his love of detail: every fight was prolonged; an extra entry was invented for Ajax; Achilles had a long pause in his last short speech to turn over Hector's body with his foot; the final departure of the Greeks was delayed while some of them picked up Hector's cloak and looked at it. After the early forcefulness the battles needed to be rapid, if they were not to disperse the charged interests; Hall's were fine pictures, but too often a dumb deflation of the drama, especially when the stage-smoke was allowed to obscure the fighters.

Added to Hall's marks of vitality, with its dependence on fine acting to avoid coarseness, of elaborate settings and of a pursuit of business, must be a slack grasp of form. All three plays were over-slow at the end, but it is probably more than a question of tempo and style. ... In *Troilus*, men and women, by satisfying their own appetites and desires, find that in time they are forced to do what they 'would not'; they learn that time has a 'robber's haste'; they foresee fate and defy fate; they swear by Diana in their licentiousness; their minds become like fountains 'troubled' of which they cannot see the bottom, and, finally, there is 'no more to say' except to triumph in an act of butchery or cover an 'inward woe' with hope of revenge. This train of actions and sentiments relating to the changes time enforces might easily have been more emphasized, by giving stature to Cassandra, by making the pledges to the future shared by Troilus, Cressida and Pandarus as boldly formal as the writing of that incident, by more relentless pressure in the battle-scenes (broken for the inevitable encounters of Achilles and Hector), by a modified style of utterance which could make isolated emphasis where the issues seem to demand it. It is possible that such attention to an idea would give a more compelling form to the plays as well as greater eloquence and fuller interest.

ROGER WARREN

ON

TROILUS AND CRESSIDA,

STRATFORD, 1976

John Barton's close involvement with *Troilus and Cressida* over several productions has its dangers. He knows it *so* well that he sometimes appears to forget that what the audience needs, primarily, is to have the main points of an exceptionally difficult text, and especially the main sense of the *arguments*, made as clear as possible. He achieved this in 1960, but his later versions have tended to lose sight of main issues in the exploration of a particular passage or detail or relationship. The result has sometimes been bewildering rather than, as he obviously intends, enriching: 'Shakespeare invites tragic, comic, satiric, intellectual and compassionate responses almost at the same time.' Quite so, but with a text so complex that it's often hard to grasp the basic sense, there is a limit to what an audience can take in all at once.

Mr Barton carried over several features from his controversial 1968 version: the Trojans were virtually naked when they went into battle, and so were the Myrmidons throughout; Achilles was showily effeminate; Thersites was covered with bleeding sores and wore a grotesque mouth-shaped codpiece with a dangling red tongue/penis; Thersites and Pandarus had a song-and-dance routine for the epilogue. My objection to these things was not that they were offensive, as some found them, but that they distracted one from concentrating on that complicated language, without being closely enough related to the text to act as visual symbols of it. His most successful innovation last time was a Helen who was not a caricatured whore but a 'glimpse of a human woman'; but Helen this time was led on by Paris, who drew her by a golden chain around her neck, and compelled to speak the unexceptional lines about un-arming Hector grimly and slowly, as if the Helen/Paris relationship was growing stale—one of the few deteriorations, surely, *not* suggested by the text: 'Sweet, above thought I love thee.'

In underlining the text's deflation of the heroes, Mr Barton has tended in fact to undermine both the possibility of characterisation and often of simple comprehension: Agamemnon carried a frying-pan to the first council, and wore a bucolic straw hat; but 'satire' was carried to the self-defeating point of sheer inaudibility in his case and of having Ulysses rise again and again during Agememnon's and Nestor's speeches in an attempt to stop the flow of senseless rhetoric and get a hearing; a similar jokiness underlined Aeneas's and Ajax's verbosity with apparently unending trumpet-calls; the balletic posturings of the Hector/Ajax duel were simply ridiculous. Shakespeare certainly satirizes heroes' feet of clay, but if Achilles, for instance, doesn't even *seem* a warrior-hero to start with, what is there to satirize? More seriously still, Mr Barton equipped Cressida with a stock courtesan mask, fitted to the back of her head-dress, which she suddenly revealed as she walked off at the end of the betrayal scene. This gross schematic ostentation flatly contradicted both the ambiguity of Cressida's feeling, and Francesca Annis's subtle presentation of it.

This device emphasized what seems an uncertainty in Mr Barton's approach. He once said in these pages, 'what happens, by the end, to Troilus and Cressida and Hector is not [black comedy]. . . . I feel a great compassion for what becomes of Troilus and Cressida'.[1]

[1] *Shakespeare Survey 25* (Cambridge 1972), pp. 67–8.

And certainly Troilus and Cressida for the first time in my experience held the centre of their play. Francesca Annis perfectly caught the 'slippery' changeability of Cressida, sophisticated one moment, the next giving intense value to the haunting solemnity with which Cressida swears truth,

When time is old and hath forgot itself,
When waterdrops have worn the stones
    of Troy.

This scene, with its magnificent juxtaposition of present and future, and of passionate seriousness and bawdy wit, was the high point of the play, superbly realized by Miss Annis, David Waller's expert Pandarus, and Mike Gwilym's coherent and unmannered Troilus.

All the more surprising, then, that Mr Barton should seem to satirize Troilus's savage outburst of disillusion by making Ulysses ironically applaud it. Perhaps the idea was to satirize Ulysses's lack of understanding, though this is unlikely since Troilus here, and only here, fell into the ranting of the conventional Troiluses; but whatever the motive, the presentation of both Ulysses and Hector reinforced my feeling of uncertainty about Mr Barton's viewpoint. It's true that there is a 'shiftingness of view . . . in the play's presentation of character', a contrast between a character's 'beliefs' and his 'actions'. But it's surely enough to make very clear (as this production certainly did) Hector's *volte-face* in the Trojan council; elsewhere the presentation of Hector was 'shifting' to the point of confusion rather than complexity. Michael Pennington achieved another of those haunting, magical moments, juxtaposing past and present, when he saluted Nestor with humanity and gravity, stilling the theatre:

Let me embrace thee, good old chronicle,
That hast so long walk'd hand in hand
    with time.

But the next moment he was ostentatiously flexing his muscles (as again in the farewell to Andromache) and appeared to be tipping the character into overt parody.

Again, it is one thing to stress the contrast between Ulysses's elaborate stratagem to bring Achilles back to the battle line, and the human motive, Patroclus's death, which actually brings him back. But you can't grasp such an irony unless you have followed the detailed arguments of Ulysses in the first place. While Tony Church certainly made all the points very clearly, with full relish for the language, Mr Barton maddeningly distracted from his Time speech by having Achilles constantly play with the book that Ulysses had been reading. I don't understand the motive for this at all. Of course we need to see Achilles's reactions; but first and foremost we need to follow Ulysses's speech, in detail and without distractions. Even if Ulysses's attitudes are subsequently undermined, they need to be established clearly first.

Yet for all these reservations it was a consistently interesting and absorbing occasion; the long evening seemed to pass very quickly. Whatever Mr Barton's over-emphasis or over-ingenuity, he enabled his cast to bring out the 'shifting' ambiguous quality of much, at least, of the play, and certainly much more than in his previous version.

DATE DUE

The Library Store   #47-0114 Peel Off Pressure Sensitive